Gun Collecting

GUN
COLLECTING

GEOFFREY
BOOTHROYD

• THE •
SPORTSMAN'S
PRESS
LONDON

This edition published in 1987 by The Sportsman's Press

© Geoffrey Boothroyd 1987
First published 1961

British Library Cataloguing in Publication Data

Boothroyd, Geoffrey, *1925–*
Gun collecting.—Rev. ed.
1. Firearms—Collectors and collecting
2. Firearms—History
I. Title   II. Boothroyd, Geoffrey, *1925–*
Guide to gun collecting.
739.7′44′09   NK6906

ISBN 0–948253–10–X

Printed and bound in Great Britain by
Redwood Burn Limited,
Trowbridge, Wiltshire

TO:
A.H.B.
S.G.B.
S.M.B.

Acknowledgements

THE pleasure of acknowledging the help and assistance which has made this book possible, although personally rewarding, would be somewhat tedious for the reader.

I cannot let this opportunity pass, however, without expressing my sincere appreciation of the guidance willingly given by Captain R. H. Walton throughout the years and to Peter A. Bedford for the helpful suggestions and comments which he made during the time this book was being written.

Many of the illustrations are of weapons now in the Glasgow Museum and Art Galleries and I am deeply indebted to the officials who provided the excellent facilities that I enjoyed during my two photographic sessions at the Museum.

Illustrations of guns from other collections are appropriately acknowledged, the remainder being from the author's collection.

Finally, my thanks are due to Moira Russell and Margaret Carnachan who did most of the typing.

Contents

Introduction

THIS book is intended for the newcomer to gun collecting. A general guide for the beginner is difficult to write since always there is the conflict between what should be included and what must be left out.

The historical section of the book attempts to cover the development of firearms from the earliest days until the opening of the twentieth century. It is designed to be of value to the present-day gun collector whose opportunity of acquiring the 'antique' rather than the 'vintage' gun has been somewhat curtailed due to the phenomenal post-war increase in the demand for old guns.

Firearms exert a compelling fascination on young and old and gun collecting embraces a scope which permits even the most sectionalized interests to be catered for. The pangs of conscience that may arise from diverting income into a hobbyist activity can be salved by the knowledge that a worth-while collection is an investment, which although subject to fluctuation, has a tendency to increase in value.

It is the earnest hope of the author that this book will be the means of introducing the reader to a fuller participation in his chosen interest and so gain the greatest possible satisfaction from the time and money which he so wisely spends.

CHAPTER ONE

Invention of gunpowder

THE invention of gunpowder ranks as one of the most important discoveries in history but it is unlikely that the inventor or inventors will ever be known. That firearms were in use by the mid-thirteenth century is indisputable but myth and legend continue to shroud the early experimenters in mystery. The use of fiery, combustible mixtures based on sulphur, fats, bitumens and charcoal for warlike purposes antedate gunpowder by a considerable period; the celebrated Greek Fire used in the Byzantine era was probably a composition based on such materials. Perhaps a seeker after an even more efficient Greek Fire had his pestle hurled out of his mortar during secret experiments and by such means the knowledge of a propulsive agent other than human bone and sinew was born.

Two men, however, due solely to the power of popular legend, stand out of the mists of time with some clarity. Roger Bacon of Ilchester in Somerset is a figure of great historical importance. The other, Berthold Schwartz, of Freiburg in Breisgau, to give him one of his many names, remains to this day, despite considerable research, a shadowy and enigmatical individual. It was Bacon in his tract entitled 'De Mirabili Potestate Artis et Naturae' (On the Marvellous Power of Art and Nature) who first made known the composition of gunpowder. Although there are no grounds for assuming that Bacon discovered gunpowder, there can be little doubt that his experiments improved the quality and power of these primitive mixtures and that such improvement was based on the increased purity of the ingredients. Similarly, there is no evidence to suppose that Bacon was aware of the propulsive power of gunpowder and its use in firearms. This discovery that the new force could be used (instead of men's muscles) to propel missiles is usually ascribed to the second, more shadowy figure, Berthold Schwartz.

Legend perpetuated in early manuscripts tells us that Friar Bertholdus was a Franciscan monk who lived in the old city of Freiburg in the district of Breisgau in southern Germany and that his name before taking vows had been Constantin Anklitzen. In 1890 the good citizens of Freiburg, confident that the fable was based on fact, erected a monument to Friar Bertholdus, but a German Historical Commission of the nineteenth century who

15

were engaged on the compilation of a large biographical work, excluded the Friar from their list of notable German historical figures on the basis that no documentary evidence as to his existence could be found.

It is unlikely that documents will now come to light that will shed further light on whether or not Friar Bertholdus did or did not invent gunpowder, but it is known that several powder mills were in operation in Germany by the mid-fourteenth century and that both powder and cannon were being manufactured in Britain in 1344. Concerning British military operations, guns and gunpowder were certainly used at the Battle of Crécy in 1346 and a form of cannon was reputed to have been used by Edward III against the Scots in 1327.

The manufacture of gunpowder in the Middle Ages was regarded with awe and suspicion as being a manifestation of the black art, but the practical value of the product for military use ensured that, despite popular misgivings, manufacture on an ever-increasing scale was carried out. Probably the most interesting contemporary document relating to the manufacture of gunpowder is the Codex Germanicus of 1350, in which many of the practical tests for ensuring the purity of the ingredients are given.

The Codex recommends the use of the wood of the lime or poplar for charcoal burning and the proportions of the ingredients were given as follows: four parts saltpetre, one of sulphur and one of charcoal.

In the hundred years that separate the Codex Germanicus from Bacon's tract of 1242, the recommended proportions of the various ingredients have already undergone some change, since Bacon advises that one should take seven parts of saltpetre, five of young hazel twigs and five of sulphur. This tendency to increase the proportion of saltpetre at the expense of the other ingredients continued through the ages until the end of the eighteenth century, when the proportions were stabilized at those in use today.

The earliest gunpowders were feeble in their power due to the impurity of the ingredients and the lack of proper mixing during incorporation, and such mixtures would probably splutter and smoulder without exploding. Once the secret of purifying saltpetre by repeated recrystallization from water was discovered, the quality of the powder improved, although since mixing was carried out dry, first of all in a pestle and mortar, and later in a primitive stamp mill, the resultant gunpowder varied considerably in particle size. The fine dust which was a necessary by-product caused considerable difficulties due to its ease of ignition and the nuisance value during manufacture and transport. The presence of this fine, easily ignitable dust no doubt accounts for the great respect with which the product was handled.

In addition to the dust problem, the fact that early powders were simple mixtures caused separation of the ingredients due to varying specific gravities, and ready-mixed powder often had to be remixed after a long journey. These problems were not solved until the discovery of wet incorporation using water, vinegar or urine to form a moist paste. In this connexion, it is recorded that a wine drinker's urine was superior to a beer drinker's and a wine-drinking bishop's best of all. The thoroughly mixed powder was then almost dried and formed under pressure into cakes, which were forced through sieves in the following granulating or corning process, producing grains which were then graduated according to size. The resultant grains were dust free. The constituents showed no tendency to separate under prolonged dry storage or transport and the corned powder was of greater power than the previous gunpowder dust or serpentine powder.

We now come to the consideration of yet another perplexing problem. When was this gunpowder first used as a missile propellant and, of more importance to the gun collector, when were the first hand guns used? The first guns were what we today would class as artillery, and from early Saracen records stone-throwing cannon were used as early as 1247 in the defence of Seville. The earliest records, whose authenticity can be established, are of Italian and Flemish origin, but whether the hand gun evolved from the siege cannon or was developed concurrently is not known and the confusion is increased since the earliest records do not differentiate between heavy ordnance and light, and we are left somewhat in the dark until later, more explicit descriptions, paintings, tapestries and drawings make it easier to follow the evolution of small arms.

In the small town of Lecetto, near Sienna, Italy, an artist, Paola Neri, worked on a series of frescoes in 1340; these frescoes are still to be seen and show contemporary warlike scenes on land and sea. A panel depicting the attack on a castle shows the besiegers using cannon, whilst the defenders are retaliating with bows and hand cannon. It is reasonable to suppose that these hand cannon are the earliest to have achieved 'immortality' through the brush of the painter, and although these paintings are badly damaged it can be seen that they are true hand cannon, being metal tubes, closed at the breech and attached to a stock. The guns were fired by one man and ignited with glowing coal.

Many records concerning the purchase of hand guns and inventories of armouries are extant and continental Europe of the mid-fourteenth century appears to have been well supplied with a variety of weapons capable of being handled by one man. By the end of the century the hand gun was well known; Chaucer, in 'The House of Fame' written in 1380, makes references which would only be intelligible to those familiar with firearms when he says:

> *As swift as a pellet out of a gonne,*
> *Whan fyr is in the powder ronne . . .*

Few of these primitive hand guns have survived the neglect of the centuries and fewer still have survived in such a way as to provide beyond a reasonable doubt proof of their authenticity. The Tannenberger Gun is one of the few and the facts concerning its preservation are such that the gun could only have been made prior to 1399. The gun, which consisted of a bronze barrel thirteen inches long, its bore just under one-and-a-half inches, secured by means of a socket on to a wooden shaft which unfortunately did not survive. Externally, the barrel is hexagonal and has a reinforced ring at the muzzle. Ignition was by means of a touch hole at right angles to the bore, the vent being provided with a shallow depression to hold the priming.

Despite the almost total lack of accuracy at anything but point-blank range, coupled with woefully inadequate ballistics, the hand gun achieved a success in warfare which can only be attributed to the terrifying effect of the smoke and noise of discharge on those who opposed it, allied to the belief that gunshot wounds were poisonous and incurable. This belief no doubt was strengthened by virtue of the lamentable inadequacy of the surgery of the period, an estimate of which can be formed by reference to one of the recipes for gunshot wounds. 'Take of oil and wine equal parts, inject them into a living dog, well boil the animal, its flesh, together with the oil and wine form the application'!

This success must have stimulated development since the hand culverin, which was designed to be used by a two-man team, made its appearance during the first half of the fifteenth century. This weapon was longer in the barrel than the hand gun and of larger calibre. It was aimed by the first man and fired by the second, who also carried the powder flask and supply of bullets.

In England, knowledge of firearms is deduced from early records and they appear to have become of military importance during the reign of Edward IV, but a dependence on the long bow perpetuated by its effectiveness mitigated against the employment of a weapon whose accuracy and rate of fire were inferior to the long bow.

The vaunted pre-eminence of the English long bow could not be disputed but many years of long and hard practice were needed to produce an accomplished archer. The disparity between the degree of training required by the archer and the hand gunner respectively, became a matter of increasing importance, and with the appearance of the matchlock and improvements in barrel boring, coupled with the provision of a means of sighting, the day of the archer and crossbowman was drawing to a close.

CHAPTER TWO

The matchlock

IN its earliest form the matchlock can be regarded as a hand cannon with an S-shaped arm attached to the stock and capable of being pivoted about the centre of the S. The lower half formed the 'trigger' (at first called a scear), the upper having a clamp or tube capable of holding the lighted fuse. By pulling back the trigger the upper arm was swung over and down, the glowing end of the fuse igniting the powder in the touch hole and so firing the gun. Such a weapon appears to have been used by the Burgundians as early as 1431.

The matchlock enjoys the same position relative to the hand cannon as does the crossbow to the long bow. In both cases mechanical means were found to reduce the element of human error, and there is little doubt that the already perfected crossbow trigger mechanism influenced the later improvements of the matchlock. Where and when the first matchlock appeared is as much in doubt as the origins of gunpowder and the subject of equal speculation. Once the principle was established, matchlocks of various types appeared throughout the second half of the fifteenth century, development being stimulated by political unrest in Europe and a change in the basic concept of war. The old system of raising troops by feudal levies was being replaced by the emergence of standing armies placed on a permanent footing and by virtue of their organization capable of being properly trained and disciplined.

Whilst a vast improvement over the hand gun, the early matchlock possessed numerous faults: inadvertent discharge could be caused by the movement of the S-shaped match holder or serpentine; a gust of wind could blow away the priming and, due to the near proximity of the glowing fuse, repriming could be a hazardous operation if the fuse were not removed and, lastly, the priming in its exposed position could be rendered ineffective by rain. Improvements were made in the fuse, since by better construction of the cord itself and by soaking in saltpetre, followed by drying, the fuse or match-cord could be made to glow evenly without fear of extinction.

By the end of the fifteenth century the serpentine had been reversed and provided with a spring to hold the match away from the priming. The mechanism, consisting of a tricker or trigger, scear and serpentine, were mounted on a lock plate which was attached to the side of the stock; the touch hole had been moved from the top of the breech to the side, and was provided with a hinged cover to protect the priming from rain or wind until the moment of discharge. The stock had become a recognizable piece of firearm furniture and extended to the muzzle, thus providing space for later ornamentation as well as increasing the robustness of the piece. Even at this stage of development, a bewildering variety of names were used to describe the various types of weapon evolved due, in some measure, to the lack of standardized spelling and, for the sake of clarity if not accuracy, the term arquebus will be used as a generic term for early matchlock long guns.

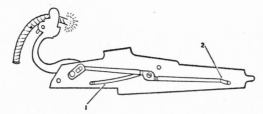

Figure 1. Interior of matchlock. (1) Scearspring. (2) Pivoted scear.

By the middle of the sixteenth century a specific type of matchlock makes its appearance—the caliver. According to Meyrick's *A Critical Enquiry into Ancient Armour* (London, 1824), the term caliver applied to an arquebus having a standard bore, which was known as 'Arquebus Calibre de Monsieur le Prince'. This unwieldy description was soon reduced to 'Calibre du Prince' and then to 'calibre' and its English corruption, caliver. The mid-sixteenth-century caliver can then be regarded with some certainty as a matchlock weapon with a 42-in. barrel, the 'calibre' or bore of which was ·76 to ·79 of an inch. Weighing in the region of ten to twelve pounds, the caliver was normally fired without a rest or forked stick to support it during discharge and, whilst effective enough against lightly armoured opponents, the increasing efficiency of the body and horse armour made an increase in fire power necessary.

The answer to the heavier armour was an even larger matchlock than the musket, the derivation of this term being attributed to the

Spanish (who developed the new gun) from the Spanish 'moschetto', or sparrow hawk. The matchlock musket had first been introduced as a form of 'secret weapon' during the wars waged by Spain in the Spanish Netherlands (1565–81), its purpose being to smash through the heaviest protective armour then devised. With a weight of up to twenty pounds, the musket required a support during use and, whilst the ball with a diameter approaching one inch and weighing one and a half ounces was capable of 'spoyling horse or man thirty score off' (Williams, *Briefe Discourse of Warre*, 1590), its undoubted range and penetration were offset by a lack of manœuvrability due to its weight and increased length.

Development was not, however, solely confined to the increase in length and calibre of the matchlock. Improvements in the lock mechanism occurred, the most highly developed being the '*lunten-schnappschloss*', the snapping, or tinder lock. With this type of lock, fire was carried to the priming by means of a small piece of tinder or match held in a tube in the jaws of the serpentine. The tinder was lighted from a glowing match immediately before firing and, on pressing the trigger, the serpentine moved towards the priming under the action of a mainspring. This then was the first of the locks where the movement of the serpentine, later to be called the cock, was mechanically propelled and this lock is considered by some authorities to be the ancestor of the later snaphaunce lock. The majority of matchlocks, however, used the common 'pressure' lock as already described, the chief virtue of which was its simplicity and cheapness.

In addition to the improvements mentioned, the late fifteenth century saw the introduction of rifling, undoubtedly one of the most important discoveries in connexion with the history of firearms, and one which was to have a profound influence on future development. Although the theory of rifling was not fully appreciated for many years after its introduction, a desire to imitate the spinning motion of the arrow or crossbow quarrel, which was known to have an important influence on accuracy, may have initiated the experiment which resulted in the spiral internal grooves known as 'rifling' (German riffeln: to groove). Another theory to account for the development of rifling is that early matchlock arquebuses are known which have eight or more straight grooves inside the barrel, the purpose of which is assumed to have been for the reception of carbon fouling. The use of serpentine powder must have resulted in excessive fouling, the accumulation of which would render reloading difficult, and have an adverse effect on accuracy. There are two claimants for the honour of the discovery of rifling, August Kotter of Nuremberg and Gaspard Kollner of Vienna. Neither of these claims has ever been fully proven but indisputably rifling was in use at the turn of the fifteenth century and the first recorded military use of the rifle was during the reign of Christian IV of Denmark (1577–1648).

Many attempts were made to devise guns which would be capable of repeating fire by use of multiple barrels, superimposed charges and even revolving arms. Weapons loading at the breech were also made, and one of these is still in the Tower of London, and is dated 1537. The practical difficulties due to inferior metallurgical and machining techniques precluded the widespread use of these weapons, and the matchlock 'arquebusier' or 'musketeer', went through an elaborate ritual each time he fired his piece.

The musketeer carried, in addition to his gun and rest, a bandolier consisting of a 'baudricke' or strap of leather slung over one shoulder from which were suspended cases of leather, copper, tin or wood, containing measured charges of gunpowder (grosse corne), a flask containing powder for priming or 'touche-box' with 'fyne corne', a bullet bag, a supply of match-cord and a sword. The shortened version of loading intructions for the matchlock, given in Grose, *Military Antiquities* (1788) is given below. 'Prime your pan.' Shake off loose powder and make certain none remains. 'Cast about your musket.' (The priming operation was carried out with the musket supported by the left hand and held across the body— muzzle to the left. On the command 'cast about', the musket was transferred to the left side, butt on the ground, muzzle upmost.) 'Open your charge'—the charge or box on the bandolier was opened by the right hand and the charge transferred to the musket. The next operation was to withdraw the 'scouring stick' or ramrod, and place a bullet in the muzzle which was 'rammed home', the scouring stick being returned to its place under the barrel. With the gun loaded and primed it was then transferred to the rest and the glowing match, which had been carefully handled by the musketeer to avoid accidents, was blown into life, placed in the jaws of the serpentine and 'tried' to make certain it was properly adjusted. The pan was then opened and the musket presented and fired.

While the more underdeveloped areas of the world managed to exist with the matchlock, and its troublesome ignition, the pressure of events in strife-torn Europe fostered the invention of the wheel-lock and, as a result of this invention, the development of yet another in the family of firearms, the pistol.

CHAPTER THREE

The wheellock

In its simplest form the wheellock consisted of a grooved and serrated wheel, similar to that of the modern petrol lighter, mounted on an axle which was supported by the lock plate of the gun. The actuating spring was connected by a small piece of flat link chain to an offset crank such that when the lock was 'spanned' or wound up with the 'spanner' (this being a key fitting the external squared end of the axle), the chain was wound round the axle. The spring tensioned until a small catch engaged in the wheel and the lock was fully wound. The upper periphery of the wheel protruded through the priming pan which formed part of the lock plate, and a spring-loaded arm, with vice jaws (the doghead) holding the pyrites or flint, was so arranged as to be capable of pivoting to place the pyrites in contact with the wheel. In use, the gun was loaded with powder and ball in a similar manner to the matchlock, the lock was then spanned, or wound up, and the priming powder introduced into the flash pan or priming pan. This pan was provided with a sliding cover, which was returned to guard the priming against damp and accidental discharge, and the last operation was to bring over the doghead with the pyrites so that the pyrites pressed against the pan cover under the influence of the 'feather spring'. Pressing the trigger released the wheel to spin round for less than one revolution and, at the same time, the pan cover was automatically withdrawn to allow the pyrites or flint to come in contact with the now spinning wheel, and ignite the priming charge. Such a mechanism was capable of infinite refinement and the variety produced culminated in complicated mechanisms containing up to eighteen separate parts. Such refinements were the invention of the 'set' or 'hair trigger' mechanism, designed to overcome the often excessive pull required to release the wheellock scear, the mechanically operated pan cover, and the 'flashguard'. Wheellocks were fitted with double locks or two dogheads and combination match and wheellocks were made for the pessimistic, who perhaps thought the 'new' mechanism untrustworthy.

In seeking some order from the amazing number of different types of wheellock, reference can be made to the lock itself as a means of classification. The visual external examination of the lock will show that there are four main types, which differ in the mounting

1. Lockplate (interior). **2.** External wheelcover. **3.** Thimble bearing for spindle (10). **4.** Support for sliding pan cover (15). **5.** Support for the spindle bridge piece (19). **6.** Support for the release scear (11) and mainspring (14). **7.** Mainspring guide and pivot and pivot for trigger scear (9). **8.** Grooved wheel with depression for release scear (11). **9.** Trigger scear. **10.** Spindle with squared end for spanning key and link chain for mainspring. **11.** Release scear and **11a** pivot screw. **12.** Double acting spring for release and trigger scears. **13.** Pan and flash guard with **13a** securing screw. **14.** Mainspring.

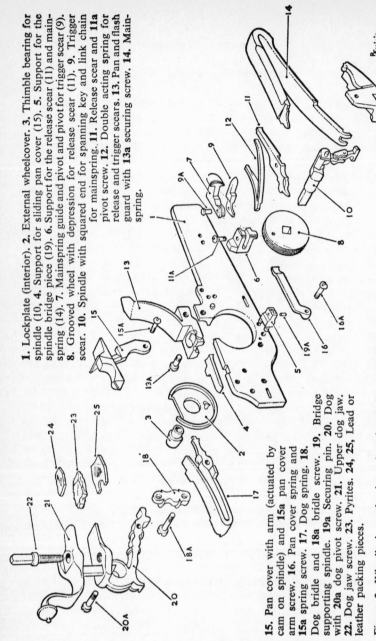

15. Pan cover with arm (actuated by cam on spindle) and **15a** pan cover arm screw. **16.** Pan cover spring and **15a** spring screw. **17.** Dog spring. **18.** Dog bridle and **18a** bridle screw. **19.** Bridge supporting spindle. **19a** Securing pin. **20.** Dog with **20a** dog pivot screw. **21.** Upper dog jaw. **22.** Dog jaw screw. **23.** Pyrites. **24, 25,** Lead or leather packing pieces.

Figure 2. Wheellock mechanism, Austrian, mid-seventeenth century.

of the wheel in relation to the plate, and in its guarding. The first type has the wheel on the outside of the lock plate and it is entirely uncovered or, in the case of some specimens, there is a narrow circumferential guard protecting the serrated edge of the wheel. The second type also carries the wheel externally but it is shielded in its entirety either with what appears to be a development of the first pattern, but having an extra flat plate to guard the wheel, as well as the edge, or a domed one-piece cover pierced to allow the axle to protrude for spanning. A third type is where the wheel is totally enclosed inside the lock plate, which may be absolutely flat or have an external plate, so that the wheel is, in fact, recessed into the lock plate from the inside. The last type not only has the wheel externally mounted and uncovered, but most of the mechanism is also exposed. This lock was invariably fitted to wheellocks of the Tschinke type, which are also characterized by the 'hinds foot' stock, which is not dissimilar to the 'hog back' stock seen on German sporting rifles of the late nineteenth and early twentieth centuries. The Tschinke wheellocks were developed in the north of Germany and the Baltic provinces in the early seventeenth century, for sporting purposes, and are light rifles capable of being carried and used without fatigue. The external mechanism was, of course, liable to accidental damage, but rendered the very necessary cleaning of the wheel and associate mechanism an easy task. The enclosed, or partially enclosed type of lock, was to a great extent free from accidental damage due to careless handling, but one wonders how much damage was caused by stripping the lock for cleaning by the probably unskilled owner. The Tschinke, with its distinctive butt stock, provided one of several clearly defined stock forms.

The earliest wheellocks have stocks obviously derived from the crossbow, such stocks being straight and provided with a cheek piece. The short, straight arquebus stock was not intended to be fired from the shoulder. It was held so that the side of the stock was in contact with the cheek, well clear of the shoulder, the recoil being taken by the arms. Early seventeenth-century arquebus stocks tended to widen slightly towards the butt and the cheek piece continued downwards, extending below the true line of the stock; the sixteenth-century stocks were parallel-sided and without the accentuated cheek piece. The lock plates on the earlier weapons are longer, the plate tending to become shorter by the seventeenth century, although retaining its angular outline.

Of the many types of wheellock arm evolved, none is of more importance than the pistol. Weapons capable of being used in one hand had appeared previously; a type of hand cannon known to the French as a petrinal, or petronel, had been used by cavalry in the mid-fifteenth century. The invention of the wheellock, however, made possible the first satisfactory one-hand gun. Since the wheellock pistol was far too heavy and cumbersome to be carried in a holster on the person, it was normally carried in holsters slung across the pommel of the saddle, and some authorities believe the term pistol was derived from 'pistallo' or 'pommel of the saddle', although others make reference to the town of Pistoia in Italy, and the fact that small gold coins called pistoles approximate to the calibre of the common pistol. One type of wheellock pistol known as a Reiter pistol or 'faustrohre' made its appearance during the middle of the sixteenth century. These pistols were carried by mounted mercenary troops known as Ritters or Reiters, and contemporary woodcuts show as many as four 18-in.-barrelled pistols with angled butts holstered at the saddle pommel. The Reiters, armed with these weapons, attacked in ranks, delivered their fire and retired to reload, an operation requiring some fifteen motions and not easily accomplished on horseback. The pistol was a short-range weapon carrying a bullet weighing twenty to the pound, the stock of which terminated in a large heavy ball which could be used as a club if the owner were surprised with an unloaded gun. Intermediate between pistol and wheellock arquebus is the 'carabin' or carbine, apparently of mid-sixteenth-century Spanish origin, and destined despite its unfortunately obscure beginnings to remain in the family of firearm descriptive terms to this day.

Due to the fantastic cost of the wheellock arm, coupled with the expense and difficulty of having it repaired in the event of failure, it is not surprising that only the most wealthy were able to afford them. Coupled with the invention of rifling already mentioned, breechloaders and multi-barrelled weapons carrying ornate decoration, often the work of highly specialized craftsmen, were made for the delectation of princes and to arm a few selected troops capable of using these costly weapons to advantage. As for the commonalty, the matchlock continued to serve for both military and sporting use until the close of the seventeenth century, when it was replaced by the flintlock, the matchlock being used by the British Army until 1690.

CHAPTER FOUR

Development of the flintlock

FOR sporting purposes the wheellock continued in use until well into the middle of the eighteenth century. However, a form of fire-arm with the effectiveness of the wheellock and the cheapness of the matchlock was destined to make its appearance and to hold the stage of history in one or another of its forms for well over two hundred years.

The new gunlock in its earliest and most rudimentary form appeared in the Netherlands during the second half of the sixteenth century and it is known today as the snaphaunce lock. Several delightful stories have come down to us through the years to account for this name, the most satisfactory of which is that the forward motion of the flint-bearing arm striking the 'steel' to produce sparks resembled a pecking farmyard fowl. To add credence to this story, many of the countries who used this lock and its later improved versions, refer to the pivoted flint-holding arm as the 'cock' and although today the pivoting firing mechanism of a revolver is known as a hammer, we still 'cock' the hammer when making ready to fire.

In addition to the cock, which was provided with vice-like jaws to hold the flint, a second swinging arm had at its free extremity a steel so arranged that when the cock, under influence of its main-spring, carried over the flint, it scraped minute red hot particles of the steel into the priming pan and so ignited the charge. Much of the internal mechanism of the snaphaunce was derived from the wheellock, particularly the separate steel and pan cover, the pan being opened immediately before discharge by a linkage connecting the pan cover with the tumbler or axle of the cock. The cock, which was mounted on the lock plate, had an extended 'tail' and when drawn back to 'full cock' it was kept in this position by a scear or catch which protruded through the lock plate under the influence of the scear spring. The separate battery (or steel) and pan cover together with the scear working through the lock plate and bearing directly on the cock are important visible signs which enable us to differentiate between the snaphaunce and later flintlock. The Dutch snaphaunce lock is easily recognizable by the extended tail to the cock and an extra piece of metal bolted on the outside of the lock

plate in front of the cock, the purpose of which was to act as a
buffer and prevent the flint and jaws of the cock from smashing
down into the priming pan. It is fortunate for the present-day
collector that, although the original Dutch locks are rare, due to

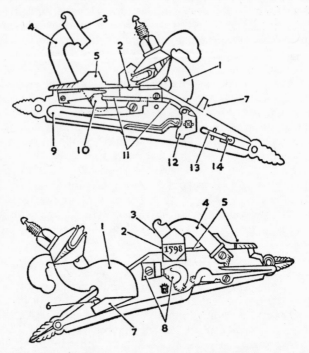

Figure 3. Late sixteenth-century Scottish snaphaunce lock. (1) Cock.
(2) Flashpan. (3) Steel or battery. (4) Battery arm. (5) Sliding pan
cover. (6) Scear nose protruding through the lockplate. (7) Tail of
the cock. (8) Buffer to arrest fall of the cock. (9) Mainspring.
(10) Pan, cover arm. (11) Lever connecting tumbler to pan cover arm.
(12) Tumbler. (13) Horizontal scear. (14) Rear arm of scear.

their use on relatively cheap arms which have long since been
relegated to the scrap heap, this type of lock had a wide geographical
distribution. Dutch type locks are to be found providing the means
of ignition on sixteenth-century Scottish long arms and pistols,
many of which have survived as examples of almost barbaric

splendour and which were the progenitors of a unique class of weapon which has excited the interest of firearms enthusiasts to the present day.

The Scandinavian or Baltic snaphaunce lock did not enjoy the same wide acceptance or the longevity of the Dutch snaphaunce, being confined to eastern Europe geographically and being replaced

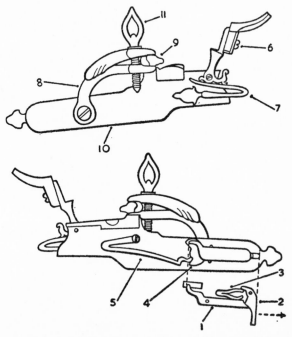

Figure 4. Scandinavian or 'Baltic' lock. Primary (1) and secondary (2) scears and a common scear spring (3) are used in a similar manner to that used on the wheellock. In this variant of the lock the scear bears on the tumbler (4) instead of passing through the lockplate (10) to engage on the tail of the cock (see Fig. 3). The mainspring (5) is attached to the lockplate by a screw and bears directly on to the tumbler. The cock (8) is provided with jaws which grip the flint (9) under pressure from the capstan screw (11). The unusual feature of the Baltic lock is the combined pan cover and steel (6) provision being made for the latter to be rotated through 90 degrees to provide a 'safety' position.

by the true flintlock in the mid-seventeenth century. As with the
Dutch lock, there is no safety or half-cock device, since the lock
can be rendered safe to carry when loaded and primed by pushing
the steel out of battery so that in the event of the trigger being
pressed or the cock snapping forward inadvertently, no discharge
can take place. An additional safety is provided by the fact that on
this lock the pan cover has to be opened by hand, there being no
internal linkage to provide automatic opening. Early forms of this

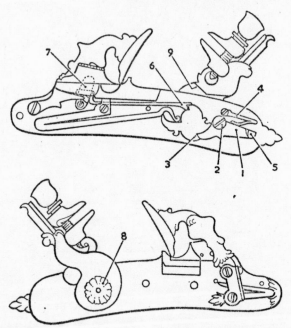

Figure 5. Late seventeenth-century Brescian snaphaunce lock. In
contrast to the locks previously described it will be seen that the
scear group pivots vertically about the pivot screw (2) the nose of
the scear (1) engaging in the 'bent' (3) cut in the tumbler. The tail
of the scear (5) is actuated by the trigger blade (not shown). In
common with Scottish locks the sliding pan cover is opened by
means of the lever (6) and the pan cover arm (7). The absence of a
buffer will be noticed, the fall of the cock being arrested by a
shoulder (9) which strikes the top edge of the lockplate. The tumbler
and spindle are formed in one piece, the separate cock being
attached by means of the cock screw (8).

lock used a horizontal scear passing through the lock plate to engage the tail of the cock. Later variants had a notched tumbler which engaged the scear, disengagement still being lateral. Even with this improvement of the mechanism a half-cock safety notch was still not provided and these later specimens have a unique additional safety feature in that the steel is attached to the arm in such a manner that it can be rotated through 90 degrees and so positively prevents the accidental contact of flint and steel.

Without doubt the most sophisticated of the snaphaunce locks was that made in Brescia in northern Italy. The development of this lock had been slightly delayed due to the Brescian gunsmiths' preoccupation with wheellocks of a type similar to those of south Germany but characterized by a particularly handsome form of pierced and chiselled steelwork, the artistry of which enhanced the later snaphaunce. In addition to the lavish care bestowed upon external ornamentation, in particular the figures chiselled in high relief, the internal mechanism showed considerable technical merit. Although retaining the separate pan and steel, the former being automatically opened, a wholly internal vertically operating scear was used acting on a tumbler formed as part of the axle whose squared end protruded through the lock plate for the reception of the separate cock. Instead of using the clumsy external buffer the inside of the cock was formed with a shoulder which bore against the lock plate, restricting forward movement. The Brescian snaphaunce continued to be used until the beginning of the eighteenth century when it was ousted by the true flintlock with combined battery and steel which had seen later but not dissimilar development. The continued use of the snaphaunce was no doubt due to the advantage gained from the absence of a safety device since the lock could be made safe when cocked and primed by pushing back the steel.

Who first combined the steel and pan cover and simplified the snaphaunce mechanism by eliminating the linkage necessary to open the pan prior to discharge may never be known. As with most discoveries, legends have arisen to account for this translation from an idea into a functioning mechanism and, in the case of the Spanish lock, credit is given to Simon Markhardt of Madrid. This Simon Markhardt was the son of Simon Markhardt, Senior, who with his brother Peter had been transplanted to Spain by that gun-loving monarch, Charles V, from their native Augsburg. Whilst it

B

is true to say that the German gunmaking brothers were responsible for the development of gunmaking in Spain, the foundations that they laid permitted Spanish gunmaking to rise to heights only surpassed by English makers in the late eighteenth century, it is

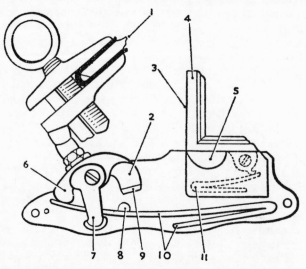

Figure 6. In the Spanish Miquelet lock the steel and pan cover are combined (4) the face of the steel (3) being deeply grooved. The combined steel and pan cover is firmly pressed against the pan (5) by means of the feather spring (11). The mainspring (10) is mounted externally on the lockplate and presses upwards against the heel of the cock (6). The cock is mounted on a pivot screw which is strengthened by a bridle (7), the toe of the cock terminating in a blade (2). In the Spanish lock the scear has two arms, both of which pass through the lockplate, the half-cock being formed as a stud (8) and the full-cock arm as a flat blade (9).

unlikely that Simon, Junior, illustrious though his parentage was, can be safely regarded as solely responsible for the invention and perfection of the miquelet. That he may have had some hand in the later perfection of the lock is undeniable and that the lock in spite of its rather odd appearance was extremely efficient, is attested to by its wide geographical distribution and undoubted longevity. The only variation on the basic Spanish theme was the Italian miquelet lock which appeared in southern Italy during the first half of the

seventeenth century. The Italian lock used the same combined pan
cover and steel as did the Spanish lock but of slightly different shape
and more reminiscent of the later French lock. An external mainspring (i.e. on the outside of the lock plate) was used, the difference
being that the mainspring of the Spanish lock bore on the heel of
the cock exerting its pressure upwards and on the Italian it bore

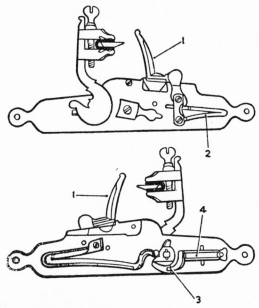

Figure 7. English 'Jacobean' lock, early seventeenth century.
The flashpan cover and steel are formed in one piece (1)
being held in the closed position by the external feather
spring (2). A horizontal scear (4) is used, the half-cock
position being obtained by the scear engaging the tumbler (3),
full-cock being obtained by the nose of the scear passing
through the lockplate and engaging the tail of the cock. In
this lock the cock and spindle are formed in one, the tumbler
being secured to the spindle by a pin.

downwards on the toe of the cock. Both types of lock used scears
which protruded through the lock plate. The Spanish had both
half- and full-cock scears in front of the cock, and the Italian had
the half-cock scear in front of the cock and the full-cock scear behind

the cock. With the combined pan cover and steel it was, of course, necessary to furnish half-cock safety devices so that the arm could be carried loaded and ready to fire without danger of inadvertent discharge.

During the early part of the seventeenth century, gunmakers in England had been perfecting a lock which in its earliest form closely resembled the Dutch snaphaunce, with the exception that it used the combined pan cover and steel of the miquelet lock. The English or Jacobean lock used the double scear moving laterally as did the wheellock, the nose of the scear passing through the lock plate and engaging the tail of the cock to hold it in the full-cock position. The cock was formed in one piece with an axle or shank which passed through the lock-plate and received the tumbler, this being pinned to the axle. The scear or releasing mechanism was entirely separate from the tumbler which had no half- or full-cock notches and merely acted as the bearing point for the mainspring. Since this lock used the combined flashpan and steel, some means of providing a safe position for the cock was necessary and this was achieved by the use of a dog catch mounted externally at the rear of the lock plate and engaging with a notch cut in the cock. Since the cock had no shoulder to arrest the forward movement, a buffer was provided as in the case of the Dutch snaphaunce. Development of the English lock was at first confined to the improvement of the scear group, the old wheellock two-piece scear being supplanted by a one-piece scear which still operated laterally and engaged the tail of the cock, but shortly afterwards a lock appeared which had half- and full-cock notches cut in the tumbler. Variants occur where the half-cock position is secured by means of a notched tumbler and the full-cock position by the use of the older method of engaging the tail of the scear. The presence of the half-cock notch on the tumbler made the dog catch superfluous but this additional form of safety persisted until the late seventeenth century. The later type of English lock which appeared in the 1640's used the vertical scear which was the main feature of the French lock and, with the demise of the dog catch, the English 'dog lock' loses its national identity. The vertical operating scear which characterized the French locks from the very beginning, eventually became the standard form in all north European countries and the true flintlock which had been developed in France by 1630 displayed all the features which were to remain unchanged, except for refinement, until the opening of the nineteenth century. In its fully developed form, the true flintlock had an entirely internal mechanism (with the exception of the feather spring) and a vertically operating scear with half- and full-cock notches on the tumbler. The tumbler was now formed as part of the axle which protruded through the lock plate to receive the cock which now had a shoulder on the inner side designed to arrest the fall against the top of the lock plate instead of the clumsier buffer, used by the snaphaunce and early English dog lock.

The end of the seventeenth century saw the pre-eminence of the French gunmaker and it is perhaps no coincidence that this supremacy corresponded with the political dominance of France under Louis XIV. The splendours of Versailles provoked universal imitation and stimulated all branches of the luxurious arts and it was appropriate that when 'le Roi Soleil' wished to make a gift to Charles XI, King of Sweden, the foremost gunsmiths of Paris were commissioned to produce a splendid series of firearms which were no doubt highly esteemed by their royal recipient. The technical perfection of the French lock, coupled with the increasing use of fine engraved ornamentation of the steel parts, resulted in a demand for the products of Parisian makers, a demand accentuated by the publication of gunmakers' pattern books, the widespread distribution of which established the traditions of Parisian style and decoration so firmly that they were emulated throughout Europe.

CHAPTER FIVE

Military flintlocks

NOT all the gunmakers of France were preoccupied with the creation of ornate and costly firearms. The manufacture of firearms as an industry had been established during the reign of Francis I in 1535 at St Étienne and it was here in 1669 that the first Government Armoury was set up. Further armouries were built at Tulle, Maubege and Charleville. Not the least of the problems which faced those responsible for supplying muskets for the armies of France was that of standardization; not only was it desirable that the bore of the weapon be of standard size but following the introduction of the socket bayonet at the close of the seventeenth century the outside diameter of the barrel, at least at the muzzle, if of standard size, would greatly facilitate the issue and fitting of bayonets so that they would not fall off when used. Apart from these considerations, the question of repair and renovation would be greatly simplified if an armourer could draw on standardized spares. France was, therefore, far ahead of other countries when in 1717 all the armouries were instructed to follow the measurements of a standard pattern and adhere, as closely as possible, to a uniform method of manufacture.

The French musket of 1717 can be regarded as the first true French musket and was of ·69 calibre, with a barrel length of 47 in., the barrel being fastened to the stock by four sliding pins, the overall length being 5 ft. $2\frac{1}{2}$ in. These muskets were of course fitted with the true flintlock lock, France being equally far-sighted in this respect since Louis XIV had been the first monarch to arm his troops with flintlocks in appreciable numbers as far back as 1660. Various modifications on the original pattern appeared throughout the eighteenth century. In 1728 the barrel was secured to the stock by three barrel bands instead of by pins which eased considerably the task of dismantling. Both of these models had been provided with wooden ramrods and, in 1746, an improved version was issued fitted with an iron ramrod. Further minor changes took place in 1754 when the sling swivels which had formerly been fitted on the left side of the musket were placed underneath and the weight of the musket was standardized at $10\frac{1}{4}$ lb.

The first major changes in design took place in 1763, when the length of the new musket was reduced to 4 ft. $11\frac{7}{8}$ in., though the bore remained at ·69 calibre. The barrel bands were now secured by spring clips instead of by friction and the cock was of the reinforced pattern. The model of 1763 was perhaps the most important of the

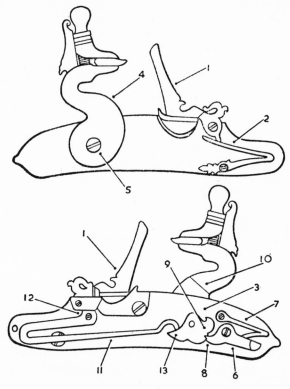

Figure 8. In the true flintlock, the steel and pan cover are formed in one piece (1) and an external feather spring (2) is used. The tumbler and spindle are also formed in one, the cock (4) being attached by a screw (5). The scear (6) moves vertically and is pressed against the tumbler by the scear spring (7) and is shown engaged in the half cock bent (8) immediately behind which is the full cock bent (9). The fall of the cock is arrested by a shoulder (10) which abuts against the lockplate. The mainspring (11) is attached to the lock-plate by a screw (12) and the long arm presses down against the tumbler at (13).

French muskets since not only did it see service during the American Revolution (when well over 100,000 muskets were imported from France by the American Congress) but it was of such excellent design that it was copied by the armouries at Springfield and Harper's Ferry when the first United States musket was put into production in 1795.

In 1777 a new model musket appeared being manufactured in five different types. Infantry, dragoon, navy or marine, artillery and cavalry musketoon patterns were produced. Design changes, which were the last of major consequence during the eighteenth century, included the provision of a corrosion-proof flashpan of brass, finger ridges on the trigger guard tang and a modified butt stock incorporating a cheek piece on the left side.

The later models are easily recognized since they bear the model dates on the barrel tang and the armoury marks are to be found on the lock plates. Muskets bearing the armoury mark Charleville or St Étienne were carried by the soldiers of the French Revolution and, by 1792, these muskets and men had gone far beyond the achievements of Louis XIV and everywhere stood on foreign soil.

Throughout the eighteenth century, constantly thwarting the designs of the French kings or the later Republic and finally of the Emperor Napoleon, were the British, armed with as many variants of the Brown Bess musket as there were models of the French musket. In order to trace the ancestry of 'Brown Bess' we must return to the Commonwealth period (1649–60) when the infantry were armed with the Service matchlock musket, the barrel of which was required to be of the regulation length of 4 ft. with a calibre of ·78 in. At the Restoration large numbers of these muskets lately in the hands of the Cromwellian armies were issued to the small standing army formed during the reign of King Charles II (1660–85). The standard calibre of No. 12 bore (·78 in.) was again specified in 1673 but barrels shorter than the original 4 ft. specified in 1631 were now permitted. Although the mass of the infantry continued to be armed with the matchlock musket until the end of the seventeenth century, in 1678 a return was made to the practice of arming selected companies or regiments with flintlocks. Mention is often made in contemporary accounts of the Civil War of troops being armed with firelocks or snaphaunces. The first of these were the North British Fusiliers who, as the name implies, were armed with the flintlock 'Fusil', a lighter weapon than the musket tracing its ancestry back to the light fowling pieces imported from Europe at the Restoration.

A typical fusil of the James II period would have a barrel 31 in. in length and would be of 16 bore (·662 in.) with the wood of the stock extending to the muzzle. The barrel would not be round in section throughout its entire length, but would be octagonal at the breech, a practice also found in the matchlock muskets of the period. Distinguishing marks would consist of the Royal Cipher 'J 2 R' surmounted by a crown on the lock plate together with the maker's name and 'J R' with the rose-and-crown used as a Government mark on the barrel.

The ignominious flight of James II to the Continent after his failure to coerce England into surrendering its constitution and its religion, resulted in Parliament's invitation to Prince William of Orange, husband of James's daughter Mary, and their joint acceptance, after some quibbling, of the throne of England. The army was poorly equipped to deal with troubles at home, let alone those which were brewing on the Continent, and William III hastened to complete the conversion from matchlock to flintlock with as much speed as possible in order to meet the threat from Louis XIV and his cousin, the exiled James. The regular contractors in London were unable to meet the vastly increased demand for arms needed for troops raised for service in Ireland and Flanders and large quantities of flintlock muskets were obtained from Holland and other sources not under the embargo of the French king.

William's plea for additional sources of arms did not go unheeded for Sir Richard Newdigate, Member of Parliament for Warwickshire, sent sample muskets to his Birmingham constituents; muskets to this pattern were completed to the Board of Ordnance's satisfaction and the first contract was completed in 1690. The standard flintlock musket of this period, many specimens of which have survived, bears on the lock plate the cipher 'W R' and the crown of King William and has a barrel some 46 in. in length. The rather crudely made flintlock was readily interchangeable with the older matchlock and is attached to the stock by three screws bearing directly upon the woodwork. With the exception of the butt plate, which was of brass, all other metal fittings were of iron, blackened or browned as was the case with the fusils made during the reign of James II.

This period, at the turn of the century, is of importance since it saw the establishment of the flintlock as the standard service arm, the development of the gun trade in Birmingham where, unfettered by corporate restrictions, it was able to grow without limitation and finally, the appearance of the celebrated Queen Anne musket, better known by the soldiers' affectionate nickname, 'Brown Bess'.

This weapon was introduced to the British Service by John Churchill, Duke of Marlborough, the ablest general England had known, to aid him in his designs against France. Intended to replace the motley collection of flintlock weapons introduced by William III, Brown Bess was issued in ever-increasing numbers and saw service during the Battle of Blenheim (1704) and Ramillies (1706) and by the time of the Peace of Utrecht (1713), it was firmly established as the standard infantry musket. Weighing ten pounds, Brown Bess had a 46-in.-long barrel of No. 11 bore (·75 in.) and was loaded with a 13½-or 14-bore ball, the windage allowed ensuring quick and easy loading. The barrel was round in section throughout its length and 'browned' by a process of artificial oxidation. The walnut stock, which extended almost to the muzzle, was stained brown and provided with heavy brass mounts consisting of a set of four ramrod pipes, trigger guard, a side plate to protect the wood under the 'side nails' which held the lock in place and an escutcheon or shield at the small of the stock behind the breech. The butt was shod with a heavy brass butt plate, the tang of which extended along the comb of the stock. Brown Bess combined a certain elegance with strength and in no other component was this better seen than in the lock.

One of the major problems of the flintlock had been the difficulty of ensuring positive operation due to the use of an extremely strong mainspring acting on an axle one end of which was unsupported. In use, the bearing of the axle in the lock plate tended to become worn and the increased friction which resulted from the canting of the axle impeded the action of the lock with the risk of misfires. The improved lock fitted to Brown Bess incorporated an extra bearing or 'bridle' which supported the axle or tumbler and ensured correct alignment of both the tumbler and scear. A similar bridle, which was forged in one piece with the flashpan, provided much-needed extra support to the pan cover screw and ensured that the pan cover and steel would snap open with the minimum of frictional resistance.

Instead of the earlier plug bayonet, a socket bayonet with a triangular blade 17 in. long was issued. As the name implies, the blade was provided with a steel sleeve or socket having internal dimensions such that it would fit over the end of the barrel. The bayonet when not in use was carried in a scabbard supported by a crossbelt passing over the right shoulder and balanced by a similar belt over the left shoulder from which hung the cartridge pouch.

The word cartridge is derived from the French 'cartouche' and was originally used to designate a wooden box containing up to 300 musket balls. Later the term came to mean a paper container

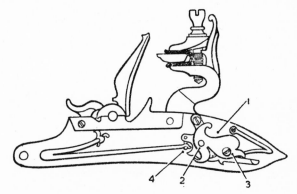

Figure 9. The fitting of a bridle (1) supported the tumbler (2) against the pressure of the mainspring and also affords a second bearing for the scear pivot screw (3). The fitting of a steel link or swivel (4) connecting the bifurcated end of the mainspring to the tumbler eliminated yet another cause of friction.

holding the correct charge of powder and by the time the use of cartridges had become more general the practice of using the same container for the bullet as well became established. Cartridges were first used for the charging of pistols or carbines by the cavalry. The difficulty of handling powder flasks, priming flasks and bullet bags as well as a pistol on horseback need not be stressed. Military insistence that the prime desiderata was speed of fire hastened the more widespread use of cartridges and, following the introduction of the military flintlock, the advantages of using made-up paper cartridges, easily and conveniently carried by the soldier in a leather cartridge box or pouch, became obvious.

The cartridges used with Brown Bess contained within a paper tube, the ends of which were closed by a few turns of pack thread, 123 grains of black powder and a bullet weighing 490 grains. It has been mentioned that the use of cartridges speeded up the rate of fire and in order to maintain this advantage it was essential that the bullet could be easily inserted into the barrel and rammed home on the powder. In spite of the improvements that had taken place in the manufacture of gunpowder, considerable fouling still occurred, and to avoid jamming the ball half-way down the barrel the diameter of the bullet was made about one twentieth of an inch less than that of the bore. In loading the musket, the soldier bit off the end of the paper tube farthest away from the bullet and squeezed a pinch of powder into the priming pan, the rest was poured down the barrel, the bullet with its attached paper as wadding being rammed home with the ramrod on top of the powder. Although these operations take some time to describe, they could be carried out by trained and disciplined soldiers as many as six times a minute, this rate being halved when deliberate shooting was called for.

This insistence on extreme rate of fire, coupled with excessive and often variable windage and powder charge (the amount used from the cartridge to prime the pan would vary considerably under stress), effectively eliminated any pretensions towards accuracy, although when loaded with a tight-fitting ball and an accurately measured charge, a well-made musket in good condition could give quite a good account of itself at 100 yards. The view that accuracy was of little account was held quite justifiably by the military authorities of the period, since in warfare which involved whole battalions moving in close formation, it mattered little if the bullet hit the man intended providing it hit the man next to him.

The service musket continued in use throughout the eighteenth century with but slight modification. During the reigns of Queen Anne and George I, the lock plates had been marked only with the name of the gunsmith supplying them and under George II the lock plate had been additionally marked with the crown and 'G R' and the barrel had been reduced from 46 to 42 in. In the reign of George III, the wooden ramrod had been replaced by one of iron and about 1770 Brown Bess had her barrel further shortened to 39 in. It was during the reign of the third George that the word Tower first appeared on the lock plate in place of the individual gunsmith's mark. This was probably due to a change in the method of purchasing arms by the Government, components being bought under contract and stored in the Tower Armouries preparatory to being issued to outworkers in the London gunmaking district of the Minories for stocking and assembly.

The House of Hanover was well served by Brown Bess. She was the equal, and in many ways the superior, of the rival muskets used against her during the 130 years of her 'reign'. This superiority, coupled with slavish adherence of the military mind to the tactics of yesteryear, resulted in the continued use of flintlock weapons by the military until a programme of conversion to percussion was started in 1840. This does not mean that attempts were not made in the preceding years to overthrow Brown Bess, since in 1747 Benjamin Robins, a distinguished mathematician, had presented his by now famous paper entitled 'Observations of the Nature and Advantage of Rifled Barrel Pieces' which for the first time clearly and concisely outlined the scientific principles of rifling.

The adoption of a rifled weapon in place of the inaccurate smooth bore musket was never even remotely considered until 1775 when the policies of Lord North, backed by his master George III, resulted in the outbreak of violence in the American Colonies. The small regular army of Britain, amounting to some 40,000 men scattered all over the world, was obviously unable to cope with such a large-scale rebellion and following the battles of Lexington and Bunker's Hill, the rejection of offers of a peaceful settlement by the Colonists by George III made it obvious that the struggle was to be fought to the bitter end. In the open, where parade ground training in rapid volley fire was of advantage, the British beat the Colonials, but much of the fighting was in wooded and broken country where the advantage was with the Americans due to their infinitely better marksmanship. Strenuous efforts were made by both sides to remedy deficiencies; Washington straining to raise and drill a regular army of the European pattern, the British seeking riflemen for employment in skirmishing warfare.

Added to the problem of fighting a war at the end of a 3,000-mile supply line, Britain, following the surrender of General Burgoyne at Saratoga in 1777, had to contend with the desire of France to avenge old defeats suffered during the Seven Years War. France acknowledged the independence of America and, in 1778, declared war on Britain. Spain, eager to win back Gibraltar and Minorca, followed suit in 1779, and Holland was added to the formidable list of Britain's enemies in the following year. Following a series of reverses on a world-wide scale, making the possibility of a break-up of the British Empire seem imminent, two great victories saved it: the crushing defeat of the French fleet in the West Indies by Admiral Rodney and the relief of Gibraltar—which had been under siege for three years by a combined Spanish and French force. Political changes in Britain made it possible for overtures of peace to be made to the Americans, which were accepted in 1783, much to the disgust of their French allies, as it left them committed to a war which was no longer going in their favour. Finally, by the Treaty of Versailles, the disastrous 'War of American Independence' was ended.

Apart from the birth of a new nation, the United States of America, the conflict had seen the first effective military use of the rifle, two of which were prominent enough to merit description. The first was the legendary American Long Rifle, more popularly known as the Kentucky Rifle and more accurately known as the Pennsylvanian Rifle. By 1735, the immigrant German gunsmiths who had introduced rifles of the continental pattern to the frontiersmen had refined and adapted their weapons to suit American conditions. The calibre had been reduced from ·75 in. to between ·40 and ·55 in. so as to conserve lead. The barrel length, on the other hand, was increased by several inches in order to extract the most from the powder charge. The long distances which had to be covered on foot demanded a light rifle and the eighteen or so pounds of the German ancestor had by 1760 been cut to an easily portable nine or ten. In place of the sliding patchbox cover found on German rifles dating back to wheellock days, the Pennsylvanian Rifle had a hinged cover usually of brass and often lavishly, though crudely, ornamented. The purpose of this box, let in to the right-hand side of the stock, was to contain a supply of circular greased leather or linen patches, the diameter of which was at least three times larger than the bore of the rifle. The patch, greased side downwards, was placed on the muzzle of the rifle and the bullet laid in the middle, patch and ball being forced down the barrel with the ramrod. This method of loading, which appears to date back to the earliest days of the rifle, considerably eased the lot of the rifleman, allowing him to load with speed and ease, contrary to the retrograde contemporary practice of using a tight-fitting ball and starting this in the rifling with the aid of a mallet. The use of the greased patch, coupled with the then small calibre, permitted muzzle velocities in the order of

1,500 feet/second, which ensured a flat trajectory and a greatly increased accurate and usable range. Against these rifles and their skilled owners, now commemorated in song and legend, the British had one native rifle, the Ferguson, which armed one small body of troops, the Light Infantry Company of the 71st Highlanders. In charge of this Company was a skilled rifleman, Captain Patrick Ferguson, who was able, such being the custom of the period, to arm his men as he wished providing that the weapons purchased were in no way inferior to the standard Tower 'Brown Bess' muskets. Should any officer be so rash as to purchase arms superior to the standard Government musket, this was quite in order providing that the extra expense was met out of that officer's own pocket. In addition to being a keen advocate of the rifle as a military weapon, an attitude greatly at variance with established military thought, Ferguson had seen military service in Germany from 1758 to 1763, being commissioned as an officer at the early age of fourteen in the Royal North British Dragoons (Scots Greys). Whether or not his ideas 'for improvements to breechloading rifles' were entirely his own or the result of having seen weapons of this nature during his continental service, may never be known, but it is a fact that in 1775 his company had been armed with a breechloading, rifled flintlock of his own design and had been thoroughly trained in its use. This rifle was by no means the first breechloader since breech-loading weapons had been made and used with some measure of success from the earliest days of firearms. Furthermore, the 'plug' system which was used was not a new idea but the Ferguson possessed two features of the greatest importance. The first was that the opening by which the rifle was loaded was on top of the breech end of the barrel and behind the charge to be introduced. The second was that the screwed breech plug was so constructed that it was not removable during the loading cycle and could not be inadvertently lost or wrongly reassembled.

To load the rifle, the trigger guard was given a complete turn and the guard, being in effect the handle of the screw plug, thus lowered the screw plug by some seven-eighths of an inch so that the top of the plug was now level with the lower surface of the barrel. The bullet was then dropped into the barrel and, providing that the muzzle was depressed, it would roll forward until stopped by the lands of the rifling. The powder charge was then introduced and the breech closed by rotating the trigger guard in the opposite

direction. It was still necessary to prime the flashpan separately
but all these operations could be carried out with surprising speed.

To demonstrate the efficiency of his rifle, Ferguson gave a
demonstration at Woolwich in 1776 and he was able to fire at the
rate of six rounds per minute, hitting a target at 200 yards con-
sistently. As a further demonstration of his rifle's effectiveness, it
was loaded and fired at the rate of four rounds per minute whilst
on the move. Despite these conclusive proofs of the rifle's undoubted merits (and further proof was forthcoming during the time
the rifle was in use in America), official apathy and the inventor's
death at the Battle of Kings Mountain in South Carolina in 1780
was the end of the Ferguson rifle in the military service.

The lessons learned by the British, although apparently forgotten
during the uneasy peace that followed the end of the American
War in 1783, were not entirely ignored, for during the Napoleonic
War (1803–14) the exploits of the 95th Regiment, or the Rifle
Brigade, during the Peninsular Campaign fully established the
value of the rifle as a military weapon.

CHAPTER SIX

Sporting flintlocks and the blunderbuss

IN order to follow the evolution of the sporting gun, it is necessary to retrace our steps to the mid-seventeenth century and return once more to France, where we have seen that the true flintlock was developed. A major factor in the rapid spread of this new means of ignition was the great interest being shown in the sport of shooting flying game as opposed to the practice of stalking birds on the ground or on water. For the business of fowling, a gun with a heavy charge to slay as many birds as possible with one shot was ideal and this practice has persisted until the present day. The difficulties of hitting a flying bird with a matchlock are immense due to the delay between pulling the trigger and the gun actually firing. The importation of the new sport from Italy into France at the beginning of the seventeenth century must have resulted in the gunmakers endeavouring by every means to devise a mechanism which would reduce the ignition time to a minimum and make it possible for the gun to be carried safely and yet brought into action with the greatest speed and facility. The development of the half-cock notch on the tumbler meant that the gun could be carried with the pan cover closed and the attached steel in position ready for firing, whilst the cock held securely in the safety or half-cock notch needed but one motion of the hand to bring it back to full cock in readiness to fire.

Although retaining traces of their wheellock ancestry in the angular outline of the lock plate, and the yet unformed shape of the cock, the early French and western European flintlock, by virtue of their relative cheapness, aided the propagation of this new pastime for the leisured classes. Many of these weapons found their way to England at the Restoration with the return of the exiled Royalists. This influx of foreign weapons stimulated the English gunmaker to produce work of comparable merit and by the time Queen Anne was on the throne (1702–14) the English gunmaker had well and truly started on the path that was, by the end of the century, to lead to a peak of such mechanical and functional perfection the like of which had never been seen before and, regrettably, is unlikely to be seen again.

The Queen Anne sporting gun was not markedly dissimilar to the Service musket in being a long-barrelled weapon stocked to the muzzle. The butt has a pronounced drop which would make it rather difficult to shoot rising game and French influence can be seen in the curved line of the comb and the knob on the heel of the butt plate which also appears to be of continental origin. The surface of the lock plate will be found to be rounded in a similar manner to that of the military musket, this style remaining in fashion until the second half of the century, long after the flat plate had been introduced by continental makers.

The barrel would, in all probability, be round in section throughout its length, the octagonal form at the breech doubtless being sacrificed for the sake of lightness, although the top of the barrel is likely to be flat for some distance from the breech as an aid to sighting. A modified form of the octagonal breech returned to popularity during the middle of the century and with the exception of double-barrel guns retained its firm hold until well into the nineteenth century. The metal furniture was likely to be of silver, brass or iron, dependent on the quality of the weapon, and the use of silver wire inlay work on the stock is a feature of early eighteenth-century sporting guns and pistols. Whilst this form of decoration was carried out in most cases with typical English restraint—unlike the productions of many continental craftsmen where the gun was merely the vehicle for exotic decoration—the fashion did not last long and, apart from a few ebullient examples, the tendency towards the end of the century was to depend on purity of form rather than applied decoration.

In contrast to the veritable stagnation of continental design and style, the eighteenth-century English sporting gun underwent many changes which improved its efficiency as a killing weapon. Decoration by the end of the century had been subordinated to mechanical perfection and whilst a study of decoration is of interest and an aid to dating a weapon, familiarity can only be gained by the comparison of actual weapons or photographs and it is with the refinement of lockwork and barrel that we must now concern ourselves.

Reference has already been made to the adoption of the flashpan cover bridle and the bridle fitted to provide an extra bearing for the tumbler and, by 1740, all well-made locks were provided with these refinements. The bridle lock, as it was called, was by reason of these improvements far quicker in operation due to the reduction of friction. In the search to provide their clients with even faster locks, two other sources of friction were investigated by the late eighteenth-century gunmaker and improvements made, one of which is still in use on certain types of lock to this day.

Nothing aided the certainty with which the flintlock would 'give fire' more than the promptness with which the pan cover snapped open when the steel was struck by the flint. Although the extra

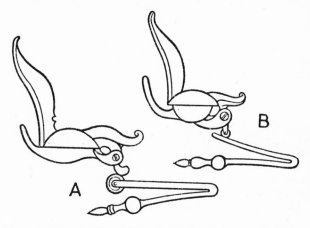

Figure 10. A valuable addition to the flintlock was the fitting of a small roller bearing to the feather spring (A) or alternatively, to the pan cover (B). By 1790 even locks of moderate quality used one of these variations to improve lock time and reduce the frequency of misfires.

bearing provided by the pan cover bridle ensured the correct alignment of the various components, the smooth operation of the steel and pan cover was hindered by friction which occurred between the feather spring and the spur of the pan cover. The cure for this problem was to fit a small roller bearing at the end of the feather spring and, less frequently, this bearing was fitted to the pan cover spur, the roller bearing against the tail of the feather spring.

The other point in the lock at which, at its best, sliding friction took place and at its worst a scraping abrasion occurred, was where the tail of the mainspring contacted the tumbler. In the improved lock, the tumbler was provided with a 'T'-shaped swivel mating with a slot in the tail of the mainspring. This excellent arrangement survived the transition from flint to percussion and is still being used on present-day sidelocks and certain revolvers.

It must not be supposed that all classes of firearms were fitted with these improvements which in any event are found but rarely until about 1780. A large class of general purpose 'self-defence' weapons were produced in the second half of the eighteenth century which lacked the finish and refinement of the sporting gun but which were nevertheless sound and well-constructed weapons. Amongst this range of weapons several can be singled out for specific mention and in progression of size, the first to be considered is the travelling or coaching carbine.

Usually made with 24-in. barrels of approximately No. 16 bore, the coaching carbine was built on the lines of the fowling piece. Equally capable of hitting a rabbit or pheasant at close quarters or discouraging the unwelcome attention of 'a knight of the road', the coaching carbine can be distinguished by the apparently bell-mouthed muzzle which, on closer examination, will be found to be only slightly larger at the muzzle internally, the bell mouthed effect being due to a heavier weight of metal and the barrel wall thickness being increased at the muzzle. As was common with weapons intended to be used in all weathers, the barrels were often made of brass, the corrosion-resistant qualities of this metal being more suitable for general use.

Equally renowned in story and legend was the blunderbuss, which was made in a variety of styles throughout the eighteenth century and into the nineteenth. The true coaching blunderbuss of the early eighteenth century usually had a barrel of 12 to 14 in. in length flaring gently towards the muzzle and lacking in any reinforce rings. Towards the close of the century the barrel length had increased to between 15 and 17 in., the flare being more pronounced at the muzzle and usually confined between two reinforce rings. The reversion to the shorter barrel of the Queen Anne period started about 1780 and continued to the demise of this class of weapon, additional features of this later period being an octagonal breech and, as if the thunderous discharge at close quarters was not sufficient to deter the aggressor, many of the coaching style of blunderbuss were fitted with spring bayonets, usually mounted on top of the barrel and arranged so as to fold back on a hinge, the tip being secured in the folded position by a catch at the breech. The release of the catch permitted the bayonet to swing over under the influence of a spring with a most intimidating 'whoosh', it being locked automatically in the forward position ready for use.

To add somewhat to the confusion among the larger type of blunderbuss, the Turnpike or Boat Gun had an equally long life but did not suffer the same vagaries of fashion as did the blunderbuss proper. These guns, with heavy 25-in. barrels up to 1 in. bore, could be fired from the shoulder although the weight, often exceeding 16 lb., made it advisable to rest the gun over some suitable object. For Naval use the large Blunderbuss or Boat Gun was highly esteemed and for this duty many were fitted with a swivel and used for boarding operations or for defence by merchant ships.

One of the problems affecting all types of flintlock had been the occurrence of misfires in wet weather. By 1750 successful attempts had been made to mitigate the results of water affecting the priming in the flash pan by recessing the edge of the pan and later by reducing the size of the pan itself so that it could be divorced from the 'flash shield' which, on the earlier locks, had by virtue of its design, directed raindrops into the pan. Although these refinements were noisily acclaimed by their late eighteenth-century inventors as being the cure for misfires caused by rain, they were but palliatives, since no modifications could prevent the priming becoming damp in heavy rain or mist and this regrettable tendency of the flintlock to misfire under these conditions had to be endured by the all-weather shooter until the detonating principle had been established.

Dedication to perfection was not confined to the lockwork alone. Refinement of the lock had resulted in improved and faster ignition and attention was now directed towards improving the combustion of the charge. Until the mid-eighteenth century, the breech end of the barrel had been closed by a simple screwed plug, a small hole in the side of the barrel serving to convey the fire from the priming to the main charge. Since only one 'corner' of the charge was ignited initially, poor combustion resulted and, in an endeavour to overcome this defect, a device known as the 'chamber plug' had been introduced. Instead of closing the breech with a flat-faced plug, a rather longer plug was fitted, having a centrally disposed hole or chamber, the bottom of which was connected to the touch hole by a narrow passage known as the ante-chamber. By this means, the spurt of flame resulting from the ignition of the powder passed directly into the centre of the main charge with consequently improved combustion resulting in a faster pressure rise and increased

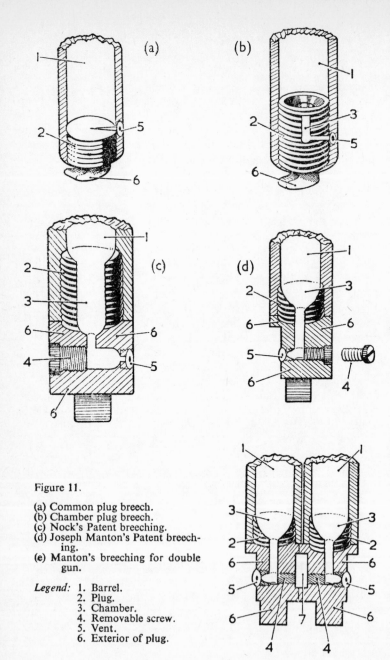

Figure 11.

(a) Common plug breech.
(b) Chamber plug breech.
(c) Nock's Patent breeching.
(d) Joseph Manton's Patent breeching.
(e) Manton's breeching for double
gun.

Legend: 1. Barrel.
        2. Plug.
        3. Chamber.
        4. Removable screw.
        5. Vent.
        6. Exterior of plug.

velocity of the missile. Apart from the improved ballistics, the faster burning rate of the powder meant that the barrels could be made shorter and metal saved at the muzzle end could be transferred to the breech to provide better balance to the weapon and give increased strength where it was most needed. Regrettably, as with most improvements, there was a price to pay, this being an increase in the time interval between pulling the trigger and the discharge of the gun. Although this may appear paradoxical, it was due to the time taken to traverse the ante-chamber and although combustion was greatly improved, it took perceptibly longer for this to happen.

The gunmakers' annoyance can well be imagined. The benefits to be gained from the adoption of the chamber breech were far too important to be ignored but it was of little use to expend meticulous care in the fabrication of a lightning fast lock if the speed obtained was 'to be lost in the ante-chamber'. Henry Nock, a celebrated London gunsmith (1772–1806), solved the problem by the invention of his patent breech, protection for which was gained in his Patent No. 1598, granted 25th April, 1787. The secret of the new breeching lay in providing a larger ante-chamber separated from the priming in the pan by a thin gold or platinum plug with a central touch hole. The ante-chamber was connected with the main breech-chamber by a narrow opening so that on ignition the powder in the ante-chamber, burning with great rapidity due to its confinement, issued as a jet into the main chamber and ensured immediate and total ignition of the charge.

By this means, total ignition time had been reduced to a minimum and the efficient combustion of the powder dispensed with the necessity for lengthy barrels. Whilst the importance of speed of ignition should not be minimized, the reduction in barrel length had important consequences. Further efforts had now to be directed towards improvements in barrel boring and, at last, the double-barrelled shotgun became a practical and desirable weapon ideally suited for game shooting.

The double-barrelled gun finally sealed the fate of the traditional full-stocked weapon with the wood extending to the muzzle. A trend towards a half-stocked weapon had appeared slightly earlier, doubtless due to desire to improve portability when the barrel was removed from the stock. The reluctance with which accepted custom was discarded can be gauged by the appearance of a few single-barrel guns, the full-length fore ends of which were cut through several inches in front of the lock plate, the severed ends being suitably mounted so as not to detract from the appearance of the gun. This permitted the conservative owner to use a full-stocked weapon, the fore end of which could be dismounted to reduce the overall length of the dismantled gun.

The single-barrel gun was by no means ousted by the double, being preferred for long shots at wildfowl where the larger calibre and longer barrel were of advantage, since the tendency was for the doubles to be made in the smaller calibres of 20, 16 and 14 bore, the single-barrel guns being of 12, 10 and larger bores. It was the double gun, however, that displayed those qualities of ultimate perfection which raised their makers to the pinnacle of their craft. It is still difficult to choose the best half-dozen British makers of sporting guns active at the turn of the century but, without doubt, the name that stands supreme is that of Joseph Manton, the younger and more famous of the Manton brothers, of whom it can be said that he established the form and style of the sporting double shotgun so truly that his influence is still seen to this day.

CHAPTER SEVEN

Flintlock pistols

THE pistol has been somewhat neglected in our chronicle since we left it in the hands of the Reiters nearly 300 years ago. The duelling pistol of the early nineteenth century was as far removed from its 'dog lock' ancestor of the English Civil War as was the Manton double flintlock shotgun from the Jacobean fowling piece. The first truly English pistol was the screw or cannon-barrelled pistol which would seem to be of native origin and was mainly restricted in its distribution to Great Britain. Pistols such as these made their appearance during the Civil War and are distinctive in that they are breechloaders. The barrel could be unscrewed from the fixed breech chamber, which contained the charge; provision being made for the reception of a ball in the form of a semi-circular depression in front of the powder chamber. The barrel was then screwed back on to the breech and after priming the pistol was ready to fire. This system of loading was slower than the common muzzle-loader but it permitted the use of a tightly fitting bullet which did not have to be forced down the barrel consequently making the pistol shoot harder and with more accuracy.

The English gunmaker was able to produce accurate, well-constructed pistols of plain design but by this time the continental maker had achieved a mastery of wood and metal such as to merit the acclaim of the world. The mid-seventeenth century provincial French and Belgian makers were producing pistols of charming simplicity of line and form, and ivory-stocked pistols, the butts of which terminated in sculptured militaristic heads were being made by the Dutch, particularly in Maastricht. The use of eccentric decorative media for pistol stocks appears to be a feature of the seventeenth century for another class of pistol made distinctive by the use of tortoiseshell veneer on the stocks made a brief appearance during the mid-seventeenth century.

Although less exotic, but by no means less interesting, are the Scottish pistols, the manufacture of which extended from the end of the sixteenth until the mid-nineteenth century. Scottish pistols are distinguished not only by the ornamentation and unique styling but by the fact that in all but the earliest specimens (and the most rare) the stocks were of either steel or brass. The reason for this

57

unusual choice of material for the stock remains unknown. Steel had been used for German pistol stocks in the sixteenth century and there is good reason to suppose that the earliest Scottish pistols were patterned after the German or western European design. Why the Scottish craftsman continued to use steel for stocking is a mystery since, as already mentioned, wooden stocks did appear but this material went out of fashion in the early seventeenth century. The rigid adherence to metal for parts elsewhere made from wood, the retention of distinctive characteristics and ornamentation, form for the collector part of the charm and mystery of this unique class of weapon.

As can be realized, pistols made during such an extended period were liable to change and the classification of Scottish pistols can be roughly made into the type of lock used, and the style of the butt. No wheellocks of Scottish manufacture have ever been authenticated, the earliest known pistols being fitted with the snaphaunce type of lock. These pistols are found with both wooden and brass stocks, rarely steel. The earliest have a flared 'fish tail' termination to the butt. Slightly later are pistols with the globular or lemon-shaped butt, reminiscent of contemporary continental wheellock pistols. During the middle of the sixteenth century an improved form of snaphaunce lock appeared, the scear acting on the tumbler instead of the tail of the cock. Pistols fitted with the improved snaphaunce lock will be found with either a heart-shaped butt or a scroll or ramshorn type butt. The scroll or ramshorn style lasted well into the nineteenth century suffering degradation into a crude copy at the hands of the Birmingham makers during the eighteenth century.

Scottish pistols fitted with flintlocks first appeared during the mid-seventeenth century and continued until the end of the flint period during the first quarter of the nineteenth century. One other form of butt appeared in the mid-eighteenth century, this being similar to the conventional contemporary wooden-stocked pistol, this type of butt being known as the lobe butt.

With the exception of the English copyists of the eighteenth and nineteenth centuries, the makers of Scottish pistols appear to be mainly confined to the Scottish Lowlands and the east coast. One locality famous for its gunsmiths who specialized in the national arm was the small village of Doune, situated a few miles north of Stirling. The rise of the village of Doune from a small agricultural community to the virtual centre of a highly specialized craft industry is perhaps due more to one man, Thomas Caddell, than to a combination of economic circumstances. Caddell came to Doune in 1646 and *The Statistical Account of Scotland of 1798* had this to say of him: 'This famous tradesman possessed of the most profound genius, and an inquisitive mind; and, though a man of no education, and remote from every means of instruction in the mechanical arts, his study and persevering exertions brought his work to so high a degree of perfection, that no pistol made in Britain excelled, or perhaps equalled, those of his making either for sureness, strength or beauty.' Those not of Scottish birth or ancestry might quarrel with these words, but argue how you will, Caddell founded a dynasty of craftsmen, the Caddells, the Murdochs, the Campbells and the Christies, who laboured throughout the 150 years that was the life of the Doune pistol.

Economic circumstances may not have had a hand in the birth of this industry but they certainly had a hand—and a crushing hand at that—in its death. The same *Statistical Account of 1798* records the epitaph of the village of gunmakers: 'There is now,' it states, 'very little demand for Doune pistols owing to the low price of pistols made in England.'

Two distinct English copies of the late Scottish pistols will be found, the first an extremely crude imitation made in Birmingham, this being issued to non-commissioned officers and men of the Highland Regiments about 1740 and an equally crude version stocked in brass which was apparently a later issue and in use until 1789 when the practice of issuing pistols ceased.

The Birmingham and London makers also supplied pistols to officers which were worn until the mid-nineteenth century and whilst of better quality the 'costume' pistol worn as an accessory to ceremonial Highland dress until 1850 cannot be confused with the true Scottish pistol. Most of them bear Birmingham proof marks and whilst many carry Scottish names and addresses these were not the makers but the vendors or, at most, the finishers of the pistol.

Scotland was not alone in the possession of such a centre of craftsmanship. The gunmakers of Brescia in northern Italy were world famous for the splendour of their steel-chiselling and, in addition to the export of finished pistols, there was a healthy trade in barrels for those who could not afford the complete pistol. Since it is usual to find the marks of both barrel and lock-maker on

Brescian pistols, the craftsman responsible can often be identified and the most famous was Lazarino Cominazzo. The Cominazzo family were barrel-makers and such was the renown of their products that other barrel-makers fraudulently inscribed the Cominazzo signature on their wares.

In southern and central Italy were produced pistols, the ornamentation of which makes even the extravagant Brescian style seem restrained. These pistols are distinctive by reason of the use of the Miquelet or Mediterranean lock instead of the Brescian snaphaunce and whilst their northern brethren later adopted the French lock the gunsmiths of Naples and Florence remained true to the Italian variant of the Spanish or Miquelet lock.

The originators of the Miquelet lock produced many pistols of high quality, both in Madrid and the town of Ripoll. Whereas the Madrid pistols in general followed European styling, the majority being fitted with the Spanish lock, those made in Ripoll were as distinctive as Scottish pistols and unlike any others made elsewhere in Spain. They are characterized by having an extremely short stock terminating in a ball butt, the stock being covered with iron, brass or silver inlays. As might be expected, the locks fitted to these stocks are of the Miquelet type but are unique in that the inside of the jaws of the cock instead of being roughened by random punch marks to grip the packing for the flint have a formalized design which serves the same purpose but with a measure of artistic merit.

On the other side of the Pyrenees, in the home of the true flintlock, the gunmakers of Paris had by the end of the eighteenth century risen to the most fantastic heights of artistic embellishment and whilst it is admitted that many of their products were never intended to be fired in anger, it is unlikely that their accuracy or handling qualities would leave much to be desired. Of the many first-class French masters, Nicholas Noel Boutet, 'Directeur Artiste à Versailles,' is perhaps pre-eminent. Under his direction the gunsmiths of the Arms Factory at Versailles produced pistols for both Louis XVI and Napoleon and it is some measure of his stature that he was able to survive the bloodbath of the Revolution when so many others who enjoyed Royal favour perished under the guillotine. His later work during the Empire was of the highest artistic merit; many of the pistols being presentation pieces for political or military figures of other nations.

Unlike the French, English gunmakers had not enjoyed any degree of fame outside the British Isles during the seventeenth and the first three-quarters of the eighteenth centuries. Many of the foremost gunmakers of the seventeenth century were French or German immigrants. Their presence raised the quality of English work but it was not long before foreign craftsmen came to Britain because it had become the centre of true gunmaking as opposed to the manufacture of arms as a basis for applied art. The screw-barrel pistol has already been mentioned as a form of pistol mainly developed and used in England and this type of pistol retained its popularity until well into the eighteenth century. The screw- or cannon-barrel pistol, is particularly associated with the reign of Queen Anne and differs from its seventeenth-century predecessors in that the lock plate and breech chamber were made as one forging eliminating the vestigal wooden fore-end required when the previous plan was in use. By 1750 this trend towards simplification had crystallized in the development of the cannon-barrel box lock. Pistols made after this pattern had the flashpan placed on top of the barrel with its associated cover and steel, the cock and action being mounted in the centre between two lock plates, forming a 'box' and thus accounting for the descriptive name.

The Service pistol at the time of Queen Anne was the long horse pistol with a barrel of No. 20 bore, 14 in. in length. During the reigns of the first two Georges the barrel length was shortened to 12 in. This tendency continued during the reign of George III, the barrel being reduced to 9 in. and the calibre increased to No. 16 or 'carbine bore'. Throughout the eighteenth century, better quality pistols had been produced to meet the demand for a superior pistol for officers' use which would take the Service cartridge. There was no regulation regarding the type of pistol worn and whilst it was of advantage to carry a weapon which would take issue ammunition, almost every type of pistol must have at one time or another been taken on active service, many of the more unsuitable types no doubt being gifts from well-meaning but unknowledgeable friends or relations.

The mid-eighteenth century saw the rise to prominence of multi-barrelled pistols, the earliest type being the side-by-side box lock. 'Cannon barrels' were again used, each barrel being provided with a separate flashpan with a common pan cover and steel. Repetitive fire was secured by providing one of the pans (usually the left) with a 'cut-off' or sliding plate actuated by a spring-loaded catch mounted on the side of the lock plate. The 'safety' was provided by pushing forward the trigger guard which locks the cock and trigger in the half-cock position. Removal of the barrels for loading was achieved by placing a plug in the muzzle, this plug engaging in a star-shaped series of grooves cut in the mouth of the barrel. The ring tool provided to unscrew single barrels could not be used on double- or multi-barrelled guns since the barrels were close together.

More popular were the 'tap action' multi-barrel pistols which dispensed with the sliding cut-off, substituting a rotating plug mounted transversely under the pan. The most common tap action pistols are those with two 'over and under' barrels and the later and more common types were fitted with plain parallel barrels. Screw-barrel pistols with three and four barrels were made during the last quarter of the eighteenth century and the versatile tap action was even used in a modified form on pistols arranged to fire super-imposed loads.

Although of high quality and possessed of considerable technical merit, it was not the screw-barrel pistol or the ingenious multi-shot pistol that raised the prestige of the English gunmaker to new and unsurpassed heights during the last years of the eighteenth century. This distinction belongs to the duelling pistol, which first appeared as a distinctive type about 1770 and which influenced the type and design of the better quality military pistol as well as holster and pocket weapons. The earliest duelling pistols are light and extremely graceful weapons with long barrels often up to 12 in. in length. Due to the high favour in which barrels of Spanish manufacture were held, many early pistols will be found fitted with barrels of the Spanish style, i.e. octagonal at the breech and round towards the muzzle, and some were even made with barrels of Spanish manufacture. The general practice, which continued throughout the period with few exceptions, was towards the use of barrels which were octagonal in section throughout their entire length. The stocks of the early duellers were often without any checkering but the sides of the butt were flattened and the fore-end, which was provided with the usual ramrod pipes, was continued up to the muzzle, some makers capping the end of the fore-end with horn.

One of the early makers of duelling pistols was Twigg, his work being characterized by the use of coarse stock checkering having an added decoration of dots in the panels. A whole series of distinctive checkering patterns arose, finally evolving into the fine checkering which is standard today on good-quality firearms. Many of the makers of duelling pistols were also renowned for their sporting guns. Alone amongst the eighteenth-century makers as a specialist in duelling pistols was Wogdon, and his early pistols were unusual in having barrels which were round in section with a flat filed along the top in the plane of sight. Although Wogdon shortly conformed to the prevalent fashion of the octagonal barrel, his original form (referred to as 'French style') will often be found on pistols made much later and in particular those of Irish origin by, for example, Rigby of Dublin.

The closing years of the century were a period of intense competition for the élite gunmakers and their ranks were soon increased, many of the newcomers having learned their skills at the work-benches of the early masters. One of the most famous was John Manton (not to be confused with his brother Joseph Manton, mentioned in the previous chapter), who had been foreman of Twigg's before establishing his own business in Dover Street, London, around 1780. Durs Egg was yet another gunmaker whose duelling pistols are justly prized by the collector. Egg was of Swiss origin and, following experience in both Switzerland and Paris, he set up shop in London in 1772, quickly rising to the peak of his profession. Pistols by this maker are characterized by their extreme neatness and he was one of those who adopted a characteristic pattern of checkering which makes his pistols easily recognizable. In addition to making pistols of superb quality, Egg probably made most of the Ferguson breech-loading rifles and, in addition, manu-factured a flintlock breechloader of his own design as well as dis-charging a number of Government contracts for flintlock muskets, rifles and carbines. Another all-round maker of first-quality pistols was Hervey Walklate Mortimer, whose shop was at No. 89 Fleet Street, London. Some Mortimer pistols have far more curve on the inside of the butt than was usually the practice and give the appear-ance of an abbreviated walking stick handle.

These then were the men whose names were borne on pistols, the like of which had never been seen before. Instead of the obvious outward display of decoration, their work was possessed of the more indefinable qualities that can only be described by the terms 'feel', 'balance', 'coming up', etc., none of which are adequate to describe feeling of 'rightness' that the pistol shot of today experiences when he handles and perhaps shoots one of these weapons. Such qualities did not appear by accident, they were the result of a painstaking empiricism, a constant search for the ultimate in perfection. Pistols made by the élite of the gunmaking craft became a natural extension of the shooting arm and, with practice, would come up to bear on the target every time.

Such perfection in any product was bound to create a cult and pistols patterned after the dueller but never intended by the purchaser for such a sinister purpose became available and serve to confuse the collector of today. At the turn of the century, the long-barrelled full-stocked dueller went out of fashion and was gradually replaced by a heavier, and in the opinion of many, a clumsier weapon. This trend was to a great extent fostered by Joseph Manton, the more flamboyant of the Manton brothers, and pistols by Joe Manton are often found with what was known as secret rifling. From an inspection of the muzzle, the barrel gave the impression of being smooth bored but in fact it was cut with shallow grooves which produced deadly accuracy. Manton also reduced the bore, which, coupled with larger external barrel dimensions, resulted in an extremely heavy barrel, the purpose of which was to correct the tendency to shoot high, a defect inherent in the style of shooting as then practised.

Several other features will be found on duelling/target type pistols, the most important being the provision of the hair or set trigger. This, as we have already seen, had been a feature of the earlier wheellocks and was so arranged by means of a system of spring-loaded levers to strike a sharp light blow upon the tail of the scear and so release the tumbler. The set triggers fitted to duelling pistols are of the single-trigger type, being 'set' by pushing forward the trigger initially. Provision was made for the adjustment of the trigger pull so that the lightest possible pressure could release the mechanism. The use of the set trigger on pistols and rifles resulted in further modification of the lock by the addition of the 'detent' which was a small triangular plate pivoted on the tumbler designed to prevent the scear from catching in the half-cock notch or bent and checking the fall of the cock. The spur trigger guard was another feature which appeared towards the end of the eighteenth century, this being a further attempt to correct high shooting. With the early spur trigger there can be little doubt that the spur was gripped with the second finger. Later pistols were fitted with modified guards

Sixteenth century
German matchlock
with chased iron
barrel and stock
inlaid with ivory and
mother-of-pearl.

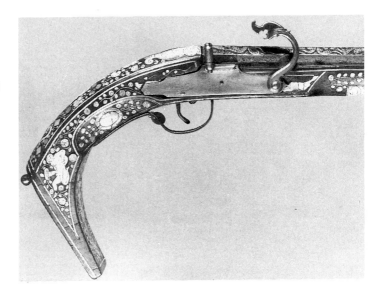

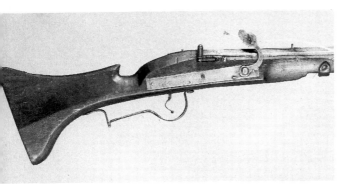

English matchlock
musket, early
seventeenth century.

The distinctive lock
mechanism and stock
of the East German
'teschinke'. Inlaid
with ivory and
mother-of-pearl, this
gun dates from the
mid-seventeenth
century.

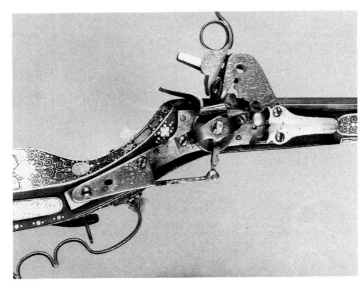

PLATE 2

The elaborately
inlaid stock of a mi
seventeenth centur
German wheellock

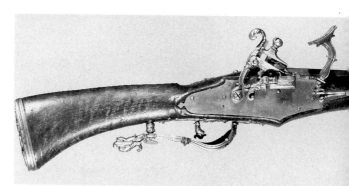

An Italian
snaphaunce gun of
the late seventeenth
century, with carved
steel mounts.

Pair of all-brass ear
snaphaunce pistols
signed AG and date
1634 on the barrel.
Note the flattened
lemon butt, rose,
strap and foliage
decoration
(Anthropological
Museum, Universi
of Aberdeen).

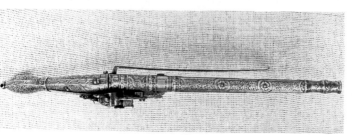

intlock pistols are
 expensive for me
 collect' is a
mplaint often
ard. You can
ways make your
n, just as James
orne did. He is not
unmaker, he is a
sel fitter!

The Ferguson
breech-loading
flintlock rifle. This
splendid example is
by Durs Egg of
London.

superb example of
e work of Boutet.
is French flintlock
stol is cased with all
cessories and
cludes a spare
rrel (Glasgow Art
lleries).

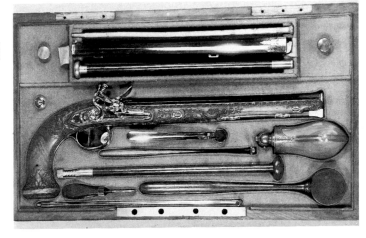

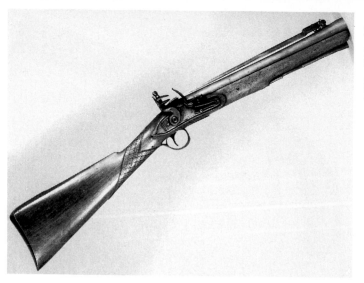

PLATE 4

Flintlock
blunderbuss by
Jones, fitted with a
folding spring
bayonet.

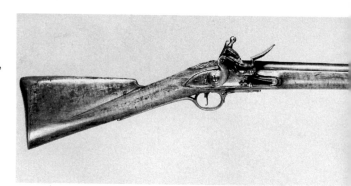

The famous 'Brown
Bess' flintlock
musket. This
example, dated 1759,
is by Galton of
London.

Very occasionally o
encounters a
'sleeper'. This is an
unused Purdey
double rifle, No.
3845, made in 1843
A 14 bore muzzle
loader, it cost £5
thirty years ago!

uble percussion
zzle loading rifle
MacLaughlan of
inburgh. This was
uired in 'as new'
ndition and is an
cellent example of
work done by the
nmakers of the
ottish Capital.

Percussion breech-
loading sporting rifle
by Durs Egg. The
barrel is shown in the
forward position to
permit the removal of
the detachable
breech chamber.

r of percussion
gle barrel pistols,
ed in the
ntinental manner
Lebeda of Prague.

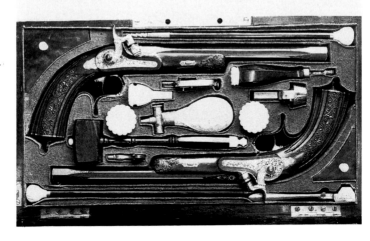

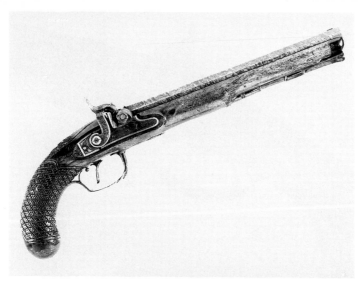

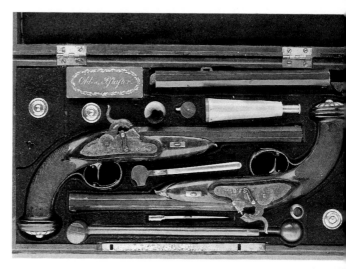

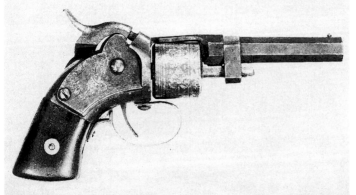

PLATE 6

This was originally made as a flintlock duelling pistol by the renowned Durs Egg. It was later converted to percussion but this is a conversion, not a forgery or fake. The conversion was carried out with the same skill as that employed by the maker and it is a highly desirable pistol.

Pair of percussion pistols by F. Ulrich of Stuttgart, with rifled micro groove barrels, complete in case with all accessories.

Percussion revolver by Massachusetts Arms Co. This pistol is fitted with a 'tape' primer.

This is the original
muzzle loading
percussion Colt
model of 1861 with
the 'creeping
rammer' under the
barrel. Also shown
are the bullet mould
and the turnscrew
and nipple wrench
combined.

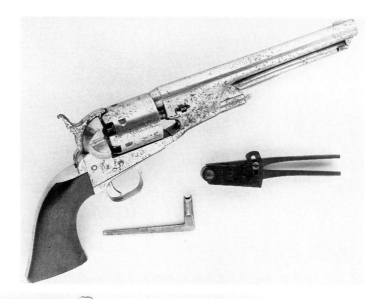

Deane, Adams,
Deane percussion
revolver, cased, with
accessories.

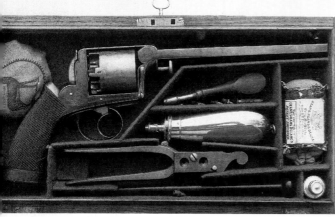

Six-chambered
percussion revolving
rifle by Holland and
Holland. Note the
wooden pillar for the
left hand in front of
the trigger guard.
(Courtesy Holland
and Holland.)

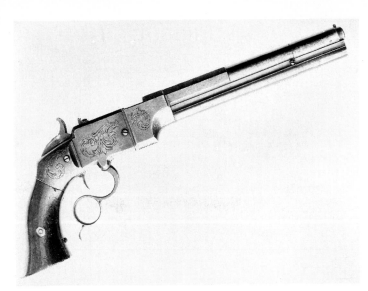

PLATE 8

Smith and Wesson
No. 2 lever action
magazine pistol.

The famous Gibbs,
Farquharson,
Metford sporting
rifle. The action was
patented by
Farquharson, the
rifling by Metford
and the maker was
George Gibbs of
Bristol.

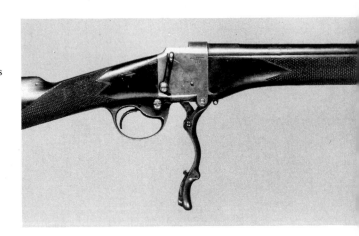

The Austrian
'Heeren' action was
used by several
British gunmakers
for their single shot
sporting rifles. This
example is by
Thomas Bland of
London.

which were incurved and permitted the user to adopt the normal full hold on the butt.

In the regrettable absence of any authoritative information on the practice adopted with set triggers and spur guards, it is difficult to make any positive assertions, and on the question of which finger gripped what, some divergence of opinion exists. Often associated with the spur trigger guard and set trigger is the saw-handled butt, which, as the name implies, resembled the handle of a wood saw in that part of the butt was continued rearward over the web of the thumb to form a point. Invariably the form of the butt of the saw-handled pistol was of the continental type, terminating in an oval, flat cut-off pommel of larger dimensions than the stock section proper and the combination of these two features made it imperative that the pistol be fitted to the user's hand.

A decided improvement was the appearance of the hook or false breech. Prior to this invention the breech plug had been formed into a tang which secured the rear of the barrel to the stock. This meant that in order to remove the barrel the long screw passing through the tang into the trigger plate had to be taken out. The improvement consisted of providing a false breech with a rectangular hole into which fitted the hooked termination of the breech plug. Thus, by removing the barrel pin the barrel could be lifted out of the stock by an upward unhooking motion. This method was of greater value when adapted to double-barrel guns, considerably simplifying breeching arrangements.

The increased weight of metal in the barrel was one of the features of the later period. Pistols are often fitted with the half-length stock terminating in a horn fore-end cap and the use of a rib became necessary to carry the ramrod. The addition of this rib emphasized the massive proportions of the barrel, particularly when combined with the saw-handled butt. The overall effect was that of a ponderous target weapon instead of the earlier snap shooting duelling pistol. Other detail changes occurred, many of which are found in other types of arms of the period. The graceful 'swan-necked' cock met with competition from two foreign styles of fashion, the double-necked cock which was a logical development to reduce the risk of fracture and the 'French' cock. This was in the form of a reversed 'C' and in a modified form continued to be used into the percussion period. Simplification of the ornateside-plate has already been referred to and, in the duelling pistol, finally

C

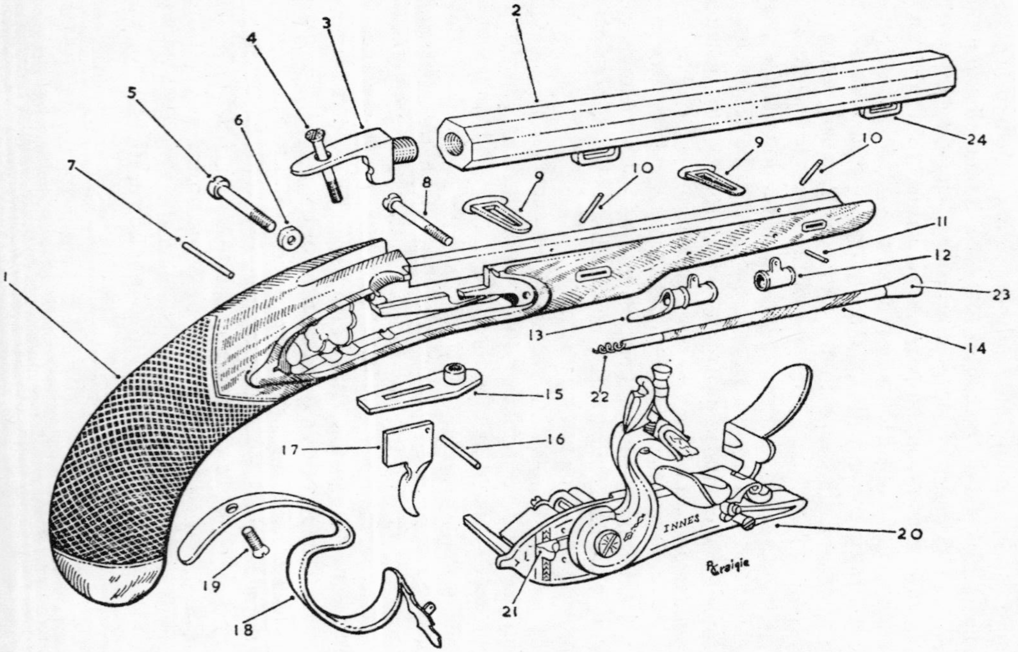

Figure 12. Flintlock Pistol. *Circa* 1800.

1. Stock.
2. Barrel.
3. Breechplug.
4. Screw passing through barrel tang and stock and into trigger plate (15).
5. Rear sidenail to secure lock to stock.
6. Sidenail cup.
7. Trigger guard pin.
8. Front sidenail.
9. Barrel pins.
10. Barrel pin retaining pins.
11. Front ramrod pipe pin.
12. Front ramrod pipe.
13. Rear ramrod pipe.
14. Ramrod.
15. Trigger plate.
16. Trigger hinge pin.
17. Trigger.
18. Trigger guard.
19. Guard fixing screw.
20. Lock.
21. Safety bolt.
22. Ramrod worm.
23. Horntip for ramrod.
24. Barrel loops.

resulted in the disappearance of the sideplate altogether. The screws or 'sidenails' which secured the lock plate to the stock were separated from the wood by recessed washers or cups often lightly engraved but in essence purely functional. It became the practice to dispense with the forward sidenail; the front of the lock plate being retained by means of a buried screw head and a small hook on the lock plate.

Despite the changes in style and fashion which occurred throughout the period of the duelling pistol, several features remained common. These were, with few exceptions, the avoidance of lavish ornamentation (the metal parts being of steel either browned or blued) and superlative quality of both workmanship and materials, the source of which was unashamedly proclaimed on both barrel and lock plate. As befitted an expensive arm of precision, a suitable case was provided of oak or Honduras mahogany lined throughout with Irish baize. English cases were invariably provided with straight partitions for the two pistols, powder flask, bullet mould, etc., whereas the French were addicted to cases with contoured recesses. The practice of providing cases for best quality pistols became the accepted form and the brightly coloured woollen bags formerly used for protection became part of history.

CHAPTER EIGHT

Forsyth and the percussion principle

THE nineteenth century is potentially the most interesting and rewarding period as far as the present-day gun collector is concerned. Three systems are represented, the flint, the percussion and the breechloading cartridge weapon, all within the compass of one hundred years.

The skill and craftsmanship of the British gunmaker had put him in a position of unchallenged supremacy at the beginning of the last century and fully able to tackle the problems which were to confront him during the transitional period which lay ahead. That a new spirit of adventure was abroad is best exemplified by the fact that that bastion of the ultimate in conservatism, the Army, had at last realized that the peculiar virtues of the rifle were worth exploiting. Following the formation of an Experimental Corps, the Corps of Riflemen was formally gazetted in October 1800. In 1801, under Lord Nelson, the Rifle Corps made its name at the Battle of Copenhagen and it subsequently fought with valour and distinction throughout the Peninsular War and at Waterloo as 'The 95th' or 'The Rifle Regiment'. The rifle selected to arm the Rifle Regiment and which was later issued to certain rifle companies of other regiments was the Baker. This rifle, made by Ezekiel Baker of Whitechapel, had been selected by the Board of Ordnance following a trial at Woolwich on the 4th February 1800 before a Committee of Field Officers. The Baker rifle finally approved by the Committee, in the face of strong competition and not without some contention, had a 30-in. barrel with a bore of ·615 in. (No. 20 bore) rifled with seven grooves making one quarter of a turn in 30 in. The stock was much straighter than the contemporary musket and, unlike the musket, the fore-end was carried to within less than an inch from the muzzle. The use of the socket bayonet on the musket required several inches of unstocked barrel, whereas the Baker was provided with a bayonet standard attached to the right-hand side of the barrel arranged to take a brass-hilted triangular bayonet. This was later changed to a sword pattern bayonet with a 24-in. single-edged blade. In the stock of the rifle, at the right-hand side of the butt, was a recess with a hinged brass lid known as the patch box (some Baker pattern rifles will be found without a patch box) and to assist the rifleman in taking steady aim, a cheek piece was furnished on the left-hand side of the butt stock and a heavy scroll type brass trigger guard was fitted. Not all the Baker rifles were made by Ezekiel Baker, many were assembled by the Government after 1804, others were made by the celebrated Birmingham gunmaking family of Ketland.

Whilst it is true to say that the breechloading rifle, in spite of its obvious military advantages, was not seriously considered by the authorities, a number of breechloading rifles of the screwplug type were made for sporting use. During the early eighteen hundreds, Durs Egg appeared to have met with a measure of success with a breechloading smooth-bore cavalry carbine using a rear pivoting breech chamber. In an endeavour to overcome the inherent fault of most of the early breechloading systems, the escape of gas from the joint between breech chamber and barrel, the 'interrupted screw' principle was used by the Sartoris breechloader which appeared in 1817. Although by this system the barrel was securely locked to the breech chamber by means of segmented external threads on the chamber engaging with similar thread cut internally in the barrel (locking being achieved by means of a sliding and rotating barrel), its own virtues were its downfall, since the accumulation of powder residues following several discharges caused difficulty in getting the breech to close.

Whilst for military purposes the breechloader made little headway during the tail-end of the flint period, the system in one or another of its various forms had a considerable following amongst sportsmen. The 'standard' pattern of sporting rifle was a half-stocked muzzle-loader with an octagonal barrel underneath, which was fitted with a rib to carry the ramrod pipes in a manner similar to the later flintlock pistol already discussed.

A feature common to many of the flintlock sporting rifles was the provision of a patch box. The Baker military rifle, as we have seen, was fitted with a patch box having a hinged lid. Most of the sporting rifles used circular steel hinged snap open lids, often engraved with sporting scenes, whilst some were fitted with patch boxes having sliding lids, this feature being of German origin and dating back to wheellock days. The lock work and furniture differed little from smooth bore practice and a few double rifles were made, although by no means in as great a quantity as the smooth bore double shotgun. Set triggers of either the double or single type were often fitted and, if so fitted, the lock would be modified by the use of the detent on the tumbler to eliminate any possibility of the scear catching in the half-cock bent or notch. It would perhaps have seemed to the early nineteenth-century user of either rifle, shotgun or pistol, that little could be done to improve the perfection of his weapons but, despite the earnest endeavours of the gunmaking giants of the day, there were faults in the flint system of ignition which no amount of ingenuity could overcome. The liability to misfire due to rain or damp had never been entirely cured, even on the most expensive guns. The patent breech, whilst a considerable improvement, left much to be desired since leakage through the touch-hole or vent reduced the propulsive force of the burning gases. Added to these annoyances was the need to adjust and change flints and the necessity of carrying a separate flask for priming and, lastly, the priming operation itself.

In an era which had already been productive of so much gun-making genius, it is remarkable that it was not a Baker, Mortimer or Manton who discovered the means whereby all these ills were cured but a Scottish minister who was not only deeply interested in chemistry and mechanics but who spent much of his time out with his gun taking toll of the local wildfowl. It had been known for some time that certain chemical substances such as the fulminates of mercury and silver could be made to explode if placed on a hard surface and struck with a hammer. It was due to the Rev. Alexander John Forsyth, Minister of Belhelvie, Aberdeenshire, that the properties of the fulminating compounds were harnessed as a means of igniting gunpowder in firearms. The first patent covering the new gun lock was taken out on the 4th of July 1807 and in 1808 manufacture of the 'fulminating lock' was undertaken at No. 10 Piccadilly, London, under the name Forsyth & Company. Since the manufacture of the new lock required the greatest precision, Forsyth secured the services of James Purdey, who had been the pupil of Joseph Manton and who was to found the famous gunmaking firm of James Purdey & Sons. The lock which was manufactured at the new premises and which came to be known as the Magazine Lock, was very expensive, costing more than a complete Birmingham-made flint gun. That this expense was to some extent justified there can be little doubt, since the greatest care had to be taken to fit the various parts of the mechanism together so as to avoid the possibility of the entire contents of the magazine from exploding. This magazine, which held the supply of detonating compound at one end, was provided with a striker at the other, the whole pivoting about a cylindrical plug one end of which was attached to the breech of the gun. By rotating the magazine a small quantity of compound

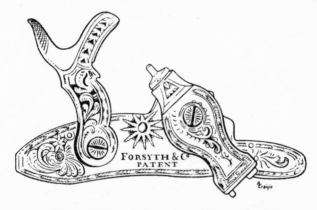

Figure 13. Forsyth 'Scent Bottle' fulminating lock.

was deposited in a small cavity provided on the upper surface of the plug; this cavity or pan was connected by means of a pin-hole vent to a powder channel in the centre of the plug. When the magazine is returned to its original position the spring-loaded striker is opposite the pan and when the hammer of the lock falls, the striker is driven into the powder so detonating it. This type of lock, known to collectors as the 'scent bottle', had all the essential features so long desired. The priming was kept dry and the gun was 'quicker', the game shot having to greatly revise his ideas of how much lead was necessary on flying game.

Some four thousand guns, pistols and detached locks for converting flintlock weapons were made by Forsyth & Company until the expiration of the Forsyth Patent in 1821. There were many who were disinclined to make the change from flint to detonator on the grounds that although it shot quicker than the flint gun, it did not shoot as hard. Interest in the new system was sufficiently high to warrant many attempts by gunmakers to evade the master patent; the most important of which was the second of Joseph Manton's percussion locks (the first, a pellet lock which involved the removal of the strikers after each shot, had not been a success). The Manton percussion tube lock utilized a thin copper tube filled with mercury fulminate, one end of which was inserted in the vent of the gun, the other resting on an anvil provided with a spring clip. When struck with the hammer, the compound exploded with great force, the flash being directed straight into the powder chamber. Similar locks were also made by Charles Lancaster and Westley Richards, although the latter was detonated by a blow on the end, the tube being inserted into a large-bore nipple. In addition to the use of loose fulminating powder contained in magazines, and separate charges contained in tubes, percussion pellets made from a mixture of potassium chlorate, sulphur and charcoal bound with gum arabic appeared. The failure of Manton's pellet lock has already been recorded but others were made by Westley Richards and Charles Moore, neither of which proved to be particularly successful. One of the advantages of the pill or pellet lock was that the user was to a great extent independent of gunsmiths since in case of dire necessity he could risk the chance of blowing himself up by compounding the detonating mixture himself, and equipment to enable him to carry out the necessary operations was occasionally provided with cased pill-lock arms.

As with many of the inventions already described, the one which was to displace all forms of pill, pellet and tube lock had obscure beginnings. The origins of the percussion cap and nipple have never been satisfactorily explained. Amongst those who have claimed the distinction of inventing the humble but all-conquering cap, Joshua Shaw appears to be the most likely candidate. Unfortunately, Shaw is somewhat of a mysterious figure and all that is definitely known about him is that he lived for a time in Philadelphia, U.S.A. Patents were taken out by him in America but, since these early patents are no longer available, his claims cannot be thoroughly substantiated. According to W. W. Greener in his book, *The Gun and Its Development*—'In England the inventors of the copper cap were as numerous as the gunmakers—nearly every armourer, London and provincial, laying claim to the invention'.

Irrespective of whether or not it was Joshua Shaw, the emigrant Englishman in America, the celebrated writer Colonel Peter Hawker, or one of the London gunmakers who was responsible for the percussion cap, this little copper cap shaped like a small thimble about an eighth of an inch in depth and diameter, quickly revolutionized all forms of shooting and swept away flint and other forms of detonator so that by 1840 the percussion principle reigned supreme. One of the reasons for the success of the new system was its simplicity. The cap, containing a small quantity of fulminate, was placed over a hollow nipple which communicated with the propellant charge. The cock, or as it was later to be called, the hammer, terminated in a recessed shielded depression which when the trigger was pulled swept downward on to the cap, igniting the fulminate and then the charge.

Once the new system was established, a considerable number of flint guns were converted to percussion and, until the availability of the copper cap became practically universal, a number of dual flint and percussion guns were made. Most of the conversions from flint to percussion were carried out during the 1820–30 period, the most satisfactory method being to fit an entirely new breeching. This was, of course, expensive and on common guns the practice was to remove the flashpan, pan cover, feather spring and cock from the lock, replacing the flint cock with a percussion hammer and filling in all screw holes. The vent or touch hole was drilled out, the gold or platinum vent (if fitted) being removed and a short hollow steel plug fitted with a nipple screwed into place.

The transition from flint to percussion was not entirely painless and in the case of shotguns a revision in the method of barrel boring was found to be necessary to ensure that the shooting performance with respect to important matters such as pattern, recoil, etc., did not deteriorate. In the case of rifles, considerable work was necessary to determine the optimum degree of twist of the rifling and since this was related to other factors such as muzzle velocity, trajectory and, what was most important, accuracy, considerable argument as to the respective merits of fast or slow twist ensued.

As in the case of both rifles and shotguns, the percussion principle was applied to pistols, conversions from flint being carried out in the manner already described. Various types of patent ignition systems were 'sold' by the London and provincial makers and the potential pistol purchaser was no doubt as easily swayed by the often extravagant claims of the maker as was the user of the shotgun or rifle. The day of the tube, pellet or pill was as brief in the pistol field as it had been in the long-gun field and the cheap and efficient percussion cap again won the day.

When the pistol was used for self-defence the natural desire of the owner to have more than one shot available without reloading was catered for by the appearance of increasing numbers of multi-barrelled weapons. The simplicity of the percussion cap system was particularly advantageous when applied to multi-shot pistols and two types gained particular favour. The first was the over and under pistol provided with two locks, the right-hand lock firing the upper barrel, the left, the lower. Pistols of this type will invariably be found with back-action locks, the mainspring being placed behind the tumbler instead of in front. The chief virtue of this lock was that the mechanism could be placed in the stock behind the barrel and, for a time, such locks were often fitted to shotguns but this fashion tended to weaken the woodwork at this point. The second important class of pistol was the 'turn over' which had the two barrels placed one over the other and pivoted on a central axis. Following the discharge of the upper barrel, they could be rotated so as to bring the nipple with its attached cap under the hammer fall. Whilst slower in action than the previous type, it had the advantage that only one lock was required. The value, both practical and commercial, of producing a pistol capable of four consecutive discharges was soon realized and four-barrelled turn-over pistols fitted with double locks made a brief appearance during the latter end of the first half of the nineteenth century.

A type of pistol which survived the transition from flint to percussion and which was made in large numbers, was the screw-barrelled single-shot pistol. Usually provided with box locks and folding triggers, many will be found bearing the names of celebrated London makers but the tell-tale evidence of the Birmingham Proof Mark indicates their true origin, and the rapid deterioration in the quality of these arms after 1850 was the precursor to the influx of cheap and degenerate continental weapons which can scarcely be dignified by the name of pistol.

As if to atone in some measure for this debasement of their art the French, German and Belgian makers continued to produce duelling and target pistols of extremely high quality. Such pistols were made up in cased pairs, provision being made in the case for ramrods, bullet moulds, powder flasks and other implements necessary to load and fire the pistol. The barrels of these pistols, whilst preserving the traditional octagonal form are often fluted and rifled. The grips on many of these pistols were also fluted, the basic stock section being diamond shaped, terminating at the butt in a dished steel cap.

Held in equal favour was the more traditional stock, oval in section, which terminated in a flared butt and it was this type of stock which became popular in Britain towards the close of the duelling/target pistol era. Fortunately, in Britain the practice of duelling suffered a decline in the years following the end of the Napoleonic Wars. Society no longer tolerated the existence of a class of 'temporary gentlemen' and the degradation of what had been an 'honoured' institution into an instrument of blackmail resulted in the traditional form of the duel rapidly going into disfavour. Some attempt was made to reduce the odds by having the duellists draw lots for the pistols, one of which would not be primed; or by drawing lots to see who would take the first shot. These stratagems and others such as 'meeting over a pocket hand-kerchief' where the contestants each held one corner of a hand-kerchief tended to deter the professional card sharp and duellist, but it was not until 1842 that duelling in the Army was forbidden, the practice continuing on the Continent and in America until much later.

The reluctance of the Army to relinquish the duel was paralleled to some extent by its reluctance to take advantage of the percussion system, and it was not until 1834 that experiments were made to decide on the most suitable type of lock for Service use. Due to the immense stocks of arms which were held following the end of the Napoleonic Wars, it is not surprising that the first percussion pistols to be issued were conversions from flint. The conversion was carried out in the cheapest possible way by brazing a piece on to the side of the barrel to carry the nipple and altering the lock by removing the flashpan and cover, the flint cock being replaced by a percussion hammer. Such conversions were only intended to be stop-gap weapons and, in 1842, new pattern smooth bored percussion pistols were issued to replace the converted flintlocks.

Several types of these pistols were made, those issued to Guards Regiments, for example, having 9-in. barrels of No. 12 bore and weighing nearly $3\frac{1}{2}$ lb. The overall length was $15\frac{1}{2}$ in. and they were fitted with heavy brass mounts and a swivel or captive ramrod. Light Cavalry Regiments were issued with a similar pistol of No. 16

bore, whilst the Navy had yet another pattern with a 6-in. barrel and provided with the traditional belt hook. The Naval or Sea Service pistol was far less clumsy, being reduced in calibre to No. 22 bore and weighing less than 2 lb.

Possessing the somewhat dubious distinction of being obsolete before it was issued, the Rifled Pistol Carbine Pattern of 1856 could be regarded as a miniature of the Enfield Rifle Pattern of 1853, being a single-shot muzzle-loading weapon of ·577 calibre and fitted with a 10-in. barrel. The ammunition used was similar to that issued for the Enfield Rifle Musket, the bullet and powder being contained in a made-up paper case. For use with the pistol, the bullet weight was reduced 390 grains and the powder charge to one dram. An 8-in. barrel version known as the Pattern of 1867, was issued to the Cavalry and to European Cavalry Regiments in India. The Rifled Pistol Carbine, as the name implies, was issued with a detachable shoulder-stock and could be used as either a pistol or short carbine. Pistols of similar pattern were used by the German, Austrian and Swedish armies, the use of the detachable shoulder-stock remaining in favour on the Continent long after it had fallen into disuse in Britain.

The Enfield Rifle Pistol was the last 'Horse Pistol' to be issued to the British Army. Manufacture was discontinued in 1864, the trooper being subsequently armed with the Snider Breech Loading Carbine. A centre-fire breechloading revolver took the place of the percussion revolving pistol which had been the preferred officer's sidearm since the Crimean War.

By the middle of the nineteenth century flintlock weapons had been almost completely replaced by percussion for both military and sporting use. Flintlock arms continued to be made in Britain up to the end of the century for export to the so-called backward areas of the world and, as an indication that the once all-conquering flint gun is perhaps down but not out, the ancient trade of 'flint-knapping' is still carried on at Brandon in Suffolk.

CHAPTER NINE

Percussion rifles and capping carbines

THE first half of the nineteenth century not only saw a revolution in the means of igniting the propellant charge but also a fundamental change in the manufacture of firearms. The traditional gunsmith was a craftsman who, with the assistance of several helpers, produced the separate parts of a gun by the use of hand tools, accurate assembly being due to individual and meticulous fitting of the various components by hand. The end of the eighteenth century had seen a measure of specialization firmly established, in that some makers concentrated on the production of barrels, others lock mechanisms. There was also a healthy trade in the supply of rough forgings and castings for trigger guards, lock plates, and other metal furniture.

Small private gunmakers, relying on hand methods, could adequately supply the market during times of peace, but the demands of war placed a severe strain on their resources. The requirements of the British Government during the Napoleonic Wars are an indication of the productive capacity of the nation since, between the years 1803 and 1815, more than two and a half million arms were manufactured. Two-thirds of this total was produced by the Birmingham makers alone. Whilst these efforts were a remarkable achievement, and fully merited Birmingham's description as 'the workshop of the world', the day of the individual craftsman was drawing to a close.

The development of machine tools, and the growth of a highly specialized machine tool industry, was responsible for the changes in firearm manufacture and the decline and virtual extinction of the individual gunmaker. The machine tool had its origins in continental Europe, being used to produce the accurate components of clocks and watches, but its practical application to industry was initially carried out in Britain. The specialized machine tool capable of being adjusted to repeatedly produce identical components, was a result of American genius and, in particular, that of Eli Whitney of New Haven, Connecticut, inventor of the cotton gin. Realizing that, due to patent litigation, the cotton gin was a lost cause financially, Whitney turned his interest in mechanics and ability to simplify manufacturing processes to the production of firearms. An American Government contract for 10,000 muskets was secured in 1798, and after designing and building the necessary machine tools, he was able to produce firearms on an assembly line basis using components made with a high degree of interchangeability. The rapid growth of the American machine tool industry, coupled with an ability to produce specialized machines for barrel-boring and rifling, and the machining of lockwork and actions, set the stage for the development of the large arms factory with a formidable mass production potentiality.

This tendency did not go unnoticed in Britain and, in 1851, American gunmaking machinery was obtained from Robbins, Kendall & Lawrence of Windsor, Vermont, to equip the Royal Small Arms Factory at Enfield, Middlesex. The decision to adopt the interchangeable mass production system of arms manufacture was no doubt influenced by a series of strikes which occurred amongst the Birmingham gunmakers during the Crimean War and which seriously affected the supply of rifles. The establishment of a Government Factory did not go unchallenged by the Birmingham gunmakers, who had already strongly resisted an attempt to establish a Government Factory in Birmingham in 1816. Continued protests were made against the manufacture by the Government of arms at factories at Lewisham and Enfield and the expansion of the Enfield facilities in 1851 was followed by the formation of the Birmingham Small Arms Company ten years later, in an endeavour to meet this competition.

The rifle that bore the Government Crown on the lock plate and which was later to carry the 'piled arm' trademark of the B.S.A. Co., eventually became the best military muzzle-loading rifle in Europe. The development of the Enfield rifle had not been without considerable teething troubles and its ultimate perfection was in no small measure due to improvements which had taken place in methods of loading and in bullet design.

The problems and difficulties which had beset the user of the Baker rifle have already been described and, in 1826, a French officer, Delvigne, in an endeavour to produce a rifle which could be quickly loaded used a loosely fitted ball which could easily be rammed down a fouled barrel. The ball rested on the edge of a smaller breech chamber and was expanded to fit the bore by means of several blows from a heavy ramrod. Two years later, Colonel Thouvenin improved on this system by using a stout central pillar or 'tige' which projected from the breech face, the powder being contained in the annular space around it. Expansion of the bullet again was achieved by blows from the ramrod.

Neither of these systems could be described as satisfactory but at least the spirit of adventure so obviously apparent in the French military mind roused the British authorities from their lethargy. A percussion rifle, the Brunswick, very similar in appearance to its flintlock predecessor, was adopted in 1836. This rifle, calibre ·704 in., was the invention of Captain Berners of the army of the German State of Brunswick. The chief peculiarity lay in the rifling, there being only two deep grooves which made one complete turn in the barrel length of 30 in. The grooves were deeply notched at the muzzle to aid the loading of a patched belted ball designed to fit the grooves. In practice, the rifle was very difficult to load in spite of the use of tallow for spreading on the patches; a contemporary account stating 'that the force required to ram down the ball being so great as to render any man's hand unsteady for accurate shooting'. The original issue Brunswick was fitted with a back action lock which tended to weaken the stocks; later patterns were fitted with the conventional bar action lock. For sporting purposes, the belted ball and two-groove system gained a number of adherents. Rifles made by James Purdey on this plan enjoyed some success, but for military purposes it was a complete failure.

In an endeavour to overcome the disadvantages of existing systems so obvious in the Brunswick, General John Jacob (founder of the Scinde Irregular Horse and the town of Jacobabad) devoted the greater part of his life to the trials of rifles and ammunition. Part of the outcome of his experiments, which were conducted at his own expense, was the development of an explosive shell and a four-groove system of rifling. Rifles made to his design by Daw of London were later adapted to use a cylindro-concidal bullet fitted with four projections to grip the rifling. Whilst the East India Company, to whom Jacob offered the fruits of his researches, rejected them on the grounds that if the Brunswick was good enough for the British Army it was good enough for service with the Hon. East India Company, Jacob's rifles enjoyed a degree of popularity amongst sporting riflemen.

Although the Brunswick rifle had been issued to the Rifle Regiments, the standard infantry weapon remained the smooth bore musket. Originally requirements were met by the conversion of existing flintlock muskets, but in 1842 new percussion muskets were manufactured. Some of these saw service in the Kaffir Wars, which started in South Africa in 1846. Since it is recorded that it took about 3,200 rounds to disable a Kaffir, the futility of continuing to use smooth bore weapons against anything but solidly massed infantry finally became apparent.

Doubtless disillusioned by the poor performance of the Brunswick, the British military authorities sought the solution to their

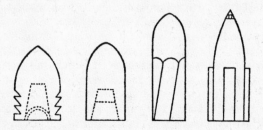

Figure 14. *Left to Right:* Minié bullet with iron cup. Enfield bullet with boxwood plug. Whitworth hexagonal bullet. Jacobs cylindro-conoidal bullet with four projections.

problems elsewhere. Turning once again to France, who had already experimented with the mechanical expansion of a loose-fitting bullet after loading and had discarded both the Delvigne and Thouvenin systems, the British found that Captain Minié, an Instructor at the School of Vincennes, had apparently solved the problem. Minié's solution, which had in fact already been anticipated by the Birmingham gunmaker William Greener, was to use an elongated hollow-based bullet with a plug. The basis of the design was that the force of the explosion would force the plug into the tapered hollow-base and expand the bullet into the rifling, without any need to hammer the bullet with the ramrod. This type of bullet was adopted by the French in replacement of the 'tige' rifle. In 1851, the British followed suit with the introduction of the 'Rifle Musket, Pattern 1851' based on the Minié system.

Apart from being the first British Service arm to employ the cylindro-conoidal bullet, it was also the first rifle in the British Army which was intended to be issued to all branches of the

Service and not to the Rifle Brigades alone. The 'rifle musket' was unfortunately not a success. The bullet, which was a retrograde modification of the original Minié design, had a deep hollow at the base in which was an iron cup intended to expand the base of the bullet into the rifling. Sometimes the iron cup was driven right through the bullet, leaving a lead cylinder in the bore of the rifle.

The Minié had a 39-in. barrel with a calibre of ·702 in., rifled with four grooves which made a complete turn in 6 ft. 6 in. The Admiralty also thought that they should have a 'rifle musket'. This was produced by the simple expedient of rifling the 1842 pattern musket with three grooves. The 'sea service' pattern as it was known had a calibre of ·758 in., the bullet weighing 825 grains and was issued to the Marines.

Only about 28,000 Minié rifles were made, for early in 1852 Lord Hardinge, Master General of the Ordnance, invited competition from the principal gunmakers in Britain and the best features of the rifles submitted were embodied in a new weapon, known as the 'Enfield'. The expansion of the Enfield factory mentioned earlier and its re-equipment with American machinery was undertaken to produce the new rifle. Due to the threat of war in Europe, and the distinct possibility that the new factory would not be in production in time, contracts were placed in Birmingham, London and Liège, Belgium. The American suppliers of the machinery at Enfield, Robbins, Kendall & Lawrence, also contracted to manufacture Enfields.

In its original form the Enfield was 4 ft. 7 in. overall and weighed 8¾ lb. The barrel, 39 in. long, was of ·577 calibre (24 bore) and was rifled with three shallow grooves which made a complete turn in 6 ft. 6 in. Later models were rifled with 'progressive' rifling, the depth of the grooves being ·005 in. deep at the muzzle and ·013 in. deep at the breech.

The origin of 'progressive' rifling was rather interesting. The French, some years previously, decided to rifle some smooth bore carbines but found that the barrels were too thin at the muzzle. In order to overcome this they decreased the depth of the grooves towards the muzzle and found to their surprise that a great improvement in the shooting resulted. They adopted this system, being followed by the British and then by the Americans, who used it on their U.S. Model 1855.

The original Long Enfield rifle first saw service in the Crimea, although most of the troops who went to the Crimea were issued with Minié rifles and many even had the old smooth bore muskets. A considerable number of Enfields were purchased by both the Federal and Confederate Governments during the American Civil War of 1861–65. Large private purchases of Enfields were also made in Britain after the founding of the Volunteer Movement in 1859, many of these rifles being specially finished to a higher standard than the normal Service issue arm.

The Enfield bullet was far lighter than its predecessors, weighing 530 grains and having a diameter of ·55 in. Instead of the iron cup used in the Minié, a boxwood plug was used, later to be replaced by one of baked clay. The bullet was made up in a paper cartridge, with a charge of 2½ drams of R.F.G. (rifle fine grained) powder, the bullet being paper patched and lubricated. It will be recalled that the circulation of a report in 1857 that the cartridges for the Enfield were lubricated with a mixture of cow's fat and lard was a contributory cause of the Indian Mutiny.

In spite of the fact that all branches of the Services were to have an arm taking the same cartridge, the patterns of the Enfield multiplied due to the curious policy of issuing a rifle of special type or dimensions to individual branches. The infantry, having been issued with the Long Enfield, Pattern 1853, presently got a short pattern, for sergeants, having a barrel 33 in. long and known as the Pattern 1856 and 1860. A similar rifle, Pattern 1858, was in general use in the Navy, differing from the 1860 pattern in that it was brass-instead of iron-mounted, and fitted with a cutlass sword bayonet. The Royal Artillery adopted an Enfield carbine with a barrel length of 24 in., Patterns 1853 and 1861, taking a similar cartridge to the rifle but with a reduced powder charge of two drams. An even shorter rifle carbine, Pattern of 1861, was the general arm of the cavalry. The cartridge was the same as for the artillery carbine but the barrel length was reduced to 21 in., the rate of twist remaining at one turn in 4 ft. There was a cavalry carbine Pattern of 1856 which used the slower rate of twist of one turn in 6 ft. 6 in., standard for the Long and Short Enfield rifles and which similarly had only three-groove rifling. The naval, artillery and later cavalry patterns all had five-groove rifling.

One might have thought that with all these variations, each suited to a particular job, satisfaction would have been guaranteed. This, unfortunately, was not the case, since accuracy varied considerably with apparently identical rifles. In an endeavour to locate and eliminate these variations, the Government referred the problem to Sir Joseph Whitworth, accounted by many to be the foremost mechanician of his day. Whitworth's speciality was accuracy, to attain which he had evolved methods of measuring and working to much smaller limits than had previously been possible. Other than a visit to the American Government Armoury at Springfield, Mass., Whitworth had no previous experience of gunmaking but, nevertheless, he agreed to investigate the problem, providing the Government would build him an enclosed range, 500 yards long, and retain the services of the well-known gunmaker, Mr Westley Richards, to act as his technical adviser.

Whitworth's experiments began in 1855 and lasted for two years. The first thing he discovered was that although identical to the eye, components of the Service arms when tested by his special gauges were not dimensionally accurate. Even when rifles were manufactured with the utmost care, the shooting performance left much to be desired and finally he decided to produce a rifle of entirely new design.

Embodying all of Whitworth's experience of precision engineering, and a standard of workmanship which was of the highest possible order, the new rifle differed not only from its contemporaries in these respects but also in a new concept of rifling. Instead of the usual grooves, the rifling was hexagonal with rounded corners. The calibre was reduced to ·450 in. and a special hard alloy bullet moulded in the same shape as the bore was employed. Comparative trials with the Enfield were arranged at the School of Musketry, Hythe, in 1857, the results of which were astonishing. A contemporary writer stated, 'that the Whitworth, as regards accuracy, was at 1,100 yards nearly on a par with the Enfield at 500 yards'.

Despite this positive demonstration of its superior accuracy, the Whitworth was never generally issued as a Service arm. A number were made at Enfield and the Rifle Brigade were for a short time armed with the Whitworth Short Rifle, Pattern 1863. This rifle weighed $9\frac{3}{4}$ lb. and had a barrel 33 in. in length. The locks of these rifles were marked 'Enfield, 1863' and although there was a Long Whitworth, Pattern 1862, these were purely experimental and never issued.

Probably the only military use of the Whitworth was during the American Civil War, a number of Whitworth rifles being brought in to the Confederacy by English blockade runners during 1862. From contemporary accounts, the Whitworth appears to have been highly prized for distribution to snipers who were able to do good work with them at ranges up to 300 yards. Whilst never used by the British for military purposes, doubtless because it was a muzzle-loader, and breechloading arms were being devised and used success-fully, a more probable reason for its rejection was the fact that the Whitworth fouled very badly after about twenty shots. Sir Joseph

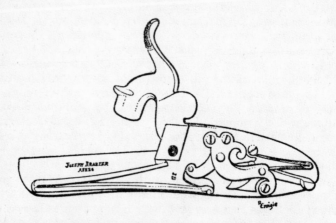

Figure 15. Interior of best quality percussion lock by Joseph Brazier, Ashes. Marked externally Alex. Henry, Edinburgh.

devised a special scraper which fitted the bore and, if this instrument was used after each shot, up to a hundred rounds could be fired without interference from fouling.

Such considerations did not influence the target rifleman who was prepared to clean out after each shot, and as a specialized form of target rifle, the Whitworth 'match rifle' was virtually unchallenged for many years. The opening shot of the first meeting of the National Rifle Association at Wimbledon in 1860 was fired by Queen Victoria from a Whitworth rifle which was mounted in a rest. It is recorded that the shot struck within one and a half inches of the centre of the target at 400 yards.

Two types of military Whitworth appear to have been made, one with three barrel bands and a shorter rifle with two bands. Although similar in external appearance to the Enfield the Whitworth was of far higher quality, the stock being finely checkered and the lock (made by Joseph Brazier, Ashes) far superior to the standard issue with regard both to finish and mechanical excellence. Many of the best-quality military rifles were supplied in cases, as were the target type match rifles. The case contained a powder flask, cleaning tools, etc., but contrary to usual practice, bullet moulds for the hexagonal bullet were not supplied, specially swaged bullets being manufactured by the Whitworth Company, Manchester. The writer has only seen one hexagonal mould for the Whitworth bullet, this being found with a cased double rifle of Whitworth pattern.

From the military aspect, the Whitworth was not a success, but the experiments which produced it and which extended to rifled and breechloading artillery had important and far-reaching consequences. Apart from the clarification of many scientific aspects of the theory of rifling, the insistence on what was then the relatively small bore of ·450 was to be fully justified in the near future, and the emphasis placed on precision machining resulted in the components of the Enfield achieving complete interchangeability by 1860.

Turning from the Whitworth with its hexagonal bore and mechanically fitting bullet to the other extreme of apparently no rifling at all, we find such a rifle being made by Charles Lancaster, the celebrated London gunmaker. Sporting rifles made by Lancaster featured his 'oval boring', the principle being to make the bore as smooth as possible but slightly oval and to give this oval a pronounced twist. This system had sufficient merit to warrant the issue of ·577 in. calibre carbines with the Lancaster oval-bored barrel to the Rifle Brigade on an experimental basis. Finally, it was adopted as the official arm of the Corps of Sappers and Miners (later to be the Royal Engineers) in 1855.

Generally similar in external appearance to the Enfield, the Lancaster carbine was brass-mounted and had a barrel 2 ft. 7½ in. in length. Not only was the rifling 'oval' but it was in addition, progressive and 'gaining', i.e. the 'grooves' were deeper at the breech than at the muzzle, and the rate of twist was slower at the breech than at the muzzle. Surprisingly enough, the Lancaster used the same ammunition as the Enfield rifle.

The mid-nineteenth century was an era of intense experimentation and the wind of change was soon to blow the muzzle-loader into obscurity. Two systems had been developed. The first, which was to challenge the supremacy of the muzzle-loader, and the second which was to supplant it. Since the first breechloading system can be regarded somewhat as a transitional development (the cartridge used containing only the propellant and the bullet), it is appropriate that it be considered at this stage. The true breechloader was the outcome of the second system in which the cartridge contained the propellant and the bullet as well as the means of ignition.

The 'capping breechloader' was the name given to arms constructed on the first system. The cartridge was made of paper, usually nitrated or treated in some manner to ensure combustion when the charge was fired. To illustrate how the system worked the Westley Richards 'Monkey Tail' capping breechloader (patented 1858) will serve as an example. Described as the best capping breechloader ever produced, the basis of its design was the use of an elongated sliding breech bolt attached to the underside of an arm (the 'monkey tail') which was hinged at the front end to the rear of the barrel. The front end of the breech bolt terminated in a specially shaped brass plug which forced the cartridge into the · breech. This was achieved by means of an extension to the rear of the barrel known as the barrel shoe which cammed the bolt forward and locked the action. To load the rifle, the specially constructed paper cartridge was introduced into the breech by lifting the 'monkey tail' lever or flap. The base of the cartridge incorporated a heavy greased wad and when the lever was closed, the brass plug forced the cartridge home and backed up the wad. The external hammer was cocked and a cap placed on the nipple. When fired, the flash from the cap passed through the paper case of the cartridge and ignited the charge. The breech wad stopped nearly all the escape of gas and was pushed forward by the next cartridge when the rifle was reloaded, cleaning and lubricating the chamber. If necessary, the rifle could be used as a muzzle-loader by inserting a metal plug and two wads in the breech.

The Westley Richards carbine was approved as the cavalry arm in 1861. Of particular interest was the form of the rifling, this being an octagonal version of the Whitworth hexagon, this choice not being surprising in view of Westley Richards' close collaboration with Whitworth. The withdrawal of this weapon from the cavalry, following the issue of the Snider breechloader, saw its transfer to the Yeomanry, in whose hands they remained until 1877.

Three other capping carbines were issued experimentally to the cavalry. The American Sharps was perhaps the most unsatisfactory. It employed an almost vertically moving breech block operated by a hinged trigger guard. The sharp edge of the block on closing the breech sliced through the base of a special paper or linen cartridge, the exposed powder being ignited by a percussion cap detonated by an external lock. Later models employed the Maynard automatic tape primer, this device being fitted to the model supplied to the British Government.

Instead of the expendable greased wad used by the Westley Richards, the Sharps employed a built-in special metal bushing; but in practice this attempt at obturation was a failure. A common practice for those armed with the Sharps was to tie a handkerchief round the breech, fire, and show the cloth cut up by gas leakage. To make things worse, the guillotine action of the breech block often cut off some of the powder, as well as the cartridge base. This powder, being ignited by the flash from the breech, added to the general feeling of insecurity felt by those who had to use it. The Sharps, as can be imagined, had a short life in the British Service although when finally adapted to a metallic cartridge in the 1870s, became the favourite weapon of the Buffalo hunters of the American West.

The second of the better-known capping carbines was the Greene, two thousand of which were purchased by the British Government from America. The Maynard tape primer was again adapted to this carbine which was fitted with a fixed breech and a forward-moving barrel, the breech and barrel being locked together by lugs which engaged by rotating the barrel. Two 'triggers' were fitted to this arm, the front trigger being used to unlock the action. Instead of slicing off the end of the cartridge, the Greene pierced the end of the cartridge by means of a hollow steel pillar in the breech face which also served to conduct the flash from the priming powder.

Employing a stout wad of greased felt in a similar manner to the Westley Richards, the Terry rifle (made by the Birmingham firm of Calisher & Terry of Whittal Street) in carbine form was also issued on trial to cavalry regiments in 1861. A simple rotating rear-locked bolt with a hinged handle was used. The coned head of the bolt, which was provided with additional leather sealing rings, abutted against the rear of the breech chamber and, when combined with the greased base wad, ensured good obturation.

A great many capping breechloaders appeared during the early part of the second half of the nineteenth century. Some, like Prince's and the Belgian Mont Storm, enjoyed a brief popularity but the others were destined for early obscurity. The major problem of the designer of these rifles was to secure adequate sealing of the breech and this difficulty was never satisfactorily overcome until the perfection of the metallic cartridge.

Since cartridges of this type contained their own means of ignition, there was considerable apprehension regarding their liability to explode in bulk and this feeling, no doubt coupled with the relative complexity of design of an effective breechloader, retarded adoption for military purposes. The transition from muzzle- to breechloader delayed by prudent governments on additional grounds of expense, was hastened by the lessons to be learned following the outbreak of Civil War in America and the rise of a militant Prussia who, as far back as 1842, had armed her troops with the Dreyse breechloading 'Needle Gun'.

CHAPTER TEN

Development of the revolver

ONE of the most important single consequences which followed the perfection of the percussion cap was the development of an efficient revolver. The possibility of using a revolving breech provided with more than one chamber in conjunction with a single barrel was most attractive and since such a mechanism would be capable of repetitive fire, an attempt to apply this principle to hand guns was made as early as the seventeenth century. Muskets made on the revolving system had appeared slightly earlier but the difficulty of manipulating a burning match robbed the revolving matchlock of much of its utility.

The evolution of the snaphaunce and the true flintlock eliminated many of the problems of the revolver-maker since each chamber could be provided with a separate flashpan and steel. In the case of the snaphaunce a single steel sufficed it being returned to battery after each discharge. Such a weapon, which may be dated approximately at 1650, is preserved in the Royal United Service Museum in London. Each of the six chambers of this weapon has a flashpan, the pan being guarded with a sliding cover. The whole of the cylinder is enclosed in an outer casing, open at the front end to permit loading. The purpose of this casing was to protect the flashpans and ensure against accidental opening with the risk of losing the priming. The most important feature of the weapon is the fact that the cylinder is mechanically revolved. Previously, it was necessary to rotate the cylinder by hand after each shot, the cylinder being locked in position by a spring catch which engaged in a series of notches cut in the cylinder.

The snaphaunce revolver with the mechanically rotated cylinder can be regarded as the ancestor of the modern revolver, and the mechanism used was, in fact, almost identical to that patented by Samuel Colt in 1836 and which is still found in that favourite arm of Western heroes, the Colt ·45 Single Action. In order to obtain mechanical rotation, a small pawl or lever was linked to the front of the cock and engaged with a six-toothed ratchet cut in the base of the cylinder. On drawing back the cock, the pawl, under the influence of a small 'V' spring, pressed against the cylinder ratchet, turning the cylinder through one-sixth of a revolution. A spring catch locked the cylinder in battery and a linkage opened the appropriate flashpan at the moment the flint struck the steel.

The design of such a pistol, displaying as it did considerable ingenuity, was far ahead of its time, since neither the machines nor the materials were available in the seventeenth century to ensure successful manufacture in quantity. That this indeed was the case is demonstrated by the disappearance of the 'self-rotating' pistol and the development of the manually rotated 'multi-barrelled' type of flintlock from the double-barrelled 'turn over' flint pistol.

Towards the end of the eighteenth century, the flintlock 'pepper-box' pistol made its appearance. This improved form of multi-barrelled pistol employed a number of full-length barrels screwed into a hand-rotated 'cylinder'. This cylinder or breeching was enclosed in a gun-metal sleeve which prevented the priming powder escaping from the flashpans provided for each barrel. A conventional pan cover and steel were mounted on an extension to the main body and so covered the flashpan of the barrel indexed in the firing position.

Undoubtedly the most interesting of pre-percussion 'revolvers' was the Collier. The first of his revolvers was developed in America in 1809, but due to the lack of interest in America, Collier came to England where he was granted Patent No. 4315, dated 24th November 1818. Elisha Haydon Collier's specifications described a flintlock revolver with a single barrel. The cylinder of his revolver was rotated by a spiral spring, similar to a watch spring, which required to be wound up periodically. Each chamber of the cylinder was provided with a recessed mouth which was pushed over the coned end of the barrel by a spring, ensuring accurate positioning of the cylinder in relation to the barrel and cutting down the escape of gas between cylinder and barrel to a mini num. Provision was made for the automatic priming of each chamber.

Although today the term revolver is generally taken to mean a hand gun, Collier's patent was undoubtedly mainly concerned with rifles and shotguns, as well as pistols. There can be little doubt that the production of pistols was but a minor activity as compared to the output of long guns.

It will be noticed that the patent described a method for rotating the cylinder by 'clockwork' but apart from possibly a few experimental models, the cylinders of all his models were rotated by hand.

An important feature of the system was the automatic priming mechanism. By means of a revolving steel plug cut with three equidistant recesses, sufficient powder was placed in the flashpan from a magazine integral with the frizzen to ensure discharge. The plug was rotated by a three-toothed ratchet and a pawl attached to the side of the flashpan, so that when the pan was closed the ratchet revolved the plug and deposited a measured quantity of powder inside the pan. Later models dispensed with the ratchet and pawl, substituting a more robust link motion. The earlier Collier revolvers are also distinctive since the cock is placed inside the lock plate instead of outside as was common practice.

Perhaps of greater importance was the means used to ensure a positive joint between the cylinder and barrel. In addition to the spring which pushed the cylinder forward so that the coned rear of the barrel entered the recessed mouth of the cylinder, a steel wedge operated by the fall of the cock ensured that this joint did not leak during discharge. The wedge was withdrawn automatically when the lock was brought to the half-cock safety position.

The Collier was probably the most perfect form of flintlock revolver but, even so, it was necessary after firing a shot to half cock the lock, pull the cylinder backwards for about an eighth of an inch against spring pressure (to disengage the mouth of the cylinder from the barrel) and rotate the cylinder by hand. The flashpan was then closed (this motion operating the priming device) and the lock brought to full cock.

Whilst it has been established that Collier manufactured percussion revolvers, no effort was made to develop this business and he apparently returned to his original occupation of 'Civil Engineer' ultimately returning to America in 1850. The true revolver was equally neglected by other makers since the percussion system was first adapted to hand guns of the pepper-box type, having hand-rotated barrels. Mechanical rotation appears to have been developed in England about 1830, one of the earliest of this type of pistol being made by Joseph Lang. Lang used the single-action system in which the cylinder was revolved by cocking the hammer using a pawl and ratchet mechanism.

By far the greatest number of pepper-boxes were made on the 'self-cocking' principle which appeared shortly after the Lang and which speedily relegated it to obscurity. The self-cocking pepper-box used the same grouping of barrels (usually six) and round a central axis the whole being made from a single block of metal. Each barrel,

provided with a nipple at the breech, was loaded from the muzzle
with powder and ball, a cap being placed on the nipple after loading.

When the trigger is pulled, the hammer is raised and the barrel
assembly rotated. These operations are so timed that when the
hammer falls, it falls on to a new cap, ready to fire an undischarged
barrel. The barrel assembly is locked in position to ensure that the
hammer falls correctly, the bolt being withdrawn after firing by
virtue of its connexion with the trigger, which returns to its original
position under the influence of a trigger spring.

The self-cocking percussion pepper-box once loaded could safely
be carried and was ready for immediate use, all that was needed
was to point it in the direction required and pull the trigger. An
equal advantage was that six shots could be fired merely by pulling
the trigger six times. As can be imagined, such a weapon achieved
immediate success as a close-quarter self-defence arm and vast
numbers were produced both here and in America until the late
1850s. In America, the 'self-cocking' or 'double-action' pepper-box
was patented by Ethan Allan and sold under the name 'Allan and
Thurber, Worcester', displacing an earlier single-action pepper-box
made at Shrewsbury, Mass., by Barton and Benjamin M. Darling.

The popularity of the pepper-box resulted in numerous imitators
and self-styled inventors, and improvers, manufacturing weapons
ranging from the practical to the pot metal. All suffered to some
degree or other from the defects inherent in the basic design.
Early pistols, due to the arrangement of the nipples, had a tendency
towards a chain reaction type of fire, the flash from one exploding
cap igniting the adjacent charge and so on. The short barrels,
excessively heavy trigger pull and the positioning of the hammer
directly in the line of sight, made it impossible to fire a pepper-box
with any degree of accuracy. This latter objection was eliminated
on pepper-boxes made on the system patented in Belgium in 1837,
the hammer being placed so that it struck the lowest nipple first.
The underhammer system also permitted an unobstructed aim along
the top of the barrel. The risk of multiple discharge was lessened by
reason of the nipple being placed in line with the axis of the barrel,
instead of at an angle and being separated one from another by
partitions. Imitations of this pistol were made in Britain and are
usually marked with the words 'J. R. Coopers Patent', although this
gentleman does not appear to have taken out a British Patent to
protect his 'invention'.

The effective answer to most of the problems which afflicted the pepper-box was developed by an American, Samuel Colt. Following in the footsteps of Elisha Collier, Colt came to England in 1835 and on 22nd October he obtained British Patent No. 6909 to protect his ideas. Unlike Collier, Colt returned to America within the year and took out American Patent No. 138 in February 1836.

The Colt patents were carefull·' drawn up and the owner rigorously fought any infringement. The first pistols made under these patents were produced at the Patterson, New Jersey, factory of the Patent Arms Manufacturing Co., in four different c libres and three main types.

As well as pistols, the Patterson factory produced revolving rifles and, in fact, the first American Government order for Colt arms was for rifles. The first production model w .s distinguished by the use of a ring lever ahead of the trigger, which was used to cock the concealed hammer and rotate the cylinder. Unlike the early pistols, which were only five-chambered, the rifle cylinder had eight and a few ten chambers. Rifles on this pattern were made between the years 1837 to 1838. A later model dispensed with the bridge over the cylinder previously featured. The barrel length of the ring lever rifle was standard at 32 in., although other lengths could be had to order.

Differing from the rifles, in that an external hammer was used and the ring cocking mechanism dispensed with, the carbine was first made in 1839. As with the later ring lever rifle, the carbine was made with an attached loading lever fitted to the right-hand side of the barrel. Rarest of all the Patterson long arms was the revolving shotgun with a calibre of approximately twenty gauge. Again using the exposed centrally disposed hammer, the shotgun could also be used as a smooth bore musket.

It was, however, as a manufacturer of pistols that Colt gained such a reputation that the name Colt became synonymous with revolver. His large 'holster' size five-chambered ·36 calibre revolvers shared with the smaller ·34 calibre belt and ·31 calibre pocket pistols the distinctive use of a folding trigger which, rendering the trigger guard superfluous, results in an outline that appears unusual to modern eyes. Although unable to obtain an eagerly sought Government contract for his pistols, despite several trials, a number were sold to the Republic of Texas and were used by the Texas Navy and the Texas Rangers in the war against Mexico.

Although financially the sales to the Texans did not benefit the Patterson factory, the favourable publicity gained by Colt arms (and put to good use by that master salesman Sam Colt himself) was of great value in the future. Continued inability to obtain major and profitable Government contracts, coupled with a ruinously expensive law suit, resulted in the failure of the Patterson factory and the Patent Arms Manufacturing Co.

At this most unpropitious moment Colt was offered by the Government a rush order for one thousand pistols. Devoid of manufacturing facilities and bereft of capital, Colt sought the assistance of that manufacturing genius Eli Whitney. After some shrewd bargaining Whitney undertook the manufacture of an improved six-chambered revolver known to present-day collectors as the Whitneyville-Walker Dragoon Colt. Whitneyville was the armoury where the pistols were produced and Captain Samuel H. Walker, Texas Ranger and U.S. Army Officer, the man assigned to the task of seeing that the Army got the type of pistol it wanted.

The Dragoon pistols made at Whitneyville were a considerable improvement on their Patterson predecessors. The calibre was increased to ·44 in., the lockwork improved and a fixed trigger with a guard replaced the earlier folding type. The barrel, rounded for two-thirds of its length was 9 in. overall and had a permanently attached loading lever.

The success of the Dragoon resulted in a further order for a thousand pistols and Sam Colt obtained his own premises and facilities in 1847 at Hartford, Conn., which were to become the best-known revolver factory in history. Early production at Hartford differed but slightly from previous practice. The barrel was reduced to $7\frac{1}{2}$ in. and detail improvements made in the loading lever. Later Hartford-made Dragoons underwent mechanical modifications, the cylinder locking slots and the cylinder bolt being rectangular instead of oval and the mainspring was altered from 'V' to a single curved leaf spring, the end of which bore on a roller fitted to the hammer instead of bearing on a plain surface.

The original Dragoon weighed 4 lb. 9 oz. and, even following the reduction in weight to 4 lb. 2 oz. that resulted when the Dragoon Colt was made at Hartford, it still remained a massive pistol to carry about. As the name implies, the Dragoon was intended for use by mounted troops or cavalry and Dragoon-type pistols, whether single shot or revolving, were usually issued in pairs and carried in double saddle holsters.

Shortly after the establishment of the Hartford factory the manufacture of a much smaller '·31 Pocket Pistol', sometimes known as the 'Baby Dragoon', was commenced. Early pocket pistols are found with straight-backed trigger guards similar in outline to those fitted on the early Dragoon Colts, and there were no loading levers attached to the barrel. One of the most popular of the entire Colt range was the later model of the pocket pistol which retained the octagon barrel but used a rounded trigger guard and which was

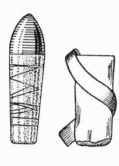

Figure 16. Eley combustible skin cartridge for Colt percussion revolver. The ribbon is used to remove the paper case from the cartridge, after which it is inserted into the chamber. Ignition was provided by the normal external percussion cap, the flash from which penetrated the skin and ignited the charge.

fitted with an attached rammer. Although known to collectors as the ·31 pocket pistol, Model of 1849, it is unlikely that manufacture commenced until 1850 or perhaps slightly later.

Occasionally encountered are the pocket pistols of Navy calibre, known also as the Model 1853. These pistols used the same basic frame as the ·31 calibre pocket models, but were of ·36 or Navy calibre and were five-chambered. Apart from the increase in calibre the ·36 pocket models are distinguished by the use of a rebated cylinder to accommodate the larger bullet used.

The year 1851 was important for two reasons; it saw the introduction of yet another model, the Navy belt pistol, or Model of 1851. Similar in appearance to the pocket pistol the Navy was of ·36 calibre and proportionately larger. The cylinder was six-chambered unlike the pocket model which, with a few exceptions made around 1860, was only five-chambered. In 1851 also, Colonel Colt was given the opportunity to display his wares at the Great Exhibition held in London at the Crystal Palace. Great interest was aroused not only in the products but also in the producer and Colt was invited to read a paper before the Institute of Civil Engineers, the theme of which was the comparison of the Colt revolver with those of the past and the advantages of mass producing them by machinery. Colt's activities in England resulted in valuable publicity stimulated by judicious gifts of presentation pistols to distinguished people but he also aroused considerable resentment, particularly amongst established English revolver manufacturers. The intentions of the Colonel were plain to see; overcome the initial prejudice which greets any new invention, establish a factory and the markets of England and an empire were there for the taking.

This threat to their supremacy was not taken lightly by the English gunmakers.

First in the lists was Robert Adams, who had already crossed swords with Colt during his famous lecture at the Institute of Civil Engineers. Unlike Colt's other English rivals, whose revolvers were essentially hand-made and consequently expensive, the Adams (known also as the Deane-Adams) was mass-produced both at the London factory and by various contractors in Birmingham and Liège, although not to the same high degree of interchangeability as were the products of Hartford. The Deane-Adams was made in three calibres, ·500 in., ·442 in. and ·32 in. (bore sizes were still used in England for even small calibre weapons and the three calibres would be given as follows, 36 bore, 54 bore and 120 bore). The Deane-Adams differed from the Colt in two important respects, it was a solid frame revolver and it could be fired 'double action' only. The Model 1851 was five-chambered and dispensed with a rammer by virtue of Adams' unique bullet which was intended to be loaded with manual pressure only. The Adams bullet was cast with a small integral spike to which was attached a greased wad intended to seal the bore and eliminate multiple discharges.

Since the conflict was not only one of design but of manufacturing methods, the rest of the English runners were handicapped by their lack of mass-production facilities and consequent dependence on high-cost hand finishing. Development had also suffered from the restrictions entailed by Colt's British Patent which did not expire until 1851 and prevented the use of partitions between the nipples and the single-action revolving mechanism. English revolvers, until the appearance of the 1851 Deane-Adams, were mainly of the 'transitional' type employing the self-cocking action of the pepper-box, a single barrel and a revolving cylinder and, as such, formed the connecting link between the pepper-box and the true revolver. Not all the transitional revolvers were of the self-cocking type, the Baker, Lang, and Witton and Daw were all single-action revolvers of high quality, the latter being used as an officers' sidearm during the Crimean War.

Colt, meantime, had not been idle. An office and showrooms had been established in London and, after some difficulty, factory premises on the bank of the Thames near Vauxhall Bridge were secured. American machinery and 'know-how' in the form of Hartford mechanics were brought to London, the machinery installed and the training of British unskilled labour undertaken. By 1853 the factory was in production, having a potential output of 1,000 revolvers per week. Manufacture was carried out on lines which would not be considered out of date today and the methods employed aroused the interest and admiration of the general public and vilification by Colt's London and Birmingham rivals whose alarm increased when it became apparent that Colt did not need their assistance and was able to produce revolvers whose quality and price defied competition.

The ·36 calibre Navy Model 1851, and the ·31 calibre 1849 Model Pocket Pistol were made at the London factory, the former with a 7½-in. barrel, the latter in various barrel lengths from 4 to 6 in. A contemporary English price list indicated that the Navy sold for £5 10s, the pocket model for £4 each, complete with bullet mould, cleaning rod and a combined turnscrew (screwdriver) and nipple key. A wooden case or alternatively a leather holster and cartridge belt were included for an extra fifteen shillings. Also sold, but never manufactured, by the London factory, was the Dragoon Colt, a number of which were specially made by the Hartford factory for export to England and which carry British Proof Marks. In deciding the origin of Navy and Pocket Colts of this period, those made at the London factory will be found with the following legend stamped on the barrel, Address: Col. Colt London, whereas those made in America and sold in this country will be found with either the stamped American New York or Hartford address or the London address which was engraved, and not stamped.

Although large orders for his pistols were obtained (approximately 25,000 pistols were supplied to the British Government), the adoption of the Adams revolver as the standard Service arm destroyed any hopes which Colt may have had of securing further

D

large orders and in 1857, after four years operation, the London Colt factory closed its doors.

The Adams revolver finally approved by the Government had undergone modification and was now supplied with a simple rammer, known as the 'Rigby', which was hinged so that it lay along the bottom of the frame on the left-hand side and could be brought into use by moving it downwards and forwards to eventually swing in a three-quarter arc and ram the bullet into the cylinder. Of more importance was the application of Captain Beaumont's ingenious modification of the original self-cocking action which permitted it to be used both single-action and self-cocking action. The Beaumont-Adams can be distinguished from its predecessor the Deane-Adams by the presence of a spur on the hammer (the Deane-Adams, being self-cocking only, did not require a thumb spur) and the more flowing general lines of the pistol, the Beaumont butt being set far less squarely to the axis of the barrel. The Beaumont-Adams was still made by Deane, Adams & Deane but in 1856 this company was taken over by the London Armoury Company, whose directors included Robert Adams and John Kerr, another well-known London gunmaker and the inventor of the Kerr revolver.

The Beaumont-Adams manufactured by the new company was fitted with a more powerful compound rammer, the invention of John Kerr, which lay along the left-hand side of the barrel when not in use. The action was modified by the introduction of a half-cock safety notch or bent on the hammer.

The L.A.C. Beaumont-Adams of ·44 calibre (No. 54 bore) was the pattern finally adopted by the British Government and was five-chambered, having a three-groove rifled barrel $5\frac{3}{4}$ in. in length.

CHAPTER ELEVEN

Percussion revolvers perfected

WITH Colt vanquished and Government contracts assured the London Armoury Company was in a strong position, but they were not without rivals. In Birmingham William Tranter had manufactured revolvers under Adams's patents and his revolver factory at Aston Cross became the most important in the Midlands. Not content with this state of affairs Tranter patented his own self-cocking mechanism in 1853 which differed radically from the Adams in that two triggers were employed. By this system, the accuracy obtainable by a manually cocked action could be achieved and, in addition, the rate of fire of the self-cocking type of action was possible.

The pistol was held in the normal manner with the index finger on the trigger. The trigger had a spur extension which protruded through the guard and the second finger was placed in position under the index finger and outside the guard. By pulling the spur trigger, the mainspring is compressed, the cylinder rotated and the hammer cocked. When the spur trigger is pulled back as far as possible a touch on the normal trigger with the index finger will release the hammer and fire the pistol. Self-cocking action was possible by pulling both the normal and spur triggers back simultaneously. Admittedly somewhat complicated to describe, it was found in practice to be remarkably effective, the double trigger action providing a rate of fire approaching that of the self-cocking Adams and yet permitting, when conditions allowed, the greater potential accuracy of a single-action revolver of the Colt pattern.

The first, or 1853 Model, Tranter had the grip set at nearly right-angles to the bore axis and in this resembled the Deane-Adams. Unlike the early Adams, the Tranter was provided with a rammer from the outset, this being entirely detachable and operating on a pin at the lower front of the left-hand of the frame. The first model Tranter will usually be found in 38 and 54 bore sizes (·500 and ·44 in.) but recently an 80 bore (·380 in.) pistol has been discovered and the smaller 120 bore (·320) might be awaiting discovery.

Shortly after the introduction of the 'First Model', improvements were made and the revolver 'streamlined' by decreasing the angle that the butt made with the barrel axis just as was done with the

Beaumont-Adams. A more powerful rammer was fitted to the 'Second Model'. The head was still made integral with the lever but it was possible to leave the rammer attached to the pistol (provision being made for it to lie along the left-hand side of the barrel) or remove it as the owner's fancy dictated. As with the earlier model, three calibres were produced, 38, 54 and 80 bore and it is possible that 120 bore pistols were also made, if so they are extremely rare.

An 'improved' later version, known as the 'Third Model', continued the fashionable trend towards increased 'streamlining', but since the angle of the butt is not always easy to interpret, identification is made easier by yet another alteration in the form of the rammer. The rammer 'head' is no longer made as part of the lever but is loose and the lever is permanently attached to the frame by a large-headed screw. Specimens of the Third Model have been encountered in 38, 54, 80 and 120 bore sizes.

Similar in outline to the Third Model and having the more pronounced 'prawl' or hump on the backstrap, the Tranter Single Trigger double-action revolver which was patented in 1856 bears a marked resemblance to the London Armoury Company's Beaumont-Adams. Fortunately for the collector, identification is possible since the Tranter has a small lug at the back of the trigger which is easily recognizable. The appearance of the Single Trigger Tranter, or Fourth Model, coincided with the adoption of the Beaumont-Adams by the British Government and Tranter was by no means the only one who hastened to produce a revolver modelled on similar lines to the favoured Beaumont-Adams. The appearance of the single-trigger model did not alienate the affections of those accustomed to the older double-trigger models, for both types continued to be manufactured concurrently.

As with any attempted system of classification, there are always those which cannot be satisfactorily placed in an orderly manner and the so-called 'Export' Model Tranter, the action of which was patented in 1856, comes under special consideration. In this patent (No. 1913) single-action, 'double-action' and 'treble-action' locks are described, the 'treble-action' lock being of the double-trigger type but with the addition of a hammer spur for manual cocking. Revolvers of the 'treble-action' type were made but were not apparently very popular in Britain, the majority being exported.

Like Adams, Tranter patented a special bullet, the feature of which was a deep groove near the base designed to be filled with a composition of beeswax and tallow. Cased Tranter revolvers, in addition to being supplied with a brass bullet mould to cast the 'patent lubricated bullet', were also provided with a small tin containing Tranter's 'Patent Lubricating Composition', which was intended to be melted, the 'grooved' base of the bullet being dipped into the lubricant which, after solidification, was ready for use.

The Birmingham firm of Philip Webley could trace its ancestry back to 1790 and as Webley & Scott Ltd is today the sole British revolver manufacturer. The first identifiable revolver made by Philip Webley & Sons was patented by James Webley (Philip's brother) in 1853 and was a five-chambered single-action revolver distinguished by an extremely long hammer spur. Unlike the Adams and Tranter revolvers the early Webleys (the Longspur Models) were open framed, i.e. similar to the Colt in having no top strap to the frame, the barrel being hinged to the frame and secured with a wedge passing through the cylinder pin. The 'First Model' Longspur had a detachable rammer, the 'Second Model' an attached one, which pivoted about the frame hinge pin. The use of the more powerful Kerr type attached rammer characterizes the 'Third Model' Webley and, in addition, the barrel group is screwed to the frame via the cylinder pin, additional security being achieved by the use of a small butterfly screw holding the barrel group to the front of the frame.

In common with other manufacturers, Webley then produced a double-action revolver which combined the single-action and self-cocking mechanism. The first of these double-action models is known as the Webley Wedge Frame since the barrel group is attached to the cylinder pin by the familiar wedge in a manner similar to the Colt. Unlike the Colt, the Webley appears to have a solid frame but on close inspection it will be found that the top strap of the frame, which is forged integrally with the barrel, is merely 'dovetailed' into an extension of the standing breech. The 'First Model' Wedge Frame had an under-barrel rammer very reminiscent of the 1851 Colt. The 'Second Model' Wedge Frame differs in minor details, trigger guard, angle of the butt, etc., but can be distinguished from earlier models by the use of a Kerr type rammer sited along the left side of the barrel. The last of the Webley percussion pistols was made with a solid frame and was fitted with a modified rammer working through a link.

The three great makers of British revolvers were undoubtedly Adams, Tranter and Webley. As we have seen, each firm made a multiplicity of models and, in the case of Webley, components were made for revolvers assembled by other less reputable makers. Webley's name is associated with a range of self-cocking open-frame revolvers which bear a strong resemblance to the earlier Longspur Webleys. Informed opinion now has it that Webley did not make these pistols, nor did they make a further series of self-cocking revolvers known as the Webley-Bentley which will be found in a wide range of quality and standard of finish, but which are distinctive by reason of the Bentley patent safety-catch fitted to the hammer nose. Apart from the complexity of model, maker, inventor, and the added difficulty that in many instances the vendor's name only appears on English revolvers, untold numbers of cheap revolvers were turned out by the 'trade' in Birmingham. Many of the revolvers bearing distinguished London names were in fact made in Birmingham; those of better quality being 'made under one roof', others by putting the work out to individual tradesmen.

In America, the loss of Colt's manufacturing facilities in London and his failure to come to a satisfactory arrangement regarding the licensing of the manufacture of his arms in Belgium was of little consequence, since the expansion of the Hartford factory resulted in sufficient manufacturing potential to meet the demands of world-wide markets. The man responsible for the efficient and economic operation of the Hartford factory was Elisha King Root. Root had joined Colt at the age of forty-one in 1849 and was responsible for the design of much of the machinery used at the Hartford factory. In general, it may be said that Colt was responsible for the design of the pistol and Root the manufacture. The influence of Root on the design side is most clearly seen in the Model of 1855 Sidehammer Pocket Pistol. Made in ·28-in. and ·31-in. calibre and in a wide variety of barrel lengths, the 'Roots' model will be found with both round and octagonal barrels. The ·28 calibre pistol has an engraved scene showing Indians on the cylinder, the ·32 the 'Stagecoach' scene found on the earlier 1849 pocket model. Notable because this was the first solid frame production Colt pistol, the 1855 pocket model was fitted with a sheath trigger and an external side hammer. The internal mechanism differed from normal Colt practice and although somewhat unreliable, the system proved to

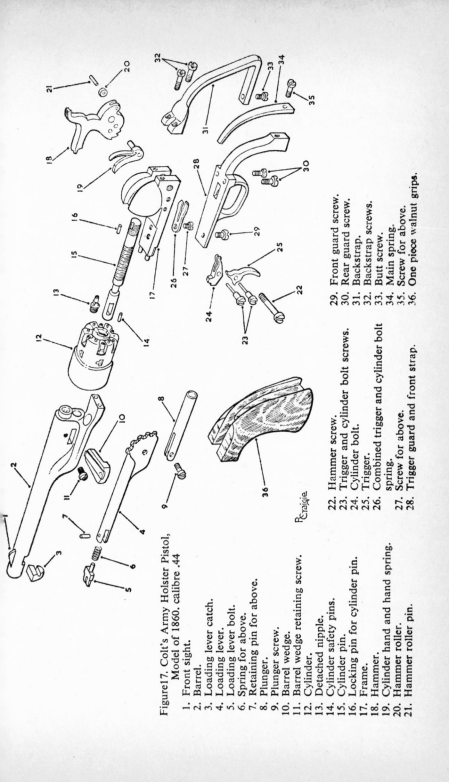

Figure 17. Colt's Army Holster Pistol,
Model of 1860. calibre .44

1. Front sight.
2. Barrel.
3. Loading lever catch.
4. Loading lever.
5. Loading lever bolt.
6. Spring for above.
7. Retaining pin for above.
8. Plunger.
9. Plunger screw.
10. Barrel wedge.
11. Barrel wedge retaining screw.
12. Cylinder.
13. Detached nipple.
14. Cylinder safety pins.
15. Cylinder pin.
16. Locking pin for cylinder pin.
17. Frame.
18. Hammer.
19. Cylinder hand and hand spring.
20. Hammer roller.
21. Hammer roller pin.

22. Hammer screw.
23. Trigger and cylinder bolt screws.
24. Cylinder bolt.
25. Trigger.
26. Combined trigger and cylinder bolt
    spring.
27. Screw for above.
28. Trigger guard and front strap.

29. Front guard screw.
30. Rear guard screw.
31. Backstrap.
32. Backstrap screws.
33. Butt screw.
34. Main spring.
35. Screw for above.
36. One piece walnut grips.

be of value when adapted to the revolving long arms, the production
of which recommenced in 1856.

Used on both the Root Model pocket pistol and the range of
military revolving rifles and carbines as well as sporting rifles and
shotguns, the Root 'creeping' type of loading lever represented a
complete departure from previous practice. The segmented cog or
'creeping lever' was used on the first of the 'streamlined' Colt pistols,
the Army Holster Pistol, Model of 1860. The calibre of this arm
was ·44 in. and it was made with 7½-in. and 8-in. barrels. Designed
to replace the famous Dragoon model, the Army model was reduced
in weight to 2 lb. 11 oz. and to many, the rounded barrel and smooth
flowing lines of this pistol are extremely attractive. Famous because
of the role it played in the American Civil War, the ·44 Army will
be found with a round cylinder rebated at the rear and an engraved
ship scene, this design being absent on a few pistols made with a
fluted cylinder. Most of the Army models will be found with cuts
in the recoil shield and a groove in the grip strap for attaching a
shoulder stock.

Featuring the streamlined barrels of the 1860 Army, the improved
Navy pistols of 1861 were of ·36 calibre and replaced the octagonal-
barrelled Navy pistol, Model of 1851. Apart from the difference in
size, the Navy Colt can be recognized from its immediate predecessor, the ·44 Army, by the fact that the Navy cylinder has no
rebate, and in all but the rarest examples, no provision for the fitting
of a shoulder stock is made. The last of the percussion Colt designs
was the Model of 1862, also known as the Police Model. Made in
4½-in., 5½-in. and 6½-in. barrel lengths, the Police Model was a
smaller version of the Navy and, although having the same calibre,
·36 in., the cylinder has only five chambers and was semi-fluted and
rebated at the rear.

The death of Samuel Colt in 1862 and the development of the
self-contained metallic cartridge brought to an end an era during
which the revolving principle had become firmly established and the
name Colt indelibly inscribed on the roll of history.

Colt's undeniable pre-eminence in the field of revolver manufacture naturally resulted in imitation and the expiry of his basic
patents in 1857 resulted in the open sale of copies of his pistols
where formerly such imitations had been surreptitiously manufactured, many of them in Belgium. This slavish imitation was not
confined to the Belgians, for on Colt's own doorstep the Manhattan

Fire Arms Manufacturing Co. and the Metropolitan Arms Co. both of New York, produced Navy pistols almost identical to the Colt original. Impelled perhaps by patriotism rather than commercial gain, the arms manufacturers of the Confederate States can be excused, since their use of the Colt design was dictated by dire necessity and the need to turn out shootable arms in the shortest possible time to meet the requirements of the arms-hungry Confederacy.

Quick to take advantage of the expiration of the Colt patents was the long-established arms company of E. Remington & Sons. The Superintendent of Manufacture at the Remington Armoury at Ilion, New York, was one Fordyce Beals, and Remington undertook the manufacture of a revolver based on Beals's 1856 and 1857 patents in an endeavour to overthrow the Colt monopoly. The Beals pocket revolvers were all five-shot single-action ·31-in. calibre weapons and are unusual in that the arm and pawl of the cylinder-rotating mechanism are exposed on the left-hand side of the frame. The First Model of 1857 was fitted with a normal trigger guard and trigger, the Second or 1858 Model had a sheath trigger and the Third or 1859 Model had a sheath trigger and was the first to have a lever rammer.

The ·44 Beals Single Action Army Model of 1860 was a man-size revolver with an 8-in. octagonal barrel and a solid frame. Identical in style, the ·36 Beals Navy Model of 1860 was produced in 7½-in. barrel length and these revolvers set the pattern of mechanical arrangement for heavy calibre Remington revolvers which was to survive until production of the 1890 Army ·44-40 ceased in 1894.

The year 1860 saw the introduction of a pocket revolver which replaced the Beals pocket models. The Remington Rider was a double-action ·31 five-shot weapon with a curious mushroom rebated cylinder. One of the earliest American double-action revolvers, it proved to be quite popular, many being used as pocket weapons during the American Civil War. Remington also manufactured the Rider single-shot 'Deringer' ·170-in. calibre pistol, in 1860. Of all-brass construction, it is estimated that less than a thousand were manufactured and, apart from its rarity, the Rider Deringer is of interest since no powder charge was employed, the explosion of the cap providing the sole propulsive force.

An attempt to improve the Beals Army and Navy revolvers, the 1861 Model Army ·44 and the ·36 Navy, incorporated William

Elliot's patent which provided a means whereby the cylinder pin could be removed without unlatching the lever rammer. This system proved impractical and the system dropped when the New Model revolvers were introduced in 1863. The 1861 revolvers can be distinguished from the Beals original by the presence of a channel in the top of the webbed rammer lever and the noticeable cut out provided to allow the forward movement of the cylinder pin wings.

The New Model Army and Navy revolvers were an attempt to correct the faults of the two previous models and are the first to use 'safety notches'. These notches, which appear on the rear radius of the cylinder midway between the nipples, provided a safe resting place for the hammer nose since it was unwise to rely on the half-cock notch, and resting the hammer on a capped and loaded chamber would be asking for trouble. Introduced concurrently, the New Model Belt Revolver was a smaller version of the ·36 1863 Navy, the barrel length was reduced from $7\frac{3}{8}$ in. to $6\frac{1}{2}$ in. retaining the traditional octagonal form. A double action version was also produced, this being based on Rider's patents and it differed in external appearance from the single-action New Model Belt revolver only in the position of the trigger and the use of a brass cone front sight instead of a German silver blade fore sight. The 'New Model Police' was built on the same general lines as the Belt model. The calibre remained at ·36 in. but the Police model has only five chambers. The last of the New Model Remingtons was the pocket model. Having a strong family resemblance to the larger revolvers, the pocket model was of ·31 calibre and five-chambered, the distinguishing feature being the use of a sheath trigger. This was the last of the Remington percussion revolvers, the story of the cartridge conversions and true cartridge revolvers will be taken up in a later chapter.

Next in popularity to Colt and Remington was the Starr made by Eben T. Starr at Yonkers, New York. The Starr was offered in both single-and double-action versions, the single-action ·44 having an 8-in. barrel, the double-action a 6-in. barrel. The double-action revolver also appeared in ·36 Navy calibre and can be identified from its larger stablemate by the nipples which are inclined outwards slightly instead of being parallel to the bore axis as are the nipples of the ·44 single- and double-action models. The basic Starr frame represented a departure from both the open-top Colt and the solid-frame Remington in that cylinder removal was facilitated by the use of a hinged frame which was secured by a large knurled screw passing through the upper rear of the frame. Removal of this screw allows the barrel group and top strap to be disengaged, the cylinder pin being integral with the cylinder.

The American Civil War, during which more American lives were lost than during World War I and World War II combined, undoubtedly established the percussion revolver as a military weapon of consequence and revolvers manufactured by Colt, Remington and Starr accounted for over eighty per cent of Government purchases. This great conflict saw the use of nearly every type of percussion revolver. The Massachusetts Arms Company manufactured Adams ·35 calibre revolvers under licence and many were supplied direct from England. From France came the nine-shot, single-action Le Mat, unique in that a ·66 calibre smooth bore barrel was provided under the rifled barrel designed to discharge shot. Large ·44 calibre percussion revolvers made by Freeman, Joslyn, Rodgers & Spencer, and Allen & Wheelock helped to swell the armouries of the North, although many were destined to be used by the South. The end of the war in 1865 was also the end of an era, since this was the last major conflict in which percussion weapons were used almost exclusively.

CHAPTER TWELVE

Early breechloaders

THROUGHOUT the history of firearms, inventors and gunmakers have diligently searched for the secret of making satisfactory breechloading arms. By the nineteenth century, the culmination of skills and knowledge made this long-sought-for ideal a practical possibility.

The first step in the evolution of the modern breechloader was to combine the paper cartridge, which contained propellant and projectile, with the means of ignition. Mention has already been made of that class of breechloading rifles known as the 'capping breechloader' (Westley Richards, Terry & Calisher, Green, Sharps) which used a combustible cartridge ignited by external means. The first to use a self-contained cartridge were the early French gunsmiths, Pauly and Demondion. It was a pupil of Pauly, Nicholas von Dreyse, who combined the self-contained cartridge with the first bolt-action breech system in his famous Needle Gun or Zundnadelgewehr in 1828. How this system, based on the common door bolt, had been overlooked for so long is difficult to understand.

The Dreyse Needle Gun was adopted by Prussia in 1841 and, due to its extremely rapid rate of fire as compared with muzzle-loading weapons, proved to be most effective. It was first used by the Prussians against Denmark in 1864 and the superiority of the breechloader was finally confirmed during the Austro-Prussian War of 1866. A leading English journal remarked at the time— 'The Austrians have been beaten in the Bohemian campaign, not because they were not as brave as the Prussians, or as well disciplined, but simply because their enemies were armed with guns which enabled the Prussians to fire five or six times whilst the Austrians fired once.'

What was the secret of this remarkable gun which had set all Europe in a ferment? Of great importance was the cartridge, which consisted of a lead bullet weighing 478 grains and ·53 in. in diameter. Attached to the base of the bullet was a wad of papier mâché in which was embedded detonating powder. Behind the bullet and means of ignition was the powder, the charge varying from 66 to 75 grains and held in a paper bag. To load the rifle, a spring catch was depressed at the rear of the bolt and the striker pulled back by hand to cock it before the bolt handle could be lifted and the bolt drawn back. With the bolt open the cartridge was placed in the breech and the bolt closed. When the trigger was pulled the striker or 'needle' was released and, under the influence of a spiral spring, it flew down the hollow centre of the bolt, passed through the powder container and powder until the point reached the detonating com-

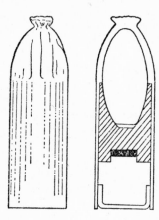

Figure 18. Prussian Needle Gun Cartridge. The shaded portion shows the wad or 'sabot' of papier mâché which contained the fulminate.

pound at the base of the bullet which ignited and set off the powder.

Although successful as a military weapon, the Dreyse suffered from two serious defects. The first was that the long striker or needle, being subjected to the corrosion of the powder gases did not last long. Secondly, since the paper case did not seal the breech properly, a considerable escape of gas took place, so much so that after the rifle had been fired a number of times it was hazardous to fire it from the shoulder, the common practice being to fire from the hip. In spite of these defects the following varieties of needle gun were issued. Infantry Models, 1841 and 1862, Fusilier Model 60, Jaeger Models, 49, 54 and 65, Engineer Model 69, Carbine Model 57 and the Needle Pistol Model 56. The needle gun remained in use until the adoption of the metallic cartridge loading rifle, Model of 1871.

The French, viewing events in Europe with some alarm, also adopted a needle gun designed by Antoine Alphonse Chassepôt. This rifle, known to the French Army as the Model 1866, used a

self-consuming cartridge and, in view of the development which
had occurred in metallic cartridges, the decision to use a rifle of
this type was unwise. Sealing of the breech was obtained by the use
of an indiarubber ring which was ineffective, and faulty obturation
resulted in fouling, and difficulty in loading. Eight years later the
Chassepôt rifle was altered to take the Gras metallic cartridge, the
Gras conversion remaining in service until 1874. It is of interest to

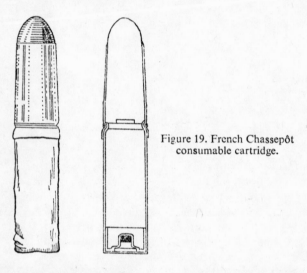

Figure 19. French Chassepôt
consumable cartridge.

record that many of these conversions were carried out in England
by the Kynoch Gun Company.

In England, the Needle Gun enjoyed a limited success for sporting
purposes, the Needham breechloader being made in both shotgun
and rifle form. The cartridge consisted of a paper cylinder with two
stout wads, the base wad being reinforced by an internal zinc cup.
The base wad and cup were pierced by a hole to permit the passage
of the needle which struck a cap containing the detonating powder.
The over powder wad went down the barrel with the projectile and
the base wad and cup were pushed ahead of the next cartridge when
reloading, the paper case being consumed. Rifles on this plan were
made by Needham in London and Rigby of Dublin, the cartridges
in 75, 90 and 110 bore being made by Eley Brothers Ltd, London.

Both the Needle Gun and the capping breechloader suffered from faulty obturation and this was not overcome until the invention and perfection of the 'gas-tight' cartridge, which expanded to seal the breech at the moment of discharge and so effectively prevented loss of gas. The gas-tight cartridge had its origins in the invention, by the French gunmaker Houiller, of the pin fire cartridge. This cartridge consisted of a stout cylinder of coiled paper fitted into a base cup of copper or brass. Through the rim of the cap protruded a pin, the other end of which ended in a point which stood clear of a standard percussion cap placed at right angles to the axis of the

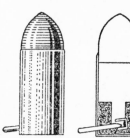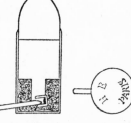

Figure 20. Pin fire cartridge. The hammer strikes the protruding pin and drives it against the fulminate, igniting the charge. The shaded portion is compressed cardboard. A brass liner was often used to provide additional support for the cap.

case. When the cartridge was loaded into the breech (provision being made for the pin by a small notch at the top of the breech end of the barrel) the pin stood proud and on being struck by a modified form of percussion hammer the point was driven into the cap, the flash igniting the surrounding charge. Sporting guns using pin fire cartridges, or 'douilles' as they were first known, were made by Lefaucheux, a French gunmaker, who succeeded to the business founded by Pauly. Lefaucheux' guns were exhibited at the Great Exhibition held in London in 1851, being introduced on the English market by the London gunmaker Lang shortly afterwards. The Lefaucheux was fitted with hinged drop down barrels and this basic system remains in use for single-and double-barrel guns to this day. The early pin fires had no extractor system to aid removal of the spent case (nor were the cases rimmed) this being withdrawn by means of the pin. In the event of the case sticking, a small tool was available to avoid lacerated fingers. In addition to the extraction problem, the locking system was not satisfactory. This was operated by a long lever pivoted at the breech end and extending forward under the fore-end. The locking system was improved by a Birmingham gunmaker by the use of the 'double grip' lever. This system, although somewhat ungainly to modern eyes, is still in use, mainly on large-bore shotguns and heavy double rifles. The lever follows the contour of the trigger guard and moved a 'two start' thread which engaged in two slots cut in the 'lumps' or downward projections from the breech end of the barrel. A quarter turn of the lever is sufficient to release the 'grips' and the barrel hinges downward on the 'knuckle pin' at the forward end of the action body. Although the double grip lever mechanism solved the problem of closing the breech, some pin fire shotguns were made using the Bastin Lepage sliding barrel action in which the barrels slide to and fro along the fore-end. A combination of the two systems, in which the barrels move forward one-eighth of an inch and then drop down on the hinge or knuckle pin, was invented by the Glasgow gunmaker, J. D. Dougall, for his 'lock fast' breech mechanism, and Dougall appears to be one of the last British gunmakers seriously to champion the pin fire cartridge.

The pin fire cartridge was restricted to shotguns, a relatively small number of rifles and low-powered 'pepper-box' and true revolvers as well as to a dubious range of double-barrelled pistols. There is only one authenticated instance of the cartridge being used for other than sporting and self-defence purposes. This was during the early 1850's when a pin fire musketoon was issued to Louis Napoleon's personal bodyguard. When the guard was formed it numbered one hundred and the musketoon was given the name, Mousqueton des Cent Gardes. Probably the only pin fire military arm ever issued, the Musketoon of the Hundred Guardsmen was also the first military small bore, leading the trend towards smaller military calibres which has continued to the present day.

It was in the field of revolver cartridges that the pin fire lasted longest. Lefaucheux exhibited a pin fire 'pepper-box' type of revolver at the 1851 London Exhibition and before long the gunmakers of France, Germany and Belgium flooded the market with 'drop-down' double-barrel pistols and pin fire revolvers, whose only dubious merit was cheapness. Such revolvers, chambered for 5, 7, 9, 12 and 15 mm. cartridges, were made until comparatively recently and the availability of these cartridges indicates their continued use to this day.

Also shown at the famous 1851 Exhibition was a rimfire copper cartridge which had been invented by Flobert of Paris and which we know today as the bulleted breech cap, or Saloon or Flobert ammunition. As originally designed, this ammunition consisted of a rimmed copper case and a round, small-calibre ball. A charge of priming composition was placed in the upset rim of the case but no powder. The explosion of the priming by the compression of the rim of the case against the breech of the barrel when it was struck by the hammer, expelled enough gas to drive out the bullet. Intended for indoor target practice, this cartridge will be encountered with spherical, conical and conoidal bullets. With a slightly longer case and a charge of black powder the cartridge then becomes the

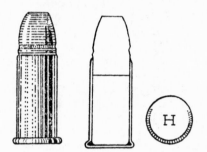

Figure 21. Rimfire cartridge. The fulminate is contained in the cartridge rim.

original ·22 short developed by Daniel Wesson and used in the Smith & Wesson First Model revolver of 1857.

Having developed the cartridge, it was necessary to design a revolver with a bored-through cylinder which could be rear loaded. Here Wesson encountered a slight difficulty. In 1854 a young American inventor secured a patent for a revolver 'with the chambers of the cylinders bored through from front to rear'. The legend goes that the inventor, Rollin White, took his patent to Sam Colt who told him that the idea was impractical and the invention was apparently stillborn.

When Wesson applied for his patents, which included a bored-through cylinder to accommodate his rimfire cartridges, he learned that Rollin White had already patented the feature so necessary for success. White was approached by Wesson and agreed to let Smith & Wesson manufacture under his patent on a royalty basis and, at the same time, agreed to defend his patent claims against infringement. Smith & Wesson, as a result of this arrangement, now held as strong a stranglehold on revolver development as had Colt previously. In effect they had an American monopoly on the feature necessary for the utilization of metallic cartridges until 1869.

The success of the famous Smith & Wesson No. 1 tip-up models (which were made until 1879) resulted in many attempts to evade the master patent of Rollin White. Colt, who had brusquely turned down White's original offer, did not live to see the results of his myopic attitude, for it was not until 1868 that the first Colt cartridge model using Alexander Thuer's conversion was produced. This attempt to evade the Rollin White patents was not entirely satisfactory and met with little success. Briefly, the conversion consisted of fitting an intricate ring, provided with both firing pin and ejecting lever, to the rear of a modified Colt percussion cylinder. The cartridge, which was metallic and self-primed, was loaded at the front of the cylinder by the loading lever in the usual way. The ring was capable of lateral movement quite independent of the cylinder and when it was moved to the right the firing pin was driven by the hammer-fall against the cartridge head in line with the barrel. To eject the cartridge, the ring was turned to the left and when the hammer was snapped, the ejecting lever gave a sharp blow to the fired case in the chamber second to the right of the hammer. Although the Thuer conversion was perhaps one of the most ingenious means of producing a cartridge revolver without infringement of the White patents, it was by no means the only attempt.

By 1862 a number of manufacturers were marketing revolvers which were clearly infringements of the patent, and, in 1863, a verdict upholding the Rollin White patent was obtained by court action. As a result of this, thousands of revolvers were turned over to Smith & Wesson which, apart from purely mercenary considerations, also served to strengthen their hold on the American market for cartridge revolvers. Since infringement had failed, the competitors of Smith & Wesson now tried evasion, the most successful of the early attempts being the Plant hinged-frame revolver. This was similar in outward appearance to the Smith & Wesson but used what is today known as a 'cup primer' cartridge, which was loaded at the front of the cylinder. The cylinder was not bored right through but a small opening was provided at the rear to permit the hammer nose to strike the inside of the hollow cartridge base. Many other attempts were made to get round the obstructive patent, some thirty or more United States patents being granted for revolvers designed to avoid infringement. Perhaps the most successful of all the 'Smith & Wesson evasions' were those designed to fire 'teat fire' cartridges, foremost being the Moore, and the National revolvers.

The teat fire cartridge revolver had been patented by Daniel Moore in 1863 and covered the use of a front loading cartridge having the fulminate contained in a teat in the base, the teat protruding through a small hole in the rear of the cylinder. Revolvers which loaded through the side of the cylinder, such as the Slocum, used standard rimfire cartridges as did the separate-chamber Pond which was patented in 1863.

The expiry of the Rollin White patent in 1869 ended what must be a unique series of picturesque and unusual revolvers and cartridges, and permitted a flood of rim- and centre-fire revolvers to fill the vacuum created by Rollin White's determined defence of his once despised invention.

In America, rimfire cartridges were made in a variety of calibres, the most famous being the ·44 Henry. B. Tyler Henry was the plant superintendent of the New Haven Arms Company which, under the presiding genius of Oliver F. Winchester, a New Haven shirt manufacturer, had acquired the assets of the Volcanic Repeating Arms Company which had failed in 1857. The Volcanic rifle represented the first really important development in breechloading repeater design since it introduced the double-toggle breechlocking mechanism.

With an ancestry dating back to the Jennings repeating rifle of 1849, and incorporating further improvements patented by Smith & Wesson in 1854, the failure of the Volcanic, made both as a rifle and a pistol, can be attributed to the inadequacy of the ammunition designed for it. The cartridge consisted of a hollow-based conical bullet having a charge of black powder in the base retained by means of a cardboard disc containing the primer. Due to the lack of an adequate gas seal and lack of space for an adequate charge, the system was unsatisfactory.

Although the New Haven Arms Company continued to manufacture the Volcanic, sales were disappointing and it was due to Henry perfecting a ·44 rimfire cartridge and devising alterations in the Volcanic that made it possible for this ammunition to be used that laid the foundations of the later success of both the Henry and later Winchester rifles.

The Henry rifle was patented in 1860. In 1862 rifles marked Henry's Patent, October 16 1860, manufactured by the New

Haven Arms Company, New Haven, Ct., using a ·44 calibre rimfire cartridge with a powder charge of 26 grains black powder and a conical bullet of 216 grains, made their début on the commercial market. The magazine of this rimfire repeater held fifteen cartridges and during the Civil War 'the gun that they could wind up on Sunday and shoot all week' earned for itself an enviable reputation.

Made only in ·44 rimfire calibre, the rifle had a 24-in. octagonal barrel and a full-length under-barrel tubular magazine. Both brass and iron were used for the receivers and the Henry can be distinguished from its later and even more illustrious offspring, the Winchester Model 1866, by the absence of a wooden fore-end. The Henry established a long and successful line of lever action repeating rifles and it is of interest to note that despite the passing of the years the name of B. Tyler Henry is still commemorated by the 'H' headstamp on every ·22 rimfire cartridge sold by Winchester to this day.

Yet another of the men who rose to fame during the latter half of the nineteenth century on the rising tide of American industrialism was Christopher M. Spencer who patented a seven-shot repeating rifle in 1860. This arm differed from its main competitor, the Henry, in having the magazine tube in the butt stock instead of under the barrel. Chambered for rimfire cartridges like the Henry, the Spencer was made in a variety of calibres, 56–46, 56–50, 56–52 and 56–56 (the first figure group refers to the case diameter above the rim, the second to the nominal calibre).

The Spencer saw considerable service during the Civil War and the ·50 calibre Model 1865 had a part in the opening of the West, Custer's famous 7th U.S. Cavalry being armed with Spencer carbines at the Battle of Washita, 27th November 1868. In the same year the Spencer Repeating Arms Company was acquired by the Winchester Repeating Arms Company—Oliver Winchester having once again reorganized his affairs—and the New Haven Arms Company in 1866 finally bore the name of its founder and majority shareholder.

The formation of the new company was an event of some importance and the first rifle to bear the Winchester name, the Winchester Model 1866, although similar to the Henry, incorporated an important new loading feature. Nelson King, Henry's successor as factory superintendent, retained the under-barrel tubular magazine but provided a hinged loading gate in the side of the receiver through which cartridges could be inserted. This feature eliminated the fragile slotted magazine tube used by the Henry rifle and greatly facilitated the loading operation as well as permitting the use of a wooden fore-end. The '66 Winchester was produced in carbine, rifle and musket style all chambered for the ·44 rimfire cartridges and can be said to have truly placed the name of Winchester firmly on the road to greatness.

Elsewhere the rimfire cartridge (with the notable exception of the ·22) did not enjoy the same run of popularity. In England, the first revolvers to employ rimfire cartridges were Birmingham-made versions of the seven-chambered ·22 single action Smith & Wesson. In 1863, however, Tranter took out the first of his breechloading revolver patents which resulted in the manufacture of a range of rimfire revolvers reminiscent of the 'improved' single-trigger Tranter percussion revolver of 1856. The 'large' calibre rimfire revolvers made in ·450, ·442, ·440 and ·380 were six-chambered and provided with a loading gate at the right-hand side of the breech, the cartridges being ejected one at a time by means of a modification of the loading lever previously used on the percussion revolvers. A range of smaller pocket pistols in a variety of calibres were also made, a common feature being the absence of an ejector and on some models, the use of a sheath trigger instead of the normal trigger and trigger guard. Tranter appears to have enjoyed a virtual monopoly of the rimfire revolver business, receiving no serious competition until the appearance of the central-fire Adams revolver in 1867.

On the Continent the rimfire cartridge was adopted by Switzerland who armed her troops in 1867 with the Amsler. This was a single-shot breechloading conversion, using an external hammer and was replaced by the rimfire Vetterli, which was approved by the Swiss in 1869, but difficulties with the early models prevented their full-scale adoption until 1881. Known as the Model 1869/81, the Vetterli was a turning bolt action repeating rifle with a magazine tube in the fore-end. Apart from the bolt action this rifle, made in ·41 in. (10·4 mm.) calibre, was similar to the Model 1866 Winchester, the cartridge elevating system and the use of the magazine tube under the barrel closely following American practice. The year 1867 saw Austria armed with a breechloading conversion, the Wanzl, which used a rimfire cartridge. This stop-gap weapon was followed by the Werndl, developed by the Director-General of the Steyr Armoury. Originally the single-shot Werndl was chambered for a rimfire cartridge of approximately ·433 in. calibre but was later converted to an 11·4 mm. centre-fire cartridge, and finally to an 11 mm. bottle necked centre-fire case. The only other continental power of consequence who used rimfire military ammunition was Belgium. Originally, the British-made and designed Braendlin-Albini breechloading conversion was chambered for a ·60 in. calibre rimfire cartridge, the calibre being reduced to ·43 in. (11 mm.) and finally a coiled brass case of centre-fire construction was adopted.

Britain did not pass through the rimfire conversion period, muzzle-loading Enfields being converted to breechloaders, using centre-fire ammunition. This action had been precipitated by events in America where, although the bulk of the fighting had been carried out with muzzle-loading arms, the Union forces had used with great effect breechloading weapons and, indeed, breechloading repeating weapons, such as the Spencer.

In 1864 a committee was appointed to consider the question of adopting a breechloader and their findings indicated that it would be advisable to convert existing stocks of muzzle-loading weapons, leaving the selection of an entirely new weapon to be decided at a later date.

Some fifty different makes of breechloader were submitted and eight systems selected for trial (one was eliminated by the inventor, who refused to fire his gun!). Five of those selected were capping breechloaders, the other three using cartridges containing their own means of ignition. Of the five finalists the breech mechanism offered by Jacob Snider of New York was approved by the committee and conversion of existing Enfield rifles and carbines commenced.

This breech action belonged to the class having laterally swinging blocks, the block being pivoted on a long pin which ran along the right-hand side of the action body. The block was opened by pressing a thumb catch on the left-hand side on the Mk II and III (the early actions had no positive lock, only a small spring stud to hold the block in the closed position) the block then being swung over to the right. This exposed the chamber and permitted the introduction of a cartridge. The action was closed and the cartridge fired by means of the original Enfield lock and hammer, the hammer striking an obliquely placed firing pin passing through the breech block instead of the percussion nipple used by the original muzzle-loading Enfield. To extract the fired cartridge, the hammer was

brought to half cock, the block opened and pulled slightly back
against spring tension. Attached to the block was a claw extractor
which withdrew the fired case, removal being achieved by turning
the rifle upside down.

This breech system was not new and its success was entirely
dependent upon the availability of satisfactory gas-tight cartridges.
Originally the cartridge used had been based on the French Pottet
patent of 1857 and the later English patent taken out in the name
of F. E. Schneider of Paris, Schneider shotgun cartridges being

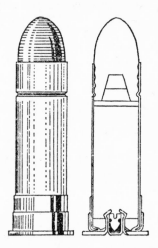

Figure 22. ·577 Boxer ca r
tridge (central fire) for the
Snider rifle.

successfully marketed for sporting purposes by G. H. Daw, a
famous London gunsmith.

Early trials with the Snider conversion showed that the cartridges,
using a case similar to the centre-fire sporting cartridge with a paper
tube and conposite head were unsuitable. The results obtained
nevertheless adequately demonstrated to the authorities that a
cartridge containing its own means of ignition was far superior to
the alternative self-consuming type. An approach was made to
Colonel Boxer, the Superintendent of the Royal Laboratory, who
produced and patented an improved centre-fire cartridge which was
approved and adopted as the Regulation pattern for the Snider rifle.

The Boxer cartridge was made of brass (·004-in. thick) which
was spirally coiled and covered with paper to keep it together. The

cap had a loose anvil similar to those used in pre-war English shotgun cases, the cap being held in a brass chamber riveted to tube, and to a black iron disc forming the outer base and rim.

Despite somewhat contentious beginnings, the Boxer cartridge proved to be successful and, indeed, started the trend towards centre-fire military cartridges which subsequently swept Europe. When stocks of the existing Enfields had been converted (by cutting off about two inches of the breech of the barrel and screwing on Snider's conversion) a completely new rifle, the Mark III, was manufactured on the same pattern, these being fitted with steel barrels, the first in the British Army.

CHAPTER THIRTEEN

Breechloading repeaters

WITH the adoption of the breechloading Snider, Britain now had a chance to sit back and consider at leisure the ideal rifle for military purposes. In America, the first military breechloading rifle manufactured at Springfield Armoury was the Model 1866, the action of which was invented by E. S. Allin, Springfield Master Amourer, as a method of converting stocks of muzzle-loading arms to breechloaders. This rifle also used a hinged breech block, lifting at the rear and hinging upwards and over in line with the axis of the barrel. The 'trap door' Springfield was adapted for a ·50 calibre centre-fire brass cartridge containing 70 grains black powder and a 450-grain, grooved, lubricated, conical bullet and earlier had used a ·58 calibre rimfire cartridge. In 1873, the calibre was reduced to ·45–70–405, i.e. ·45 calibre, 70 grains black powder and a 405-grain bullet. Bullet weight was then increased to 500 grains, the ·45–70–405 cartridge being retained for use with the carbine model. The last model of the Springfield was the M. 1888 which saw service with the Volunteer and Militia forces during the Spanish-American War, remaining in use with the regular U.S. forces until 1894. The early Springfield ·50 calibre cartridge differed from the British Boxer in that it was solid drawn from copper and not built up like the Boxer. This cartridge used a bar anvil which proved unsuitable and it was replaced in 1868 by a centre-primed cup anvil cartridge designed by Colonel S. V. Benet, then in charge of the Frankford Arsenal.

During the 70's and 60's considerable experimental work was carried out at the various Government Arsenals in America and many were the visitors who called and extolled the virtues of their particular inventions. Prominent among these visitors was Colonel Berdan, who, so the story goes, saw the Benet cartridge and applied the principle of continuously forming the head to his own cartridge. Thus apparently was born the Berdan primer which differs basically from the Boxer in that the anvil is formed as part of the case and does not require a separate anvil. The American type with integral anvil is now standard in Europe and the British Boxer separate anvil in America. The Boxer type of primer with the single, central flash hole has the advantage of being easier to de-cap and more readily permits reloading and is, of course, more simple to manu-facture.

The Berdan cartridge in ·42-in. calibre was adopted by Russia in 1868 and used in the Berdan I single-shot rifle. The Berdan I was similar to the Springfield in that it used a lifting hinged block but instead of an external hammer an internal striker was used. Three years later the Berdan II was adopted, this being a single-shot ·42 calibre rifle using a turning bolt system. This rifle was often used with the 'Krnka Quick Loader', a device for holding cartridges which was attached to the rifle to permit rapid reloading. This Austrian gunsmith with the almost unpronounceable name was also responsible for the Krnka Model 1869 which had been a stop-gap lifting block conversion system for muzzle-loading rifles.

Not content with arming the Russians, arms of American design and manufacture were sold to Spain in 1869, Sweden in 1867, France 1870–71, Egypt 1870 and numerous South American Republics. The rifle that was sold in such quantities was manu-factured by the Remington Armoury at Ilion, New York, being based on a lock mechanism invented by Leonard M. Geiger, improved by the Armoury's Superintendent Rider. The Remington-Rider Rolling Block rifle has one of the simplest and strongest breech actions ever developed. To load, the external centrally disposed hammer is cocked and the rolling breech block, which carries the firing pin moved back by pulling on a projecting handle. This operation also operates the extractor. When the cartridge is inserted the block is pushed forward against the breech face, being supported, but not locked, by a flat steel spring. The hammer is so shaped as to lock against the breech block on falling, locking taking place before the hammer strikes the firing pin. The most widely used cartridge for this rifle was the 11 mm. or ·433-in. Remington Spanish cartridge, which was adopted by Denmark, Sweden and Norway as well as many of the South American Republics.

Mention has already been made of the Sharps rifle (patented by Christian Sharps in 1848) which saw service in the American Civil War and which had been experimentally issued to the British Cavalry as a capping breechloader. The introduction of the metallic cartridge solved the problem of gas escaping from the breech and the early side-hammer Sharps chambered for the ·40–90–370 cartridge accounted for many of the buffalo roaming the western plains of America, one particular model being known as the

'Buffalo Gun'. Converted to 'hammerless' style by Hugo Borchardt, a naturalized American citizen, the Sharps-Borchardt took on a new lease of life and chambered for the heavy ·45 and ·50 calibre cartridges it became the most powerful black powder rifle ever designed in America. In 1881 the Sharps Rifle Company closed, due to want of capital but the Sharps action lived on as the progenitor of a number of breech actions differing only in non-essentials from the original.

From America came yet another of the original single-shot breech mechanisms, the Peabody. Developed by Henry O. Peabody of Boston, this was the earliest action to employ a breech block hinged at the rear and above the axis of the bore. Manufactured by the Providence (R.I.) Tool Company, the Peabody, with its large external hammer and falling block action, was offered to foreign markets: Canada, Switzerland, Roumania, France and Denmark purchasing this rifle.

In Switzerland, Frederich von Martini modified the Peabody action by replacing the external hammer with an internal firing pin inside the breech block. This was the rifle, the Peabody-Martini, which was submitted for trial as a result of an advertisement issued by the British Government dated 22nd October 1866, calling for a replacement for the Snider. One hundred and four rifles were submitted and amongst those which were rejected in the early stages was a breechloading Whitworth, adapted for his famous mechanically fitting bullet (the cartridge case for this round was also hexagonal) the ·44 rimfire Henry, and several bolt-action weapons. Of the latter class, the Carter Edwards bolt-action breechloader was provided with a hinged cover over the bolt and the Lindner which used a consumable cartridge, the bolt being locked by an interrupted screw thread. Two other bolt-action rifles were submitted, one by Cooper, the locking action of which was reminiscent of the later Lee, and a bolt-action weapon offered by Tranter, the famous Birmingham gunmaker.

It was, however, the opinion of the selection committee that bolt-action weapons were unsuitable, since the jamming of a cartridge might produce a premature explosion and, in fact, the Bacon action went off accidentally when tested with defective cartridges specially provided for the trial. This decision left only the 'block' rifle and in the rapidity trials the first three were the Westley Richards (elevating block), the Martini and the Henry. The latter rifle had been submitted by Alexander Henry, a noted gunmaker of Edinburgh, and was yet another variant of the versatile Sharps vertical block action.

A number of trials had been devised to thoroughly examine the serviceability of the rifles submitted and by the time the exposure tests had been completed the competition had been reduced to the Henry and the Martini. Based on the consideration of the number of parts in each rifle, ease and cost of manufacture and facility in use, the Henry was finally rejected and the Martini emerged triumphant. None of the rifles came up to the standards required and it was advised that a combination of the Martini action and the Alex Henry barrel be adopted. It was recommended that the Henry barrel, having shown itself to be the most accurate, be wedded to the most suitable action, the Martini 'marriage' being consummated at Enfield Lock, Middlesex, the Government Small Arms factory.

The Martini-Henry, as finally adopted in 1869, weighed 9 lb., had an overall length of 48½ in. and a ·450 calibre barrel 33·2 in. long rifled with seven grooves, right-handed twist, making one complete turn in 22 in. Four different 'Marks' or improvements were issued, the Mark IV having an extended operating lever, following complaints of difficult extraction received during use in Egypt. The patterns issued to the various branches of the forces were cut down, the same rifle being issued to the Infantry, the Rifle Regiments and the Royal Navy. A carbine was issued to the Cavalry and the Royal Artillery, the artillery carbine having a sword bar and sling swivels.

The ammunition for the Martini-Henry was produced with the collaboration of Mr Henry, and the original cartridges, of ·450 calibre, were of Boxer construction and parallel sided. In order to provide sufficient space for the powder charge, the cartridge was longer than the ·577 Snider. The increased length and relative fragility of its construction made it liable to damage if dropped or roughly handled. In order to overcome this difficulty, it was decided to adopt a shorter cartridge of bottle-necked construction and, in effect, the ·577 Boxer case for the Snider was 'necked down' to accept the ·450 Henry bullet. These early Boxer ·577/450 cartridges, although satisfactory under normal conditions, were replaced by a cartridge with solid drawn case following difficulties encountered with extraction during the Sudan campaigns of 1882. Two types of cartridge were issued, one for rifles and one for carbines. Case dimensions were similar so that in an emergency the cartridges were interchangeable, the rifle cartridge having a powder charge of 85 grains black powder and a bullet weight of 480 grains; the carbine charge being 70 grains black powder, bullet weight 410 grains. The bullet of the carbine cartridge was patched with red paper instead of white for identification.

Two men who were to revolutionize military thought, and whose arms eventually sold in the tens of millions, were the brothers Paul and Wilhelm Mauser. Paul, the younger brother, was the dominant partner, and after working in the Government firearms factory at Oberndorf in the Kingdom of Wurtemburg, he developed a bolt-action single-shot rifle in 1867, a later version of which was adopted by Prussia in 1871. The important features of this rifle were as follows:

1. The lock was self cocking (previous bolt actions had to be manually cocked before the bolt could be opened).
2. On opening, the striker is retracted so that the tip of the firing pin is behind the bolt face. This effectively prevents the possibility of premature ignition when the cartridge is pushed forward by the bolt into the chamber. (The lack of this feature condemned the bolt-action systems submitted to the British Small Arms Committee.)
3. The provision of an effective extractor suitable for metallic cartridges as well as an ejector.
4. An efficient safety catch mounted on the cocking piece which locks the bolt and prevents the striker from reaching the cartridge.

The first Mauser factory was burnt down in 1873, but due to substantial orders from Prussia and Wurtemburg, the brothers Mauser were able to buy the Oberndorf factory and manufacture started here in 1874. In 1876, 26,000 Model 71 rifles were sold to China, this being but the first of many orders which were to arm the smaller nations of the world and eventually develop into the largest and most complex organization of arms interests in history.

Although the most important of the bolt actions developed, the Mauser was by no means the only contender. Mention has already been made of the American Berdan I adopted by Russia and the

Swiss Vetterli which led the field in being not only bolt action but capable of magazine fire also. For the record, the Austrian Fruwirth bolt-action rifle with tubular magazine was employed in quantity before the Vetterli but since the Austrians were already heavily committed to the Werndl single-shot rifle, the Fruwirth saw but limited use by the Austro-Hungarian Gendarmerie.

France, watching affairs in Europe closely, adopted the 11 mm. Gras rifle in 1874. As far back as 1866 conversions of the Chassepôt rifle, which used a consumable cartridge, had been made using the Gras system and many conversions of the Chassepôt to use metallic cartridges had been undertaken in Britain by the Kynoch Gun Company of Aston, Birmingham.

A variety of repeating arms were tested by the French as early as 1874 when trials with the Vetterli-Gras combination were carried out. A limited issue of Kropatschek 11 mm. bolt-action rifles were made to the Marines in 1878, this rifle having an under-barrel tubular magazine, the patent of Colonel Kropatschek of the Austrian Army. Known as the Gras-Kropatschek, the rifle had a magazine capacity of seven rounds and used the 11 mm. Gras cartridge slightly modified by flattening the nose, a precaution necessary when using tubular magazines.

One defect of the tubular magazine was that the centre of gravity of the rifle altered as the cartridges were used; another was that only single cartridges could be loaded, one after the other. A successful attempt to preserve the balance of the weapon was the introduction of the Spitalsky rotary magazine in 1879 which was developed at the Steyr Armoury in Austria. This type of magazine was further developed by Otto Schoenauer (later a director of the Austrian Arms Co.) and was used by Ferdinand Ritter von Mannlicher in the Mannlicher-Schoenauer which was to gain fame as a sporting rifle in later years.

An alternative approach to the problem, and one which was to be almost universally adopted for military use, was the invention, also in 1879, of the box magazine. This device was first introduced on the ·45–70 Lee U.S. Navy Rifle. James Paris Lee was born in Hawick, Scotland, in 1831, and educated in Canada, being an American by adoption only. The Lee rifle was submitted to the American Navy but before production commenced manufacture was turned over to the Remington Arms Company, ever eager to welcome new ideas. Modifications were necessary to remedy faults in the action and in 1884 Lee entered into an agreement with Remington to manufacture and sell his rifle on a royalty basis.

Back in Germany, Paul Mauser added the benefits of repeating fire to his Model 1871 bolt-action rifle and in 1884 the Infantry Repeating Rifle M.71–84 was officially adopted by the German Government using the standard 11 mm. (·433) military cartridge. The rifle was loaded with eight cartridges held in the standard tubular magazine, a ninth could be placed on the 'carrier' and a tenth placed directly in the chamber. Large numbers of this rifle were manufactured, 550,000 in 9·5 mm. calibre being delivered to Turkey alone. The Mauser factory at Oberndorf was not entirely responsible for the manufacture of all Mauser rifles and many will be found bearing the marks or names of the Government arsenals, Amberg, Danzig, Erfurt or Spandau. Mausers marked 'Oesterr, Waff. Ges.' being made at the Austrian Arms Company factory at Steyr.

The Austrian Arms Company is, however, more renowned for its association with Mannlicher, whose 11 mm. Austro-Hungarian rifle Model 1885 was the forerunner of a new class of bolt-action weapons which were to see world-wide use. Mannlicher's design differed in that the bolt was operated by straight backwards and forwards movement, no turning being necessary. Although theoretically faster than turning-bolt designs, the lack of a camming primary extraction nullifies some of the advantages of the straight pull action in practice. Coupled with the straight-pull action was a box magazine with a most important innovation, clip loading. With this system a sheet steel clip is inserted into the magazine, the clip holding five cartridges. When the magazine is emptied and the bolt opened the clip is automatically ejected upward and a fresh clip and cartridges can be inserted. (This system is used in the U.S. M. 1 Garand semi-automatic rifle.)

The Model 1886 replaced the earlier rifle but differed only in the magazine and loading clip. Instead of being ejected upwards when empty the M.1886 clip falls out of the bottom of the magazine. This system was used in many of the later Mannlicher models and also by the German M.1888, the French Berthier, and the Italian Mannlicher-Carcano.

So far, emphasis has been placed on mechanical improvements. The next major step was in the field of ballistics. In general, the repeating rifles which had been adopted for military or sporting purposes had used large-calibre black-powder cartridge designs already available. A minor alteration already mentioned was the need to flatten the nose of cartridges used in tubular magazines to avoid accidental discharge of the preceding cartridge, a modification not required when box magazines were used. It was left to Portugal to make the first move by adopting the Guedes rifle manufactured at Steyr. Although mechanically backward since it was a single-shot falling-block action, the Guedes rifle is important since the cartridge used an 8 mm. copper-clad bullet weighing 264 grains.

Rubin and Hebler in Switzerland appear to be the first to have developed a satisfactory technique for 'cladding' bullets in 1878. Colonel Rubin and Colonel Rudoph Schmidt, Director of the Swiss Federal Arms Factory, worked on the development of a straight pull rifle, officially designated as the Swiss Repeating Rifle Model 1889, or the Schmidt-Rubin, which was adopted by the Swiss. The calibre of this rifle was 7·5 mm. (·295 in.). Rubin was responsible for the ballistic developments and it is his work on clad bullets which provided the second necessary feature of the modern high-velocity cartridge, a metal envelope which would resist the increased friction caused by high velocities. The first feature was the solid drawn case and the last the development of non-fouling powder.

Prussian Dreyse
edle-fire' military
e.

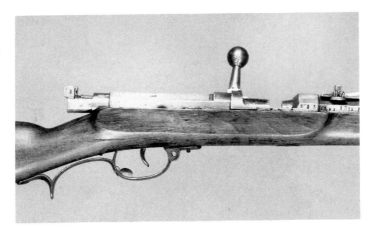

Close up of the action
of the rifle above.
Look carefully and
you can see the
needle.

e Martini-Henry
7/.450 military
e. The action by
artini, the rifling
ented by Alex
nry of Edinburgh.
is is the first
oduction model
m the RSAF at
field and was
sented to Alex
nry himself.

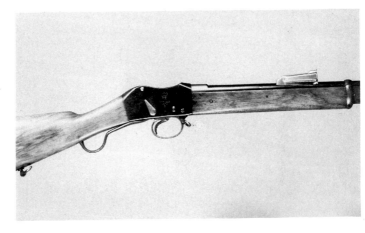

PLATE 10

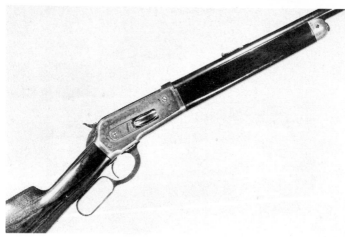

The Winchester
Model 1886. This i
the rifle style with
half-length magazi
in .45–90 calibre.

The Winchester lever
action shotgun. I
cannot ever conceive
of using a device like
this in the company
of other guns.

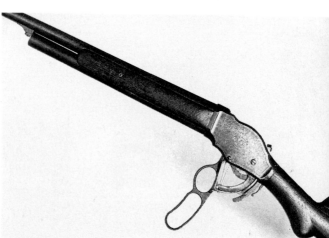

One of the early
British shotgun
actions, the
Lancaster. This is
one of the 'move
forward and drop
down' type; here th
barrels have been
moved forward to
illustrate the
amount of moveme
obtained. Early
versions fired a
special Lancaster
'base-fire' cartridge
surviving examples
of which cannot be
traced.

The early
...echloading
...tguns are very
...ectable and are
...available in an
...ost bewildering
...iety. This
...mple of a central-
... hammer gun is
...George Daw of
...ndon with his
...sh forward'
...derlever action.

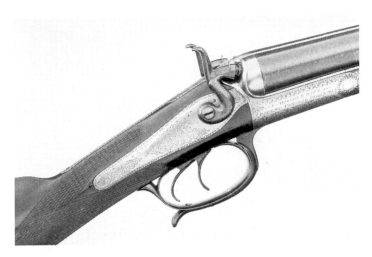

Pin-fire shotguns can
still be found
although not at the
low prices they used
to fetch. This
unnamed example
shows the classic
layout with the rotary
underlever and back
action lockwork.

...vented by James
... Dougall, the
...asgow gunmaker,
...s special action
...ves the barrels
...ward slightly
...fore they drop
...wn. Known as the
...ockfast' action it
...l be encountered
...a rifle, shotgun
...d in pin and
...atral-fire. It is an
...mensely strong
...ion.

PLATE 12

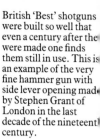

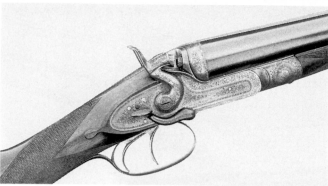

British 'Best' shotguns were built so well that even a century after they were made one finds them still in use. This is an example of the very fine hammer gun with side lever opening made by Stephen Grant of London in the last decade of the nineteenth century.

Things are not always what they seem to be. A Dickson central-fire hammer double shotgun was originally made as a pin-fire and later converted to a central-fire. The owner submitted the gun for nitro-proof and the action cracked; it was just too much for an already modified 'old lady'.

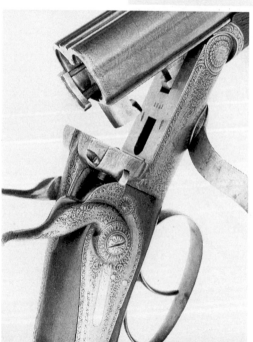

A double 12 bore hammer shotgun by Thomas Horsley of York, showing the Horsley patent striker retraction mechanism operated by the cam surfaces on the hammer breast.

PLATE 13

Truly a 'one off'. The very first
Anson & Deeley box lock shotgun
and to ensure there is no mistake the
gun is suitable inscribed. (Courtesy
Westley Richards Ltd.)

The less rare three barrel Dickson
with the barrels arranged side-by-
side-by-side! Square back guard
and pistol hand with side-lever
opening.

e Colt No. 2 with the
rrel swung to the side
loading. The
esight is brass and a
rsight notch is cut in
hammer spur.

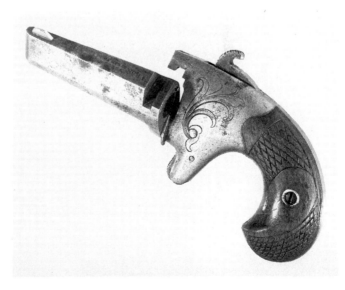

PLATE 14

Made in almost endless profusion and variety, the pin-fire revolvers ar of interest to collectors since such a wide range has survived.

The famous Colt Single Action Army Model. This one with wooden stocks, long barrel and a foresight designed by the famous American target revolver shot Ira Paine.

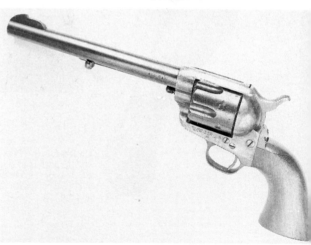

Something out of the ordinary. A .380 Trant central-fire double actic revolver. This example engraved and plated an would have made a nice retirement gift for a Chief Constable in the late nineteenth century

PLATE 15

Webley's No. 5
Revolver showing the
'Winged Bullet' trade
mark. A compact and
powerful weapon.

This is the first of the
hinge frame
simultaneous
ejection Smith &
Wesson's, the .44
calibre Model No. 3.

French Lebel Model
92, dismantled.
The cylinder swings
out to the right to
load instead of the
left, and the revolver
has a quick
dismantling feature.

PLATE 16

Detail of the engraving on the patch
box of a double 10 gauge muzzle
loading Dickson percussion rifle.

Accessories also form an
interesting field for the
collector. Here are
several nineteenth
century items amongst
which are a crimping tool
for all brass cases, a
decapper, chamber
brush and a special
crimping tool for all
metal cases.

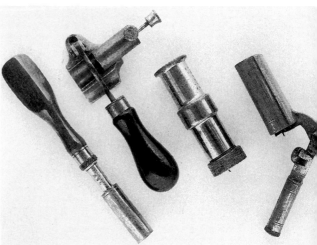

The true collector overlooks
nothing. If the actual weapons are
too expensive then ammunition can
be a rewarding collecting activity.
In particular the paper case shotgun
cartridges often bore the name of
the vendor and, for the very young,
empty cases can be collected to start
with!

CHAPTER FOURTEEN

Smokeless powders and their influence on design

THE supremacy of black powder, the propellant used for some three centuries, was first seriously challenged when the French adopted the Lebel Rifle of 1866. The rifle was undistinguished, but the cartridge used a solid drawn case with a solid bronze alloy bullet and, most important of all, 'smokeless powder'.

The development of smokeless powder had been hastened by the interest shown in smaller calibre cartridges possessing a higher velocity and a flatter trajectory. In addition, fouling caused by black powder became troublesome in the smaller bore rifles, with their increasingly complex breech mechanisms, interfering with both loading and accuracy.

As far back as 1838 Pelouze had obtained a highly inflammable material by treating cotton with nitric acid, Schönbein improving this process in 1845, using a mixture of nitric and sulphuric acids for the nitration of cotton. The product, guncotton, was a satisfactory 'shattering' explosive, but it was left to the French chemist, Vieille, to produce a suitable nitrocellulose propellant.

Vieille's smokeless powder, 'Poudre B', named after the French Minister of War, General Boulanger, was loaded into an 8 mm. bottle-necked case, the result being the first satisfactory small bore military smokeless cartridge. General Lebel of the French Ordnance gave his name to the rifle which was to use the new cartridge. The 1886 Lebel used a turning-bolt action with a two-piece bolt based on the 1874 Gras rifle, and retaining the tubular under-barrel magazine. Four years later the Berthier bolt-action carbine, using a three-shot Mannlicher type clip was adopted for cavalry use and in 1907 the Lebel was altered to take a similar magazine. In 1915–16 the magazine capacity was increased to five rounds.

Whereas previously the race had been between nations adopting magazine arms repeating fire was no longer the sole aim. The day of the old black powder low-velocity cartridge had passed, Germany being the next country to change to the smaller calibre smokeless cartridge. Their new cartridge was an outstanding development, the 7·9 mm. design being the basis for all military cartridges used by

Germany until the end of World War II. The rifle introduced to handle this cartridge was a hybrid design known as the 'Mauser and Commission', or more properly the German Infantry Model of 1888. The action was an alteration of the original Mauser design, the clip magazine being a modification of the Mannlicher.

By this time Great Britain, America and Russia were the only major powers who had not adopted a magazine rifle of some type. Britain had considered a reduction in calibre from ·450 in. to ·402 in. and a number of Martini-Henry rifles chambered for this smaller cartridge, using barrels rifled with 'ratchet grooving', had been produced. The decision regarding rifling was, however, changed and a shallow seven-grooved rifling developed by William Ellis Metford, one of the foremost ballisticians of his day, was finally adopted. In 1886, 70,000 Enfield-Martini ·402 rifles with Metford barrels were manufactured, but never introduced to the Service, being subsequently altered to ·577/450 Martini-Henry and issued as a Mark IV pattern. The reason for this action was, of course, developments on the Continent. Despite considerable disapproval from many sections of 'informed' opinion, trials with magazine weapons were carried out under conditions of some secrecy, quite unlike the publicity that had attended the earlier trials prior to the adoption of the Martini-Henry.

Three rifles passed the preliminary trials. The Lee, and an improved Lee with the Bethel Burton magazine and the Owen Jones magazine rifle. The Owen Jones rifle was eliminated on the grounds of cost and complexity, and final trials, using ·402-in. calibre barrels and cartridges eliminated the Bethel Burton hopper magazine.

In 1888, following further trials and yet another reduction in calibre, influenced by foreign trends, the Magazine Rifle, Mark I, based on James Paris Lee's patent of 1879 and much modified by the Small Arms Committee appeared, only to be greeted by storms of abuse and criticism. The original ·303 calibre cartridge for this rifle was replaced by yet another black powder cartridge of ·303 calibre with a powder charge of $71\frac{1}{2}$ grains, giving the 215-grain nickel-jacketed bullet a muzzle velocity of 1,850 feet per second. Two years later the Mark I cordite cartridge was introduced with a 31-grain powder charge. The bullet weight remained the same, but the velocity was increased to 1,970 feet per second. After a further two years the Mark II cordite cartridge appeared, the main changes being connected with the case and primer design, Mark I cartridges using the Boxer primer and one central flash hole, the Mark II version having the Berdan primer and two smaller flash holes.

The year 1891 saw the name of the rifle changed to Lee-Metford Magazine Rifle Mark I. A year later the first of many modifications was incorporated, the rifles being known as the Mark I*. This mark had the safety catch omitted and following the adoption of the Mark II rifle a ten-round two-column magazine, instead of an eight-round single column magazine, was introduced. The safety catch was reintroduced on the Mark II* rifle, introduced in 1895, being mounted on the cocking piece and a year previously a carbine version for mounted troops was approved. The carbine had an overall length of 3 ft. 4 in., a six-round magazine and the bolt was altered so that it lay closer to the stock.

Although conferring many benefits, the introduction of smokeless cordite cartridges resulted in a greatly reduced barrel life. To combat this problem a new form of rifling was developed at Enfield with deeper grooves and wider lands. Rifles with the new Enfield barrels were introduced in 1895, being known as the Lee-Enfield Magazine Rifle Mark I.

Concurrently, large numbers of Martini-Henry rifles were converted from ·577/450 to ·303 calibre. This conversion was followed by the introduction of the Martini-Enfield Artillery Carbine towards the end of 1895. The cavalry were then issued with Lee-Enfield Mark I Carbines to replace their Lee-Metford Carbines. As the century drew to a close, minor modifications made their appearance and reports concerning the performance of the Lee-Enfield reached the Mother Country from every part of the globe under the British Flag.

In 1899 the Boer War broke out and the Lee-Enfield was matched against the Mauser. The majority of the Mausers used were the Model 1895 pattern, being similar to the Mauser 93 used by Spain during the Spanish-American War. The Model 93 traces its ancestry back to the Model 1889 adopted by Belgium. The Belgian Army had requested manufacturers to submit magazine rifles which could be loaded with the Mannlicher type 'packet' loading clip. They had also specified that the magazine should be capable of being loaded with single cartridges, a feature not possible with the Mannlicher system.

The 7·65-mm. calibre Model 1889 fulfilled these conditions and more besides. Loading of the magazine was accomplished by the

use of the now familiar cartridge clip or 'charger'. Each clip held
five cartridges which were stripped from the clip into the magazine,
the clip being discarded. The clip did not form, as was the case with
the Mannlicher, a necessary part of the magazine system. The first
Mauser rifle to use a box magazine, the M.1889, is of importance
since a forward-locking one-piece bolt was used, the design of which
has undergone only minor modifications to the present day.
Another innovation was the use of a barrel jacket to protect the
hands of the user from the heat generated during firing. This jacket
was discarded in the next Mauser design, the 7·65 mm. Model 1890,
adopted by Turkey. Once again a box magazine extending below
the stock with a capacity of five cartridges was used and unlike the
Belgian Mauser a cut-off is provided so that the magazine can be
held in reserve.

Variations of the Turkish pattern Mauser were adopted by
Argentina in 1891 and Spain in 1890. Minor modifications were
made in the 7 mm. Spanish Model of 1892 but in 1893 the external
single-column box magazine was replaced by a more compact
double-column magazine which did not extend below the bottom of
the stock. With but minor modifications Mausers based on the
M.93 were sold to Sweden (6·5 mm.), Transvaal and the Orange
Free State (Model 95, 7 mm. cal.), and to many of the South American
states.

The last major design change took place in 1898 when a third
safety lug was introduced at the rear of the bolt. The 1898 Mauser
was adopted by Germany in the same year and formed the basis
for all Mauser military and sporting model bolt-action rifles made
since. In addition to rifles made by the Mauser organization in
Germany, rifles based on the 98 action were made by F.N. in
Belgium, Steyr in Austria and at Brno in Czechoslovakia. China,
Poland and Spain also made copies of the Mauser '89. The Italian
M.1891, 6·5 mm. and 1935 7·35 mm. Carcano rifles were based on
Mauser designs as were the Japanese 6·5 mm. Model 1905 and the
7·7 mm. Model 1939.

All of these rifles, as far back as the original Belgian M.1889,
use the basic Mauser magazine system, the first official tests of
which took place in England being rejected by the War Office. The
practical demonstration of the value of charger loading given to
the British during the Boer War could not be ignored and, in
December 1902, the Short Magazine Lee-Enfield, reduced in length

to 3 ft. 8½ in. and modified to permit the use of chargers on the
Mauser system, was introduced as the rifle for both infantry and
cavalry.

Shortly after the short rifle had been issued, a further series of
trials took place. Their purpose was to improve accuracy and to
eradicate faults which had arisen in the charger magazine loading
system. In 1907 the result of these trials was finalized as the Short
Magazine Lee-Enfield Mark III. Apart from being shorter than
the Lee-Enfield, the S.M.L.E. introduced a full-length wooden
handguard on top of the barrel, a 'double' trigger pull to avoid
accidental discharge during rapid magazine fire, and charger guides
(which on the Marks I and II had been mounted separately on the
bolt head and action body) mounted on the action body arranged
so that the action of closing the bolt ejected the charger clip. The
cover over the bolt had been discarded but the magazine cut-off
retained.

In 1910 a new cartridge was introduced, the Mark VII, having a
lighter bullet, weighing 174 grains, against the 215-grain bullets used
for the previous Marks. Following German practice, the bullet was
pointed (spitzer) instead of having a rounded nose, and was to
remain in the British Service throughout two World Wars.

British Service rifles were all of the conventional turning-bolt
type but in 1914 the Canadians arrived in France bringing with
them their own Service rifle, the Ross. Designed by Sir Charles Ross,
and manufactured by the Ross Rifle Company of Quebec, Canada,
the Ross Mark I model 1905 was adopted as the official Canadian
Service arm. A later modification was known as the Mark II
Model 1907 and the final type the Mark III Model 1910. All models
used a straight pull type of bolt similar to the Mannlicher. The
Marks I and II having solid bolt lugs, locking horizontally, the
Mark III 1910 Ross using an 'interrupted thread' type of lug which
locked in the vertical position. Difficulties with extraction, inherent
with the straight pull action and aggravated by Flanders mud,
resulted in the withdrawal of the Ross rifle, and its replacement by
S.M.L.E.'s. This decision was no doubt speeded by reports of bolts
flying out of the rear of the Mark III rifle, with disastrous consequences to the firer, it being proven that the bolt could be reassembled incorrectly so that it did not rotate into the locked
position. Regrettably the rifle could still be fired and although the
Ross is capable of excellent accuracy, the rifles being extremely

well made, this design weakness relegated them to the gun racks of collectors and gun cranks. With the exception of the Ross, the only other aberrant form of bolt action was the 'inclined' bolt systems which, as far as can be discovered, are of British origin only. The best known is the Norman-B.S.A., designed and patented in 1911 by George Norman, Chief Designer to the Birmingham Small Arms Company Limited. The idea behind this system was to incline the bolt by about ten degrees so that when the bolt was operated it slid backwards into the comb of the stock under the shooter's face. The face of the bolt was non-rotatable and at right angles to the bore.

The originator of the inclined bolt principle appears to be J. B. Thorneycroft who, in 1901, patented a rifle with an inclined bolt, the action body of which was attached to the stock to the rear of the conventional position, the scear being connected to the trigger by a linkage. No specimen of Thorneycroft's rifle has apparently survived, but two rifles made under Major Godsal's patents of 1902 are in existence. Godsal was responsible for a number of patents relating to firearms taken out between 1887 and 1922 and appears to have been a fervent exponent of the inclined-bolt system which had, when allied to the rear positioning of the action body, the advantage of producing a rifle of reduced overall length, and yet retaining the barrel length of the original Lee-Metford. The adoption of the shortened S.M.L.E. must have been quite a blow to the hopes of those interested in the unique and short-lived inclined-bolt rifle.

The British Military authorities placed their trust in the much-modified Lee action and the British sportsman in one of the many variants of the Mauser action chambered for British cartridges and barrelled and stocked by British gunmakers. If he could afford it, the Englishman venturing abroad in search of large and dangerous game would buy a double rifle and in the days before the adoption of high-velocity cartridges such rifles reached fantastic proportions, some being chambered for four bore cartridges loaded with up to fourteen drams of black powder. Such rifles, weighing up to 18 lb., gave way to the lighter eight bores and the need for a good all-round sporting weapon resulted in the appearance of 'rifled' shotguns and 'oval' bored rifles which would handle both shot and ball cartridges with equal facility.

The Holland & Holland 'Paradox' and the Westley Richards

'Explora' were perhaps the best examples of 'rifled' shotguns. In both these examples the barrels were smooth bored except for a few inches at the muzzle which was rifled. An alternative system was to use 'oval' boring, Charles Lancaster building his 'Colindian' ball and shotgun on this principle.

Yet another attempt to provide the 'all-round' gun was the combination weapon, one barrel of which was bored for a standard twelve-bore game cartridge, the other being rifled and taking perhaps the ·303 rifle cartridge. Combination weapons were not greatly favoured by British sportsmen but on the Continent this class of weapon became highly developed and resulted in not only double but three- and four-barrelled combination rifle-shotguns.

Figure 23. Combination Rifle-Shotguns. Left to Right, Top to Bottom: *Doppelflinte*—double shotgun. *Büchsflinte*—side-by-side rifle-shotgun. *Doppelbüchse*—double rifle. *Drilling*—three barrel gun, two shot barrels above a single rifled barrel. *Flintendrilling*—Three barrel shotgun. *Doppelbüchse drilling*—two rifled barrels above one shot barrel. *Vierling*—four barrel gun with two rifled barrels and two shot barrels. *Bock-büchsflinte*—over and under combined rifle-shotgun.

The availability of smokeless powder led to the further development of the 'Express' rifle. The term 'Express' had by 1860 come to mean a high-velocity black-powder muzzle-loading rifle possessing a long point blank range and low trajectory. Many such rifles firing bullets which had two 'wings' diametrically opposed and fitting the 'two-grooved' rifling used, became popular in South Africa and were known as 'Cape Rifles'. The high-velocity principle continued to gain in popularity when used for black-powder cartridge rifles and later, when allied to smokeless powder, resulted in the 'High Velocity Express' or 'Cordite Express' rifle. Rifles of this class with muzzle velocities in excess of 1,600 feet per second revolutionized sporting shooting and whilst many double rifles were made for the high-velocity cordite cartridge in calibres up to ·600 nitro Express, the introduction of high-velocity ammunition led the way for the recognition of the smaller calibre magazine rifle and its use on heavy and dangerous game.

In America, the lever-action rifle was the favourite for both self-protection and sporting purposes, its popularity not being seriously challenged until the adoption by the United States of the Krag-Jorgensen bolt-action rifle. This rifle had been adopted in 1889 by the Danish Army in 8 mm. calibre, the American Krag using a ·30-calibre cartridge loaded with 40 grains of black powder. Shortly after the adoption of the Krag it was decided to investigate the potentialities of the Mauser action and, following the payment of royalties to the Mauser company, Springfield Armoury started to manufacture a slightly modified American Mauser which became known as the U.S. Rifle, Calibre ·30, Model 1903. Unlike the ·30/40 Krag the new Springfield 1903 rifle cartridge was rimless. It was only in service for a short time being replaced by the rimless ·30–'06 Springfield cartridge adopted in 1906 which used a lighter 150-grain pointed bullet instead of the 220-grain round-nose bullet used in the 1903 cartridge.

Although the bolt-action rifle gained in popularity in America, particularly after the First World War when many became accustomed to its use, the lever action rifle was the arm carried by Lawman and Badman, Cowboy and Indian Fighter. The name of Winchester, having risen to prominence by virtue of the success of the Model '66, became almost synonymous with the term repeating rifle, following the introduction of the Model of 1873. The '73 was stronger than its predecessors, having the frame made of iron instead of brass until 1884, when steel was used. Differing from the Model '66 in being a centre-fire rifle, the '73 was chambered for the Winchester ·44–40 cartridge. Such was the success of this combination of rifle and cartridge that Colt's chambered the Single Action Army revolver for the ·44–40 in 1878, the advantages of having both arms taking the same calibre cartridge being obvious. The most famous of the '73 variants was undoubtedly the 'One of One Thousand' model and 124 of these specially prepared rifles were produced. Since some 720,600 Model 1873 rifles were made until the model was discontinued in 1924, simple arithmetic shows that the special models were rarer than supposed being, in fact, more nearly 'One of Six Thousand'.

The action of the '73 was based on the previous Model '66 and consisted of a sliding breech block locked by a toggle. The full-length tubular magazine in ·44–40 calibre arms held fifteen rounds. In addition to the sporting rifles, carbine and musket styles could be had and, on sporting rifles, both round and octagonal barrels could be furnished in various lengths.

The design and dimensions of the '73 action limited the cartridges that could be handled and the rifle was not effective beyond 100 to 150 yards. For longer range shooting the Remington or Sharps single-shot rifles were preferred and it was no doubt with the intention of breaking into this market that Winchester redesigned the '73 action to take a more powerful cartridge.

The new rifle was the Model 1876 and won many enthusiastic users, being adopted by the Royal Canadian North West Mounted Police in carbine style, remaining their official weapon until the adoption of the bolt-action Lee-Enfield Carbine in 1914. As with the Model 1873 the '76 could be had in a variety of styles and in the following calibres: ·45–70, ·50–95 Express, ·45–60 and ·40–60 WCF. Despite its imposing appearance, the Model '76 never became really popular due to the inherent limitations of the toggle link action.

The desire to produce a rifle capable of handling the more powerful ammunition becoming available, led to the Winchester Company's long and profitable association with John Moses Browning. In 1879 Browning took out a patent for a single-shot rifle which was first announced by Winchester in 1885. Made in a bewildering variety of styles and calibres until 1920, the single-shot Winchester was one of the most successful single-shot rifles manufactured.

The first lever action designed by Browning for Winchester was the Model 1886, considered by many to be the strongest and smoothest lever action ever made. This action dispensed with the toggle locking arrangement, being locked instead by two vertical bolts, each fitting into a slot in the receiver and into similar slots in the breech bolt. Originally this Model was chambered for the ·45–70 U.S. Government cartridge and, shortly afterwards, became available in the following black-powder calibres: ·38–56, ·38–70, ·40–65, ·40–70, ·40–82, ·45–90 and ·50–110. With the availability of the Model '86 the production of the Model '76 ceased and the new rifle became very popular for dealing with the larger American game, particularly in ·45–90 calibre.

A new rifle, almost identical in appearance to the '86 but smaller in conception, appeared in 1892. The Model 1892 retained the same breech locking mechanism but was simplified in detail to reduce production costs and to make the rifle lighter. In effect, the '92 was intended to replace the old Model '73 and was chambered for such short-range cartridges as the ·32–20, ·38–40 and ·44–40. It became available in ·25 W.C.F. in 1895 but without doubt the carbine style in ·44–40 calibre was the most popular and found use by trappers in the frozen north of Canada and by rubber planters in the steaming jungles of Brazil.

The most widely used and perhaps the most famous of the Winchester line was, however, the Model of 1894. Based again on Browning's patents, this rifle was similar to the Model '92 but was the first Winchester to be adapted for smokeless cartridges. Initially, the rifle was made for two black-powder cartridges, the ·32–40 and the ·38–55, but with the introduction of the Winchester ·30–30, the new rifle and the 'thutty-thutty' cartridge revolutionized American sporting shooting. Loaded with smokeless powder this cartridge with its flat trajectory and light recoil became the most popular American game cartridge and the Model '94 outsold all the other rifles ever made by Winchester.

The last of the 'vintage' lever-action Winchesters was the Model 1895. This rifle was the first box magazine, lever action, placed on the market and was designed to handle the more powerful military cartridges such as the ·303 British, the U.S. ·30–40 Krag and ·30–'06 Springfield. Especially popular among American big game hunters, the '95 was made available in the specially designed Winchester ·405 calibre. In spite of several disadvantages, one of which was a reputation for not feeding correctly, this model had many advocates, perhaps the most famous being Theodore Roosevelt who, on his celebrated trip to British West Africa, took with him two Model '95's, one chambered for the ·30–'03, the other for the Winchester ·405. The Model '95 was an official U.S. Army weapon for a short period and was also used as a military rifle by Russia.

The Winchester was by no means the only American lever-action rifle. The Savage, which employed an interesting revolving box magazine, was first made in 1889. The use of an enclosed breech mechanism and 'hammerless' action represented a departure from the traditional in lever-action rifles. To Winchester, however, must go the credit for participating in the earliest practical experiments in self-loading or 'automatic' rifles. Winchester Model '66 and '73 rifles were used by Hiram Maxim in producing a recoil operated semi-automatic rifle. These early experiments in recoil operation resulted in the Maxim Machine Gun and can be said to have started a train of development which greatly speeded up automatic rifle design and which will no doubt produce yet another 'period' to intrigue and confuse the Gun Collector of the Future.

CHAPTER FIFTEEN

Revolvers and automatics

THE availability of a suitable smokeless propellant for revolver cartridges did not have the same far-reaching results on design as had the smokeless rifle cartridge on the development of the shoulder arm. Revolvers adapted for use with central-fire black-powder ammunition rapidly reached perfection, the mechanisms being in most cases based on previous practice. As with the muzzle-loading progenitor, lockwork can be divided into two types, the single or cocking action, and the double or trigger action. The main problem which occupied the revolver manufacturer was the means by which fired cases could be ejected and several designs were evolved.

Earliest in the field were the solid-frame rod-ejection revolvers typified by the Colt Single Action Army Model of 1873. Without doubt the most famous of all centre-fire revolvers, the Colt Single Action, was manufactured in over twenty different calibres ranging from ·22 short rimfire to ·476 Eley, ·45 Colt being the most popular calibre. Except for the period 1941–1955, this legendary revolver has been in continuous production without major design changes from 1873 until the present day. Chambered for six cartridges, these were introduced by means of a loading gate on the right-hand side of the frame, the empty cases being extracted singly by half cocking the hammer, opening the loading gate and pushing back the rod ejector mounted below the barrel, the cylinder being rotated by hand to bring each chamber in line with the ejector rod. Early Single Action revolvers had a round ejector rod head, this being altered about 1883 to a shape which conformed to the barrel contour. A number of Colts were made without provision for ejector rods, the majority of which being the short-barrelled 'Storekeepers' Model. Ejector-less long-barrelled Colts are considerably rarer. Another minor design change occurred during the early 1890's when the original cylinder screw was replaced by a spring-loaded transverse bolt, the system being based on Mason's patent of 1874. In 1896 the Single Action Army was adapted to use smokeless cartridges by improving the quality of the steel and standardizing on cartridge head space. Only pistols having a serial number higher than 165,000 should be used with modern ammunition.

Standard barrel lengths were $4\frac{3}{4}$ in., $5\frac{1}{2}$ in. and $7\frac{1}{2}$ in., longer or shorter barrels being obtained from the factory on special order. The first extra long-barrelled Colts were displayed at the Philadelphia Exhibition of 1876 where they were seen by Edward Z. C. Judson, who wrote some of the earliest 'Wild West' fiction under the name of Ned Buntline. The purchase, by Buntline, of what came to be known as 'Colt Buntline Specials' started one of the most colourful of all Colt legends. The true Buntline had a special frame to accommodate a folding-leaf adjustable rear-right and provision was made for a detachable shoulder stock.

Commonly known, and referred to, as the Colt Single Action Army Model, it was advertised as the 'Frontier Six Shooter' in 1878 when chambered for the ·44–40 cartridge used by the Winchester rifle. The name 'Peacemaker' was used only for those revolvers chambered for the ·45 Colt Cartridge.

An interesting variation of the Colt S.A.A. was the Bisley Model which was discontinued in 1912 after an estimated 45,000 of this model had been produced. Differing from the standard model in that new designs of hammer, trigger and grip straps were used, the Bisley was designed with the target-shooter's needs in mind, and was developed from earlier target models which had been supplied with special stocks and flat top frames to permit more readily the use of adjustable sights. Target arms were blued overall. The Standard Model was supplied with a case-hardened frame, loading gate and hammer, the remainder being blued. Stocks originally were one piece walnut and almost identical to the percussion Colt Navy stocks. After 1882, two-piece hard rubber stocks were furnished, but de-luxe walnut, ivory and pearl stocks could be had on special order, as could engraved and specially finished nickel or silver-plated arms.

The Colt Single Action Army has been described in some detail due to its historical importance. The basic extraction system was widely used, one variant being employed by the Webley Royal Irish Constabulary revolver. Adopted by the R.I.C. in 1867, in ·442 calibre, this solid-frame double-action revolver became widely used and copied. The extraction system differed from the Colt in that the rod was housed in the hollow cylinder pin being withdrawn and pivoted before it could be thrust into the cylinder chamber. Prior to the introduction of the R.I.C. revolver, Webleys had made a ·577 calibre weapon, the cylinder of which had to be removed for loading. It was the R.I.C. revolver, which used a loading gate similar to the Tranter, that firmly placed Webleys ahead of all other British competition, both Adams and Tranter disappearing from the scene before the end of the nineteenth century.

Many extraction systems had been developed from the rammer systems used by percussion revolvers. The first major design improvement took place in 1869 when Smith & Wesson introduced the ·44 S. & W. American Model. Deprived of their commercial advantage by the expiry of the Rollin White patents, Smith & Wesson produced the first simultaneous extraction revolver in an endeavour to retain ascendancy over their rivals. The ·44 American was a hinged-frame revolver, the barrel being forged in one piece with the top strap, the rear of which was provided with a latch locking over the standing breech. Raising the latch permitted the barrel and cylinder assembly to be hinged down, simultaneously forcing the extractor from its seat in the centre of the cylinder. The star-shaped extractor ejected all six cases from the cylinder and returned automatically to its seating to permit the introduction of new cartridges. The ease and speed with which this type of revolver could be reloaded far surpassed that of the solid-frame rod-ejection type, and although Smith & Wesson were able to interest the American Government in their revolver, 1,000 of the improved American Models being sold in 1870, the first major sale was to the Russians who purchased some 200,000 of a slightly altered version known as the ·44 Russian Model. Following the success of the Russian Model, some 6,000 of an improved model known as the Schofield were sold to the American Government in 1875. Similar in appearance to the 1869 American Model, the Schofield was chambered for the ·45 Smith & Wesson cartridge, which could be used in the ·45 Colt S.A.A. The ·45 Colt cartridge could not, however, be chambered in the Smith & Wesson due to its length. Trials with the Smith & Wesson, Schofield Model, and the Colt took place in 1876.

A decided preference for the Colt was shown by the U.S. Board of Ordnance, possibly because of the greater complexity of the Smith & Wesson. Undeterred, Smith & Wesson brought out a line of single-action ·38 pocket models and, in 1880, a similar series, using the top latch breech fastening but employing a double-action trigger mechanism. Basically similar to the ·38 double-action revolvers was the hammerless 'Safety Model' introduced in 1887, incorporating a safety lever which projected through the back strap and arranged to prevent discharge of the revolver unless properly held in the shooter's hand.

Smith & Wesson were the only manufacturers who produced a quality revolver of the hinged-frame, barrel-latch type, although Harrington & Richardson and Iver Johnson manufactured small-calibre weapons of similar type.

Possessed of far greater strength, the hinged-frame revolvers, using a stirrup latch made by P. Webley & Sons of Birmingham, had been developed from the previous Webley-Pryse revolver, first manufactured in 1876. The locking system used was based on

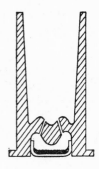

Figure 24. Rimmed revolver cartridge with Berdan primer, anvil integral with case.

two separate thumb-pieces pivoted at either side of the standing breech. This system will also be found on the massive ·45 Montenegrin revolver. The Pryse system was dropped for the 1882 revolver, a stirrup-shaped lock pivoted to the standing breech and provided with an extended thumb-piece being provided instead. This system proved so successful that it was used on the Webley Mark I, eventually adopted by the British Government in 1887.

Official adoption of the Webley had been delayed by the appearance of the Government-sponsored ·476 Enfield, the extractor mechanism of which had been patented by O. Jones, a member of the staff at the Enfield factory. Neither the revolver nor its peculiar extraction system, which was based on a hinged barrel and a forward-sliding cylinder, combined with a fixed extractor, proved successful and with the adoption of the Webley Mark I the stage was set for the development of a virtual monopoly by Webley of the English trade in revolvers. The Mark II or Webley Government revolver, differing only from the Mark I in the shape of the butt, was adopted in 1889, being replaced by the Mark IV chambered for the ·455 cordite cartridge. The continued reliance placed on the Webley system, despite the appearance of the later solid-frame, swing-out cylinder revolvers, is ample testimony to the strength and utility of the stirrup locking system.

The third of the basic revolver systems is the solid-frame, swing-out cylinder type first successfully introduced by Colt in 1889 as the Colt Double Action Navy Revolver. Experience in the manu-facture of double-action pistols had been gained during the market-ing of a range of double-action weapons based on William Mason's patents. Bearing a superficial resemblance to the Single Action Army, the double-action revolvers were first marketed in 1877 in ·38 calibre, and later in ·41 calibre. The early D.A. pistols were made with separate grip straps in a similar manner to the S.A.A. Model but the appearance of a ·45 calibre D.A. military revolver in 1878 heralded the introduction of the one-piece strap formed as part of the frame. Although possessing the advantages of the double-action system, Colts still lacked the important simultaneous ejection feature of the Smith & Wesson and this problem was solved by William Mason. The first swing-out cylinder Colts were produced in 1889. The cylinder was locked by a latch on the left-hand side of the frame which, on being disengaged, permitted the cylinder to swing out to the left on a pivoted crane, ejection of the spent cases being effected by a manually operated spring-loaded ejector. This system permitted the retention of the solid frame and the simple manual ejection feature eliminated the complexity associated with automatic ejection. Available in both ·38 and ·41 calibre, the Model 1889 was short-lived, being replaced by the 1892 Model which incor-porated locking notches on the cylinder and which was successively improved until the appearance of the Colt 'New Service' Model, manufacture of which commenced in 1897 and continued until 1943.

Success invariably results in emulation and in 1896 the first swing-out cylinder Smith & Wesson appeared. Differing mainly in the locking system from the Colt, the S. & W. Hand Ejector was produced in a variety of models. The first important design change occurred with the introduction of the forward cylinder lock on the Military and Police Model of 1902. The number and variety of Smith & Wesson models almost defies description and, as with the later Colt models, the reader must be referred to specialized literature and catalogues for detailed information.

Both the Colt and S. & W. swing-out revolvers have been widely imitated, particularly by Belgian and Spanish makers. Two swing-out systems, one French and the other Belgian, do, however, have special features which merit consideration. The French 'Modelle D'Ordonnance' (Lebel) 1892 uses the Colt swing-out cylinder principle, the cylinder swinging out to the right instead of the left. The cylinder latch pivots and an unusual feature is the hinged side plate which facilitates cleaning and dismounting. Chambered for an 8 mm. cartridge, this was the official French Army revolver. The second swing-out cylinder revolver is the Belgian Pieper chambered for the 7·62 mm. Nagant cartridge. The unique feature of this weapon is that when the hammer is cocked the cylinder moves forward, causing the special Nagant 'gas seal' cartridge to enter the mouth of the barrel to minimize gas leakage. The cartridge is bottle-necked and the bullet is seated entirely within the case. The swing-out version of the Nagant was developed to overcome the slow loading feature of the standard model which was of the solid-frame, rod-ejector type, and as such had been officially adopted by Russia, being manufactured both in Belgium and at the Tula Arsenal in Russia.

Many attempts have been made to provide automatic ejection of empty cases from revolvers without success, but one 'automatic' revolver, more properly called a self-cocking revolver, was manufactured in Britain by Webley & Scott Ltd (prior to 1897 known as P. Webley & Son) and invented by Lt-Colonel G. V. Fosbery. The barrel, cylinder and upper frame form a unit which slides back and forth in grooves in the lower frame, which comprises the trigger group and stock. The barrel lock is the standard Webley stirrup and the cylinder holds six cartridges. The weapon must be cocked by hand for the first shot, the recoil of which drives back the barrel-cylinder group, cocking the hammer and rotating the cylinder. The trigger can again be pressed for the second and subsequent shots, the hammer being cocked and the cylinder rotated automatically. Made in two calibres, ·455 and an eight-shot, rimless ·38 version the Webley-Fosbery was first manufactured in 1901 and for a time enjoyed a vogue as a target revolver at the Bisley Meeting. Although the system of cylinder rotation by means of a stud operating in zigzag grooves formed on the cylinder has been employed by several others, the only similar revolver to the Fosbery was brought out by the Union Arms Company of Toledo, U.S.A., in 1904 and, as with its more illustrious parent, enjoyed only a limited success.

Although the development of the metallic cartridge, smokeless powder and metal-jacketed bullets caused no major technical advance in revolver design, these inventions combined permitted the exploitation of the automatic system, i.e. the utilization of some of the energy of discharge to reload, recock and discharge the

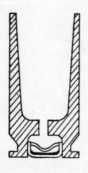

Figure 25. Rimless automatic pistol cartridge with Boxer type primer, using separate anvil.

weapon. In the fullest sense, the automatic system finds application only in machine guns, fully automatic hand guns being comparatively rare and generally unsuccessful. The term Automatic Pistol is now firmly established as a description of what should more properly be referred to as a 'self-loading pistol', since such weapons require a separate and independent pressure on the trigger to fire each shot.

In the space available, it would be impossible to describe the various automatic systems, let alone the types of pistol that have been manufactured. Several, however, are of considerable historical importance and, as such, are of interest to the collector. The first practical self-loading pistol to be sold commercially was the Austrian Schonberger, made in 1892 by the Osterreichische Waffenfabrik at Steyr. A Mannlicher-type clip containing six 8-mm. cartridges is used in conjunction with a fixed magazine placed in front of the trigger guard. The pistol fires from a locked breech, unlocking being achieved by 'primer setback'. This system has not since been greatly exploited and depends on the use of a deep-seated primer cup. On discharge, the primer is forced rearward by gas pressure and unlocks the breech mechanism.

Next to appear was the Borchardt, manufactured by the Deutsche Waffen-un Munitionsfabriken in 1893. A considerable number of these pistols were made, complete with a wooden detachable stock, and the Borchardt is important since it was the first pistol to use a detachable magazine inserted in the butt from below. The breech was locked by a toggle link, also used in the Luger-Parabellum, a more famous direct descendant.

The year 1894 saw the appearance of the first Mannlicher pistol, operating on the 'blow back' system. To be strictly accurate, the Mannlicher was a 'blow forward' pistol, being unusual in that the breech was fixed solidly to the frame, the barrel moving forward against spring pressure to eject the fired case. The 'blow back' system, using a fixed barrel and sliding breech, is widely adopted for small calibre pistols and relies on the inertia of the recoiling parts to delay the opening of the breech until the pressure has fallen to a safe limit.

Theodore Bergmann produced the first pocket automatic pistols in 1894, followed by two military automatics which appeared in 1897 and 1903. The magazine on all the early Bergmanns was ahead of the trigger guard and access to the magazine was by means of a pivoted side plate. The cartridges, held in a light clip, are placed in the magazine, the side plate is closed and the clip withdrawn by means of a small loop formed for this purpose. The clip can be left in position or alternatively the magazine can be loaded with loose cartridges. Some models of the Bergmann were fitted with extractors and some without. Due to this practice, rimless or grooved cart-ridges and cartridges without either rims or grooves may be en-countered.

The 7·63 Mauser automatic pistol of 1898 was the first really successful automatic pistol and was carried by Winston Churchill at the Battle of Omdurman and later saw extensive use during the Boer War. Using a locked breech action and a magazine holding ten cartridges ahead of the trigger guard, the Mauser is a clumsy weapon to fire with one hand but becomes an effective 'carbine' when used with the detachable shoulder stock. The action is the earliest to incorporate a feature now considered essential for military purposes, this being provision whereby the breech remains open when the last cartridge has been fired. This effectively eliminates the embarrassment of presenting an unloaded pistol at an adversary in the mistaken idea that ammunition is still available.

The first of the Browning automatic pistols patents was obtained in 1897. John Moses Browning must rank as one of the most successful and prolific of all firearms inventors. Mention has already been made of the lever-action Winchester rifles designed by him. In addition, he designed pump-action rifles and shotguns, automatic shotguns and rifles, and machine guns.

By 1900, Browning had developed two types of automatic pistol, one for low-powered cartridges, using a straight blow-back action, the other a short-recoil locked action, for high-powered cartridges.

The 'blow back' pistol was made by Fabrique Nationale of Liège, Belgium, and produced in 7·65-mm. calibre. As with all Browning-designed arms, the magazine was in the butt in the form of a detachable box and different from all other Browning arms, the slide spring was mounted above the barrel giving the impression of two barrels. The F.N. Model 1900 Browning was never produced by Colt in America but the later 1903 Model was made by Colt as the Pocket Model and by F.N. as the 1903 Military Model. In America, this model was chambered for the ·32 ACP and ·380 ACP or Browning 9-mm. short cartridge, the Belgian-made Military Model being chambered for the 9-mm. Browning long cartridge. A vest pocket model in 6·35-mm. Browning calibre followed in 1906, an identical model made by Colt in America was chambered for the Colt ·25 ACP. The 1910 Model again departed from previous practice, the 1900 pistol had the slide return spring above the barrel, the 1903 below the barrel and the 1910 used a spring which surrounded the barrel. Identical except for size, the 1922 Browning had been developed at the request of the French Government and many will be found bearing German markings, since this model was made right through World War II by the F.N. factory under German control. Colt did not make either the 1910 or the 1922 models.

With the exception of the last of the pistols designed by Browning, the Model 1935 Hi-Power, all the short locked-action weapons were manufactured in America by Colt. The first of the short recoil pistols appeared in 1900 and was chambered for the ·38 ACP. In this, as in later designs, the barrel and one-piece slide are locked together by recesses cut in the barrel and slide. In recoil, both move rearwards for a short distance, the barrel then being pulled down-

wards to disengage the recesses and permitting the slide to move
backwards to its full extent. Similar models were produced in 1902,
1903, 1905 and 1908. All of these models used the parallel-ruler
locking principle of the 1900 version in which the barrel moved
downwards in such a manner that the axis of the bore remained
parallel to its original position. In the Model 1911, adopted by the
United States, the parallel-ruler principle was abandoned in favour
of a toggle link at the rear, and a loose barrel bushing at the muzzle,
which permitted realignment of the barrel. Alterations were made

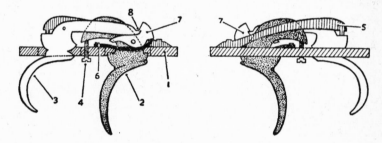

Figure 26. Typical double set trigger mechanism. (1) Trigger plate. (2) Front
trigger. (3) Rear trigger. (4) Capstan screw. (5) Mainspring. (6) Trigger spring.
(7) Auxiliary lever. (8) Notch. This mechanism can be 'set' by pulling the set
or rear trigger against the main spring pressure until the long arm engages in
the notch. An extremely light pull on the 'fire' or front trigger then releases
the bar which flies upwards to release the scear (not shown). Adjustment of
trigger pressure required for release is obtained by turning the capstan screw.
With this type of mechanism, the front trigger will also fire the gun but trigger
pull is long and abnormally heavy.

in the external appearance of the pistol in 1920, the result being
known as the 1911 A1 Model. The last of the Brownings, the
Model 1935, dispensed with the linkage, substituting camming
surfaces, and variations were adopted by the French, Belgian and
Roumanian Governments. Large quantities were made in Canada
during the last war and the basic Model 1935 design has more
recently been adopted by the British to replace the ·38 revolver.
   Many variants, copies and imitations of Browning's pistols have
been manufactured since 1900 and these, in addition to the genuine
Browning arms, whether made by Colt in America, or F.N. at
Liège, form a most fascinating facet of but one aspect of automatic
pistol collecting. Regrettably, many restrictions hamper the collector

of automatic pistols and whilst few have been made whose lavish decoration will delight the collector of the future, at least during the first half of the twentieth century automatic pistols have been manufactured in such wide profusion of design to ensure that future gun collectors, at least, will be intrigued and possibly mystified by this, the latest outcome of many centuries of labour and effort.

CHAPTER SIXTEEN

Collecting guns

HIGH on the list of questions which any gun collector finds himself called on to answer repeatedly is: 'Where did you find all those guns?'

Firearms of almost any age can be acquired from gunsmiths. There are several who specialize in collectors' arms. Many do not, but find that they are offered antique weapons because the seller cannot be bothered to seek out an alternative means of disposal. Quite often the gunsmith regards antique weapons as an embarrassment to his regular line of business and is reluctant to trade in such weapons. The collector has then to build up a state of mutual trust and many visits may be made before the gunsmith relents and produces a desirable piece.

As well as the gunsmith who may trade in old weapons as a sideline, a number of dealers in antique weapons have appeared in recent years. These people specialize in old guns, many finding this to be a full-time occupation. There are, as well, the part-time dealers, who find in gun trading a profitable means of augmenting their income or of augmenting their collection. Another source of old weapons are the salerooms. These vary from the periodic general sale where occasionally an antique weapon can be purchased to the sales which specialize in firearms alone. Attendance at the latter, even if a purchase is not made, is of the greatest value to the collector since many guns are displayed and the indication of values which can be gained is of the greatest importance. Such salerooms publish catalogues with price lists which are of interest to the collector, who may not, for geographical reasons, be able to attend in person.

In your search for old guns you will experience many disappointments. It may be that your territory has been 'milked dry' and in such circumstances greater reliance will have to be placed on personal contacts. Even if your search for firearms proves abortive, there is the very distinct possibility that you may find something of perhaps greater importance, a fellow gun collector. Gun collecting has been described as a constructive, educational and relaxing way of spending one's leisure time. In addition to these benefits, it also affords splendid social contacts. Many collectors value the friendships that have developed over the years far higher than the valuable

arms that they have acquired. Most advanced collectors can recall
how during their early days the friendship of an older collector
broadened their outlook, increased their knowledge and guided
them past mistakes and unwise acquisitions.

The majority of collectors are only too anxious to have the
opportunity of both discussing and displaying their collection to
fellow enthusiasts. If you have been invited to view a collection,
remember that your host has a right to expect proper conduct from
you, both to safeguard his feelings and his property. Etiquette in
the gunroom, whether this be a special room set aside, or merely
the kitchen with the table cleared and the children out of the way,
is based on sound reasons which are framed to avoid embarrassment to both host and guest and to protect persons and property.

Most of the rules are designed to protect your host's property;
some to protect his feelings. Regarding the latter, remember that
for most people values and financial transactions are somewhat
touchy subjects and unless comment is volunteered, questions on
what was paid for a specific item are out. Do not put your host in
the position of having to tell you that his collection is not for sale.
A desire to sell or exchange duplicate items must be volunteered by
the host.

It is reasonable to assume that you have been invited to see only
those pieces in which the owner feels some pride. The reason for
his sense of pride may not be apparent and deprecatory gratuitous
comment may not be well received. A candid comment may be
requested on some particular weapon, particularly if the visitor is
thought to possess specialized knowledge that the owner lacks.
Even when called for, your remarks should be factual and in no
way derisive.

Normal good behaviour will safeguard your host's pride during
conversation—it is of equal importance that you safeguard his
property. Never pick up any weapon without first asking and
obtaining permission. The way that the piece is mounted may be
such that damage to the gun or support could result from clumsy
handling. The weapon may be unsound and any disturbance will
mean further damage or the loss of some component. Many of us
suffer from what the German gunsmiths call 'poison hands' and the
owner may not have the opportunity to examine his collection after
your departure and re-oil those weapons which have been handled.
The temptation to pick up and fondle weapons is present in most

of us and is greatest of all in gun collectors. Resist it until permission has been given. Once this permission has been granted, hold the weapon by the wooden furniture and, if it is necessary to touch metal parts, use the side of the fingers, not the tip.

Now you have the gun in your hand. Do not try and operate the mechanism. If the owner wishes to demonstrate some mechanical peculiarity, he will either do it himself or show you how to operate it without risk of damage. Remember that there may be weak springs or unsound parts which might break. Never snap a flint or percussion weapon, the neck of the cock may break and with percussion weapons damage to the nipple will result. Do not demonstrate your familiarity with Western fiction by 'spinning' revolvers—however skilled you may be in this 'art', accidents will happen. Whilst on the subject of spinning, revolver cylinders should not be 'spun', since the finish of the cylinder can be marred. Roughly flicking open the action of cartridge revolvers can result in strain or damage.

Any cartridge weapon should be examined to see if it is loaded, regardless of any assurances that you may have received. If you are unfamiliar with the action, get the owner to prove that it is unloaded before you handle it. Rifles and shotguns, because of their length, often present additional problems. Long arms with attached bayonets may hazard the safety of light fittings, ornaments or other people. Shotguns have relatively thin barrels; avoid accidental contact with other objects which might result in dented barrels. Finally, if you are a family man and have gained your release on the understanding that you will take the children with you, please keep them under control.

A long and forbidding list of rules, perhaps, but their observance will ensure that your first visit will not be your last and the feeling of confidence and respect that results are sure to form the basis of a sound and lasting friendship of mutual benefit.

The opportunity of increasing your knowledge of some aspect of collecting, or of widening the scope of your interests, should not be restricted solely to contact with other collectors. Many important collections formerly in private hands are now housed in National or the larger Provincial Museums. Every effort should be made to see such collections, as even the smaller local museum often contains important weapons perhaps the gift of some now forgotten collector. Such items may not be on display and a word with the curator may bring forth a piece, 'held in reserve', which has not seen the light of day for many a long year.

In addition to taking every opportunity of examining firearms, the collector should endeavour to build up a collection of books. No one book can provide coverage of all aspects but by careful selection a gun library can be acquired at moderate cost.

Along with an increased awareness of the vast range of firearms available will come a gradual appreciation of values. The value of any article is often difficult to assess and in the last analysis depends on how much the potential purchaser is willing to pay for ownership. Closely allied to values is the question of condition and its accurate description. The seller has a natural tendency to overrate the condition of his wares, the purchaser to depreciate. The seller may endeavour to improve the 'condition' of a weapon by refinishing. Such work badly carried out is ruinous and at the best will only improve the appearance, not the condition. Since many firearms are bought unseen a universal scale of 'condition standards' is long overdue, the best and most recent attempt having been made by the American National Rifle Association Gun Collectors Committee. The term 'condition' not only covers the appearance of the weapon (and here it is important for the collector to learn how to differentiate between an original finish and a 'reblue job') but also whether or not the stock has been repaired, a new lock fitted or the gun converted from flint to percussion.

There is a considerable difference between an honest attempt at repair and work carried out with the intent to mislead the purchaser. As the values of antiques and vintage arms increase, so does the temptation of the unscrupulous. The problem of 'faked' weapons is a real one and the detection of the spurious at times difficult. To the beginner, a request for a second opinion is some insurance and such a request would not offend a reputable dealer or collector. An added safeguard is to obtain a receipt which clearly establishes what the seller represents his goods to be. Where replacement parts have been used to improve appearance, this should be admitted.

A full understanding of values cannot be gained easily, one must have a thorough knowledge of arms and it follows that every serious collector should also be a student.

Any gun worth owning is well worth learning about. In order to gain greater detailed knowledge, some thought must be given to specialization. All of us would like to have one of everything, but with the exception of the very rich or the very foolish, whose sole delight would be in the number of guns they possessed, specializing in one particular aspect of gun collecting has many advantages to offer. Such a decision must not be made rashly nor must your interests be too strongly canalized, but it is well to concentrate on a period, on certain makers, or some other classification that might appeal to you.

Less demanding on both money and space are cartridges. Recent years have seen a phenomenal increase in the number of cartridge collectors and even in this field the collector could limit his interests to either metallic or sporting cartridges, the latter making up for their greater uniformity by possessing visual attraction due to the rainbow-hued variety of their paper cases.

If you intend to obtain real and lasting pleasure from your activities direct your energies into some single purposeful channel. If, with the resources at your command, this can best be achieved by specialization, this is the course to take. If you are able to cast your net wider, do so by all means, but always set before you some goal. It does not matter if you never reach it, for you will have enjoyed the added pleasure of striving to complete something with meaning and value, rather than merely satisfying an urge to acquire.

CHAPTER SEVENTEEN

Shooting old guns

SOONER or later the owner of an old gun will ask himself, 'Can I shoot it?' If the gun is an early cartridge model the answer may well be no, since suitable ammunition may be so rare that each round is, in itself, a desirable collector's item. Furthermore, even if ammunition has been obtained that will chamber satisfactorily, this is by no means proof that the gun will handle it safely. Cartridges loaded with smokeless powder and used in black-powder arms may damage or destroy a valuable firearm and injure the shooter.

With muzzle-loading arms the difficulties and dangers are considerably less. With patience, bullet moulds can be located or as a last extremity, manufactured. Black powder, and here it must be stressed that only black powder, and nothing else, must be used in muzzle-loading arms, is still available, as are flints and percussion caps.

Merely because you have heeded the above advice and have obtained a supply of black powder this does not mean that any muzzle-loading gun you may have acquired can now be loaded and fired with safety. Muzzle-loading guns charged with modern smokeless nitro powders have blown up and so have M.L. guns when loaded with black powder when the load has been excessive or the gun in poor condition.

Guidance on loads for muzzle-loading shotguns and rifles is given in the Appendices but no hard and fast ruling can be given concerning the advisability of loading up some item in your collection and letting it off (assuming you have safe facilities for shooting). One of the most important ingredients required is plain common sense. It would be foolish to risk damage to a valuable gun by yielding to the urge to shoot it, since damage can occur during examination prior to shooting, by reason of having tried to fire it and also during the dismantling necessary to ensure thorough cleaning before the gun is returned to the rack.

The safety factor of any muzzle-loading gun, despite outward appearance, is an unknown quantity. Irrespective of how good the gun looks, there may be invisible rust pits or other internal bore damage which cannot be detected by an external examination. Muzzle-loading double shotguns and rifles may have defective ribs and corrosion may have taken place under the ribs and weakened the barrel but since the damage is hidden by the rib once again a cursory external examination will not bring to light such dangers.

Ideally, antique or vintage arms which are to be returned to service should be examined by a competent gunsmith who has the necessary experience and facilities for examination and, should defects be discovered, advice is available concerning the possibility of repair. It must be understood that there is considerable difference between the efforts of the amateur to renovate arms purely for display when his ignorance or lack of skill might merely reduce the value of a gun and similar endeavours to render a gun suitable for service where mistakes may well cost him his life or result in serious injury.

Should the services of a competent gunsmith be unavailable for any reason, and the work have to be undertaken, the barrel or barrels must be dismounted from the stock, the breech plug removed and the barrel thoroughly cleaned prior to inspection. The clean dry barrel should then be held up to a strong light and it should be carefully inspected from both muzzle and breech ends. The gun should be reassembled and enjoyed purely as a collector's item, if any serious pitting or corrosion is found; if, on the other hand, no obvious defects are apparent the plug can be replaced and the barrel set up for test firing.

Loads indicated in the Appendices can be used for proof firing, the barrel being loaded as will be later discussed. Some means of anchoring the barrel during 'operation test fire' is necessary to avoid damage which might occur as a result of the barrel being thrown about due to recoil. The barrel can either be lashed to a stout plank or supported on sandbags. Whatever means is used. make certain that there is no possibility of any obstruction at the muzzle. So that you can be well out of the way when the charge is fired, lay a powder train at least five feet in length, one end terminating at the nipple vent (the nipple having been removed) or touch-hole, the other on a piece of paper which you light before retreating to a place of safety. If the barrel is still intact, the operation should be repeated and the barrel dismantled and again examined. If the proof firing has not brought to light defects, the barrel can be considered safe for normal use and the gun reassembled.

Accidents can be caused by defects other than those found in the barrel and it is very necessary thoroughly to check lock and trigger mechanisms to make certain that abuse has not resulted in some malfunctioning that would cause accidental discharge if, for example, the butt is allowed to strike the ground thus jarring off the lock.

A careful check on the stock to make certain that no flaws or cracks are present (which under the strain of firing might result in a broken stock) is a wise precaution since early repair might prevent costly damage.

With the gun test-fired and fully checked—lock, stock and barrel —it can now be loaded and used. It will be assumed that a 20-bore single-barrel flintlock shotgun has been selected. From the Appendices it will be seen that if the gun is a true 20 bore the barrel diameter will be 0·615 in. This figure is a guide only since one hundredth of an inch either up or down will not seriously affect matters. A supply of felt wads of approximately barrel diameter will have been obtained either by purchase or by being made with the aid of a wad punch. The thickness of the felt wads should be at least half the bore diameter and it will aid loading if they are carefully greased on the bearing surfaces. Card wads of the same diameter should also be acquired and loading is helped if the card wad is pierced in the centre with a small hole or the circumference 'nicked' so that the build-up of air pressure as the wad is forced down the barrel is relieved.

Formerly a wide range of sporting gunpowder was available, made in a variety of grain sizes. This is no longer the case and, in Britain, for shotguns less than 10 bore grain size No. 4 will be found suitable. For rifles and larger shotguns No. 6 powder is recommended.

Shot, fortunately, is still available over the counters of many gunmakers and No. 6 will be found to answer for general sporting use. Modern English No. 6 shot is approximately 0·102 in. in diameter and 270 pellets weigh 1 oz.

Measures for both powder and shot are required, the powder measure being calibrated in drams. This measure can easily be checked for accuracy with the powder being used, one dram equalling 27·3 grains avoirdupois. From the Appendices it will be seen that the service charge for our 20-bore shotgun is 2½ drams and with the measure set to throw this, the powder should be scooped up from a large bowl with a single motion, the excess being struck off with a card. Powder charges can be measured and kept in small containers, if a proper powder flask is not available. Do not forget to check the charge thrown by weighing.

The shot measure is calibrated in ounces and from the table the recommended shot charge is $\frac{7}{8}$ oz. Set the measure to throw this weight and either weigh the charge or count the number of pellets (1 oz. No. 6 shot containing 270 pellets). If no shot flask or shot belt is available or if the measure is grossly inaccurate, once again the shot charges can be made up in small containers ready for use.

Lastly, we have to consider the ignition of the charge. Since we are using a flint gun, priming powder and flints are required. Priming powder is finer in grain than that used for the main charge and FFFG will serve. This fine-grain material should not be used for the main charge. Flints are still made at Brandon and a size commensurate with the size of the cock should be selected. It is important that the flint be provided with a leather packing which serves to cushion the shock of the flint striking the frizzen or battery and also helps to hold more securely the flint in the jaws of the cock. Try the flint with an empty gun to see that it is the proper size and correctly fitted. When the trigger is pulled copious sparks should be produced and the battery or steel thrown smartly open.

With the flint securely fixed and all components ready, the gun butt should be placed on the ground or the toe of the left shoe. The pan should be closed and the muzzle held in the left hand, inclined away from the body. Withdraw the ramrod and hold this also in the left hand and with the right hand pour into the barrel a measured quantity of powder. Place a thick felt wad on to the muzzle and press it into the barrel with the thumb of the right hand. Drive it home on to the powder with the ramrod, the rod being held between the fingers of the right hand. Do not use the palm of the hand since a premature explosion could drive the rod through the hand. With the wad seated firmly on top of the powder, withdraw the ramrod and hold it once again in the left hand. Pour in the shot and place a card wad into the barrel, seating it on top of the shot with one firm stroke of the rod. Withdraw the rod and return it to the ramrod pipes, bringing the gun to waist level. Hold it horizontally, pointed in a safe direction, and flip open the pan cover, drawing the cock to the half-cock position. Priming powder is then introduced into the pan, first making sure that the touch hole is clear. Excessive priming should be avoided since when the pan cover is closed, caking of the grains may take place. Close the pan cover after priming and give the gun a sharp rap with the hand on the left side to fill the touch hole. The cock can then be drawn back and the gun fired.

Practice these operations with an empty gun until proficiency has been gained and never hurry the loading operation or vary the procedure once it has been standardized. Misfires should be treated with extreme caution. Always keep the muzzle pointed in a safe direction and count up to fifteen before examining the gun. Check flint and priming and prick out the touch hole. See that the steel is free from moisture or oil. Flints are normally fitted flat side uppermost but in an emergency it can be reversed and may produce sparks where before none resulted.

The procedure with a percussion gun is similar. It is generally advisable to snap at least one cap through an empty barrel before loading. Hammers during loading can be kept at half cock but the cap must not be placed on the nipple until you are ready to fire. The cap should be a snug fit and since cap sizes are now somewhat restricted, new nipples can be made to suit the available size of cap. Difficulty in loading may be due to oversize wads which can be reduced in diameter by rolling them on edge between two boards. Excessive fouling will also result in difficulty, and if the barrels cannot be cleaned, spit down the empty barrel before loading with powder when it will be found that the wad can now be seated.

If it is intended to use the gun for sporting purposes it should be patterned either against a large sheet of brown paper or against a white-washed wall. Alteration of powder or shot load may be found to improve the regularity of the pattern and the selected load should be adhered to. The old adage, 'little powder, much lead, shoots far, kills dead' should be remembered. Excessive powder charges are wasteful of powder and produce blown patterns.

Loading procedure with rifles follows the same general pattern. With round ball, it is essential to patch with either thin leather or linen. The patches should be between two to three times the bore diameter. Leather is not normally recommended on the grounds of cost, but the increased thickness may permit the use of a bullet the size of which when patched with linen or cotton is too small for accurate shooting. Linen is preferable to cotton purely on the grounds of strength, since cotton patches can be torn when ramming home the bullet.

Patches should be greased and for speed of operation are best cut using a circular punch. If the supply of cut patches runs out

simply place a roughly patched bullet in the muzzle and trim round
the edges with scissors. Cylindro-conoidal bullets are either
greased or used with lubricated paper patches. Lubricated
paper patched bullets are advisable if made-up paper cartridges
are to be used.

Bullets used for muzzle-loading rifled weapons should be cast
from pure lead. The bullet mould should be free from water or oil
before casting is commenced and the lead should be at the correct
temperature. The mould must also be at the right temperature and
preheating is best carried out by casting bullets, rejects being returned
to the melting pot. As an indication, if the bullets cast are wrinkled,
a cold mould, cold bullet metal, or the presence of oil on the mould
may be suspected. Bullets not properly 'filled out' can also be caused
by cold mould or metal. A frosted appearance indicates overheating
of the mould or metal. It is advised that gloves and safety glasses be
worn during casting operations, since molten lead can inflict
dangerous burns and at all times keep moisture away from the scene
of operations.

As with the shotgun, the powder charge can often be varied to
provide improved accuracy and to those experimentally inclined,
muzzle-loading shooting offers a wide and rewarding opportunity
for research. Misfires with percussion arms are not as frequent as
with flint weapons and often the source of the trouble is a blocked
nipple. Fine wire for clearing the nipple orifice should always form
part of the muzzle-loader's extensive outfit and if this does not
prove effective, a few grains of fine powder carefully placed in the
nipple orifice may well do the trick.

One other class of muzzle-loading arm that provides great enjoy-
ment in shooting is the revolver. With the majority of good-quality
revolving pistols, it can be said that providing black powder and
pure lead are used, the chambers can be loaded to the brim without
any trouble occurring. If, when the chambers are loaded, it is
impossible to cock the gun, i.e. the cylinder will not rotate, then an
excessive charge has been used and the chambers must be unloaded
first of all to 'untie' the gun and secondly, so that a reduced powder
charge can be used.

Once again it is assumed that a gun in good condition is being
used and after a thorough cleaning and check up, powder can be
loaded into each chamber. The charge for ·44 calibre weapons may
be taken as 40 grains black powder, the ·36 calibre 20 grains, and

F

14 grains for the ·31 calibre pistols. Fine-grain powder is recommended and this must be black powder, not smokeless.

Cased percussion revolvers are usually found complete with the appropriate bullet mould but round ball can be used providing that it is a good fit in the chamber. Pure lead without any alloy constituent must be used for casting bullets which are seated one at a time ahead of the powder by means of the lever rammer. After all chambers have been loaded the bullets are lubricated *in situ* with grease to reduce fouling troubles and to eliminate multiple discharges. With the rammer secure and the hammer at half cock, the nipples are capped and the gun is ready to be fired.

After use black powder guns must be thoroughly cleaned. Excess fouling can be removed by a brush, this to be followed by copious quantities of cold water applied to the inside of the bore. Any part of the mechanism which has been fouled, hammer nose, nipples, etc., must also be washed with cold water. In the case of rifles and shotguns, the barrels can be removed from the stock and, if percussion, the nipples removed. The barrels are then placed breech down in a bucket of cold water, polythene preferred, and a tight-fitting patch drawn up and down the bore. This 'pumping' action is easier to carry out and more effective than pouring water down the barrel. After cleaning, the barrels are rinsed in cold water and the buckets refilled with hot. The same procedure is carried out until the barrels are too hot to hold, all water is expelled and they are allowed to dry by virtue of their retained heat. The use of a good dewatering oil such as Young's ·303 Cleaner is then recommended before the gun is put away.

Muzzle-loading guns are lethal weapons, so handle your gun with care. This care should be observed not only when firing but when loading and cleaning also. The way you handle a gun in the company of others tells them in a plainer language than words how familiar you are with firearms. Finally, when shooting, always wear shooting glasses.

CHAPTER EIGHTEEN

Cleaning and repairs

NOT all the acquisitions of the gun collector will be in a state of pristine newness. The degree to which time and past abuse have taken their toll will vary greatly, some items retaining nearly all their original finish, others being a broken, rusty, worm-eaten travesty of past splendour.

What are the means available of restoring those items which, but for their appearance, would grace any collection and, of equal importance, what are the ethics of such restorations?

Every collector at one time or another encounters a rusty and decrepit firearm which could be made into a handsome specimen. The extent to which such work can be carried out depends almost entirely on the patience and skill of the restorer.

When the latest addition to the collection is borne home in triumph and it is possible to assess the weapon dispassionately, the first action should be to make sure that it is not loaded. (With muzzle-loading guns pass a cleaning rod down the barrel to ensure no charge was left by a past owner.) Follow this by a rub down with an oily rag to remove surface dirt which will make it possible to see, to some extent, the amount of work necessary to repair the ravages of the past.

To carry out even the cleaning operation effectively, the weapon will have to be dismantled. For this, a number of good tools are essential. Of primary importance are screwdrivers. These should be available in a variety of blade widths and thicknesses. The end of the blade should not terminate in a knife edge and, since many screw slots have parallel vertical sides, the blade should be formed appropriately. Most modern screwdrivers lack this feature and, if necessary, the blade should be carefully altered, so that the working surfaces suit. Obtain a set of steel pin drifts or punches and at least one gunsmith's mainspring cramp. Unfortunately genuine mainspring cramps are difficult to come by but it will be found that a toolmaker's clamp will make a satisfactory substitute. A selection of cleaning rods, with appropriate brushes and jags, a supply of clean flannel, some fine steel wool and a range of emery paper down to '000' grade should also be obtained. Two types of oil, one fine lubricating, the other a rust preventer such as Young's

·303 Cleaner, should form part of the gun collector's tool kit. Although not essential, a small bench vice with fibre grips will be found to be of great value. The use of a hammer is often necessary, the normal householder's all-purpose 'tool' should be avoided. Buy a light 4-oz. pin hammer and keep it, as with the rest of the equipment, solely for gunsmithing.

The first task is to remove the barrel. Great care should be taken to avoid any damage to the woodwork either by reason of the working surface used (which can be padded), or when driving out the pins securing the barrel to the stock. If these pins (which may be round or flat) are rusted to the barrel loops, or in the wood, removal should be delayed until they have been loosened by doses of rust solvents, such as Plus-Gas, Formula 'A', or oil. The breech end of the barrel may be secured by the use of a 'false breech', in which case the barrel merely unhooks or the common barrel tang may be found and any attempt to 'unhook' this will result in damage.

With the barrel removed it should be possible to decide how far it is possible to restore it to its original condition. Often the original finish has been protected by the wooden furniture and can be compared with the exposed portions of the barrel. If any of the original finish has been retained, the cleaning procedure adopted should be such that this finish is preserved and not removed by attempts to clean other less fortunate parts of the barrel. On blued or browned barrels marked with slight rust patches, repeated soakings in rust solvent and oil, followed by polishing with flannel, will remove rust without damage to the surrounding areas, and steel wool or a scraper should only be used as a last extremity. In the case of badly rusted common guns, where all traces of the original finish have vanished, the surface should be soaked with rust solvent or oil and emery cloth used. Even if the finish has disappeared, important markings may still be present and these should not be rendered illegible through the over-energetic application of abrasives. In the case of octagonal barrels, every effort should be made to preserve the original flat surfaces and sharp corners and the abrasive can be placed on top of a piece of plate glass, the polishing paper being stationary and the barrel or other flat surface moved to and fro. As an alternative, the paper can be wrapped round a flat piece of wood.

Before restoration has been completed, an attempt should be

made to remove the breech plug, particularly if the owner intends to fire the weapon. Before starting, check once again that the barrel contains no long-forgotten charge and then firmly secure the barrel in a vice. It is often wiser to anticipate trouble with this operation so allow time for a rust solvent or penetrating oil to do its work. If possible obtain access to a large bench vice and make certain that the barrel is adequately padded to prevent damage. Normal engineer's tools will in many instances serve, but in the case of double-barrel guns or rifles, special tools may have to be made to fit the breech hooks. If a particularly stubborn breech plug is encountered, the barrel can be heated, but only if all traces of the original finish have been lost, since heating will destroy both blueing and browning. The nipples on percussion guns should be removed for cleaning and inspection if the gun is to be used and if damaged and rusted solid, removal can be achieved by carefully drilling out the remains. The threads should be cleaned up and a new nipple fitted.

The inside of the barrel can now be tackled using conventional cleaning rods and attachments. At this stage the barrel can be gauged from both the breech and muzzle ends and, if rifled, a note taken of the number of grooves and style of rifling used. Before the barrel is laid aside, make a note of all barrel markings for future reference and record purposes. Lastly, ensure that the work that has been put into cleaning is not wasted, by wiping down with an oily rag before placing aside to prevent rusting.

Attention should now be directed to the lock. Removal on the normal sidelock gun will be effected by unscrewing the side nails or screws which pass through the stock into the lock plate. If the lock plate is retained by the inletting, replace the side nails loosely, and tap the heads with a soft mallet. Do not attempt to prise out the plate, or damage to the furniture will result. Before stripping the lock, soak in penetrating oil overnight and then remove the mainspring. The lock should be brought to full cock, the mainspring cramp fitted, and the cock or hammer lowered. The mainspring, complete with cramp, can then be removed. Great care must be taken and the use of makeshifts avoided, since, if the mainspring is allowed to spring open unhindered, it will probably break. Removal of the scear follows, the tail being held against the pressure of the scear spring to avoid damage to the scear pivot screw. With the removal of the scear the remaining screws should present no difficulty. It is advised that a note be taken of the position of each screw so that it can be replaced in its original position.

Where possible, the remaining metal furniture should be removed from the stock for cleaning. The trigger guard, ramrod pipes and butt plate must be taken off the gun if at all possible so that cleaning can be carried out expeditiously and without damage to the surrounding woodwork. Large screws that do not yield to the normal well-fitting screwdriver can often be removed by the use of a carpenter's brace fitted with a screwdriver bit. Iron furniture which has suffered excessive corrosion can be cleaned quickly by chemical means and the use of an inhibited phosphoric acid derusting solution is recommended since adequate inhibition will effectively prevent any attack on the sound metal. The parts can either be immersed in this solution or treated by brush application. If proprietary materials are unavailable, 10 per cent phosphoric acid used at a temperature of 180°F. can be used or, as an alternative, 10 oz. citric acid per gallon of water to which has been added ammonia until the solution is alkaline to litmus paper, the solution to be used at boiling point.

Brass furniture which is heavily corroded can be cleaned by immersion in sulphuric acid, 8 per cent by volume and ferric sulphate 8 per cent by weight. This solution can be used between 120° and 180°F. For silver, 60 per cent by volume of nitric acid at room temperature, can be used or several other solutions based on the use of sodium cyanide.

When using any chemical solutions, have them made up by a reputable person. The bottles must be properly labelled with instructions regarding use and any safety precautions that have to be taken. The practice of storing dangerous chemical solutions in lemonade bottles cannot be too strongly deprecated. As a precaution, rubber gloves and safety glasses should be worn when handling corrosive chemicals.

Strong chemical cleaning agents and power tools must only be used when all other methods have been explored, otherwise an antique weapon with a twentieth-century finish will result.

These remarks apply equally to the prevalent practice of re-browning or reblueing components. The examination of a variety of weapons will demonstrate that the 'blueing' applied varies considerably in colour, depth and quality. There is, for example, a vast difference between the finish found on English percussion revolvers of the better class, and modern cartridge weapons. The finish obtained depends on the type of steel and its heat treatment as well as the blueing technique. Of prime importance is the quality of surface finish and the recolouring of unpolished or pitted parts cannot give satisfaction.

The processes available for metal colouring are extremely varied, ranging from the simple to the complex. Some are demanding in time, others in consumable chemicals and equipment costs. For small screws, heating the shank in a gas flame until colour builds up on the polished head and quenching in oil, will serve to colour insignificant parts which, if left 'in the white', would cause disharmony in the finished weapon. Adequate colour control cannot be obtained by this method on larger items and proprietary cold blueing solutions such as 'Comet' gun blue can be obtained from Messrs. Parker-Hale Ltd, Bisley Works, Birmingham.

If it has been decided fully to refinish and a discordant result is to be avoided, the information contained in *Firearms Blueing and Browning* by R. H. Angier (see Bibliography) will be of the greatest value and a choice of a suitable process which can be carried out with the facilities available can be made. Before starting to use an untried process or formula, trials should be carried out on similar material in order to see if the results come up to expectation. A badly or incorrectly blued weapon is an abomination, and if satisfactory results cannot be obtained on trial, reblueing should not be attempted.

The restoration of the woodwork, which has now to be considered, is of equal importance. Here again, where possible, the original finish should be retained. Since much of the metal furniture will have to be removed for cleaning, the stock can be carefully examined and a rub down with raw linseed oil will greatly facilitate such an inspection. In many instances application of linseed oil will be all that is required and periodic attention will restore the appearance of the stock. If dents are present, these can be raised by 'pressing', using water-soaked cloths and a hot iron, the generation of steam swelling the damaged fibres and eliminating the damage. Where damage to the stock has resulted in the removal of wood, thought will have to be given to the use of inserts and, in order to ease this operation, a supply of small pieces of wood should be available so that matching pieces can be selected for repair work. The introduction of modern adhesives has greatly simplified stock surgery and cracks can be repaired with far less difficulty than formerly.

Major repairs inevitably result in the need to refinish the stock, either in the region of the repair or in its entirety dependent on the general appearance. The removal of old finishes can best be achieved by the use of small pieces of glass. Used glass photographic negatives provide a convenient source of suitable scrapers or these can be made to suit the individual. Where possible the scraper should be used with the grain and far less damage to the stock is caused than by the use of coarse sandpaper. Following the removal of the old finish, the stock should be 'whiskered' by wetting and then raising the grain by careful heating. The whiskers are then removed by fine sanding. This operation should be repeated until no further whiskers can be raised.

Oil finishing at this stage will rarely provide a first-class result since it is necessary to fill the pores of the wood to prevent sinkage and loss of gloss. Fillers based on silica are preferred, and following application the excess should be removed by rubbing with a coarse cloth. A final light sanding and the first coat of raw linseed oil can be applied. This coat should be allowed to oxidize fully before further coats are put on since an excess will not dry and the result will be a sticky mess. Oil should be applied and rubbed well in by hand until the darkening of the wood is satisfactory. Too many coats of oil will result in excessive darkening and the loss of figure. Speedier results can be obtained by applying raw linseed oil followed by a 2 to 1 mixture of terebine and linseed oil, the latter mixture applied by a felt pad. When a satisfactory finish has been built up, all that is needed to maintain the finish is occasionally to rub the stock with a small quantity of linseed oil, the palm of the hand being the best means of application.

If the results obtained are not completely satisfactory, the fully hardened oil finish can be polished, using rottenstone. For this operation a small felt-covered block of wood must be made, the felt to be at least $\frac{1}{4}$ in. thick. The rubbing pad is soaked in water and then dipped into rottenstone, this being previously placed into some convenient flat container. The surface of the stock is then lightly rubbed with the pad, a careful watch being kept for caking or gumming of the pad with oil. Pick up can be avoided by washing the pad in water and reapplying rottenstone. Smooth, long strokes should be given, the pad being moved with the grain, never across it.

After rubbing, the stock can be lightly hand rubbed with linseed oil/terebine mixture.

As an alternative, the rottenstone can be applied to a stitched muslin wheel. The polishing carried out by using a hand power tool. This method is speedier but great care must be taken to avoid burning the stock and some form of stock support is advisable.

Throughout every operation, care must be taken to avoid damaging any decorative work or chequering. In the latter case, following the application of oil to the stock, a stiff brush can be used to remove excess oil and the chequering can be sharpened by the careful use of a needle file of the appropriate shape.

The reconditioning of old arms requires considerable forethought, many parts which are broken can be made or repaired and in the last extremity a facsimile copy of the part can be reproduced by modern techniques. A modern copy is not the thing to grace any collection and a part taken from a contemporary piece is to be preferred to the modern replica. Consequently, no arm should be turned down, however decrepit, since it might prove to be a useful source of spares. A carefully preserved, though perhaps battered, original is preferable to a varnished and highly buffed 'rebuild', the only purpose of which is to serve as a testimonial to the skill or otherwise of the modern 'expert' renovator.

CHAPTER NINETEEN

The law and the collector

In Britain, the collector who restricts his interest purely to the collection of flintlock and percussion muzzle-loading arms is unlikely to encounter any problems with the Law unless he uses them for their original purpose. If, on the other hand, his interests lie in the collection of breech loading weapons firing 'fixed' ammunition (i.e. containing the propellant, the projectile and the means of ignition) he undoubtedly will!

The reason, in Britain, is the Firearms Act 1968 and 1982.

The three important sections of the Act are as follows,

Part 1

Section 1 (1) Subject to any exemption under the Act, it is an offence for a person

(*a*) to have in his possession, or to purchase or acquire, a firearm to which this section applies without holding a firearms certificate in force at the time, or otherwise than as authorised by such a certificate;

(*b*) to have in his possession, or to purchase or acquire, any ammunition to which this section applies without holding a firearm certificate in force at the time, or otherwise than as authorised by such a certificate, or quantities in excess of those so authorised.

(2) It is an offence for a person to fail to comply with a condition subject to which a firearm certificate is held by him.

(3) This section applies to every firearms except:

(*a*) a shot gun (that is to say a smooth bore gun with a barrel not less than 24 inches in length, not being an air gun), and

(*b*) an air weapon (that is to say an air rifle, air gun or air pistol not of a type declared by the rules made by the Secretary of State under Section 53 of the Act to be specially dangerous).

(4) This section applies to any ammunition for a firearm, except the following articles, namely:

(*a*) cartridges containing five or more shot, none of which exceeds .36 inch in diameter;

(*b*) ammunition for an air gun, air rifle or air pistol; and

(*c*) blank cartridges not more than one inch in diameter measured immediately in front of the rim or cannelure of the base of the cartridge.

Section 2 (1) Subject to any exemption under this Act, it is an offence for a person to have in his possession, or to purchase or acquire, a shot gun without holding a certificate under this Act authorising him to possess shot guns.

Section 3 (1) A person commits an offence if, by way of trade or business, he

(*a*) manufactures, sells, transfers, repairs, tests or proves any firearm or ammunition to which section 1 of this Act applies, or a shotgun; or

(*b*) exposes for sale or transfer, or has in his possession for sale, transfer, repair, test or proof any such firearm or ammunition, or a shotgun, without being registered under this Act as a firearms dealer.

The extract from the 1968 Act which covers most of the provisions of the Act (except that, oddly enough, it has no definition of the term 'firearm') can be purchased from H.M. Stationery Office for £4.70. The later Firearms Act of 1982 refers in general to imitation firearms, i.e., those which have the appearance of firearms or those which are constructed so as to be readily converted to be used as firearms. It is, I suppose, conceivable that a collector of toy and replica arms could well encounter problems given the very realistic nature of today's replica weapons and for this reason he should be aware of the provisions (and the penalties) of the 1982 Act.

Chapter 27 of the 1968 Act, referred to above, is 46 pages long and before you think how badly those of us with a legitimate interest in firearms are served in this country, spare a thought for the American gun collector. The American guide to Federal Firearms regulations is twice the size of ours and has nearly twice as many pages and this is backed by additional legislation contained in a booklet, the same size as our 'guide book' in the U.K. but which is well over two hundred pages long!

In Britain an application for firearm and shot gun certificates must be made to the chief officer of police for the area in which the applicant resides. Whether or not the application is approved is entirely at the discretion of the local chief officer of police. His interpretation of the Act can be the deciding factor in the granting of a firearms certificate and also in the conditions which may be applied in an individual case. The conditions, subject to which the certificate is held, may be altered or varied at any time by the chief officer of police and he may revoke the certificate at any time.

For this reason any dogmatic pronouncement regarding the operation of the Act in practice is of little value. Those collectors whose interests lie in firearms to which the Act might apply are advised to write to the chief officer of police in their area and request an interpretation of the Act as it would apply to them.

As a general guide firearms which employ fixed ammunition and which are rifled, and smooth bore shotguns with barrels less than 24 in. in length, require a firearm certificate. Smooth bore weapons with barrel(s) in excess of 24 in. in length require a shotgun certificate.

Any comment on the value of the Firearms Acts or indeed, upon its interpretation, is outside the scope of this book. Nevertheless, such an Act is in existence in this country and since each Act has been more draconian than its predecessors, it is extremely unlikely that any Government will ease the restrictions which govern the activities of the modern 'Gun Collector'. As the cost of flintlock and percussion muzzle loading arms continues to escalate the collector has to turn increasingly to the later breech loading weapons. It is, of course, far easier to shoot muzzle loading weapons than it is to fire many of the early breechloaders, the ammunition for which is far scarcer than the guns in which it is intended to be used. It is in this area where a liberal interpretation of the Act might well allow a collector with no intention of using his breech loaders, and with no intention of obtaining ammunition (even if this were possible), full rein to his desires. This is where a frank and full discussion with your local police of your collecting ambitions could prove beneficial.

In addition to the purchase or acquisition, the ownership and possible use, the Act also covers the disposal of firearms, their testing and repair and the ownership and use of certain classes of air weapons which could present problems for the airgun collector.

There are, in addition, further Regulations which govern the import and export of firearms and, in particular, those firearms which do not bear valid proof marks.

If, incidentally, the collector decides to find out exactly how the original owner of his flintlock rifle or shotgun loaded and used the weapon he should check whether the local officer of police requires the gun to be 'on ticket' or not. Until half way through the nineteenth century major wars were fought with muzzle loaders and today, correctly loaded, they are still lethal weapons!

CHAPTER TWENTY

Proof and other marks

PROOF in Britain dates back to 1637 when the Gunmakers' Company of London was granted its Royal Charter. The intention was to protect the public against the many unsound arms then being sold which were not only a source of danger to the user but which also tended to discredit the reputable gunmaker. Later, a second Proof House was established by the Act of Parliament in Birmingham in 1813 which replaced earlier private Proof Houses operated by the Birmingham Gun Trade. Since 1813, it has been an offence to sell or offer for sale an unproved arm anywhere in the United Kingdom.

In what way is the gun collector in Britain affected by the Gun Barrel Proof Act? If only muzzle-loading weapons are concerned and the owner does not intend to use them, the Act need not concern him. On the other hand, if he intends to use his muzzle-loading rifle, pistol or shotgun, the existence of the two Proof Houses might well be the means of his avoiding serious injury since submission to proof is an excellent guarantee that the gun will not blow up in use. Common sense will dictate whether or not any antique firearm should be fired or submitted to Proof. Obviously extremely rare or valuable weapons should not be called upon to undergo the stress of firing nor should weapons which are unsound. Since, however, in recent years considerable interest has arisen in the use of both flint and percussion weapons for sporting and target purposes, the facilities of the two Proof Houses should not be overlooked. Anyone who wishes to submit firearms for proof or reproof should first seek the opinion of a competent gunmaker and should in any case submit weapons for proof through a gunmaker instead of direct to the Proof House, since many firearms require attention before they are acceptable for proof.

At this stage, we can leave the legal jungle and regard the whole question of proof from the special viewpoint of the gun collector. Proof dates back to the earliest days of gunmaking and was also used by swordsmiths and armourers as a guarantee of the excellence of their work. Unscrupulous makers who capitalized on the general good name or high reputation for quality which had been painstakingly built up in some area or region by lowering quality in order to increase their profit, resulted in the reputable makers banding together in guilds. The regulations that they enforced to protect their good name from exploitation were later reinforced by local or national governments anxious to protect their valuable markets. By 1500, the practice of impressing marks on barrels by a responsible authority indicating satisfactory quality was becoming more widely used and many thousands of these marks can be found reproduced in Støckel's *Haandskydevaabens Bedømmelse* (Analysis of Handshooting Arms). The first country to establish an official Proof House was England. Prior to the London Gunmakers obtaining their Charter of Incorporation in 1637, a system of inspection had already been established. Such systems of inspection had their

London proof marks. *Left to right: c.* 1700; 1637 type; 1672 type.

origins in the early Craft Guilds or Incorporations. The ability to turn out good work was tested by the craftsman making a proof piece or essay piece, the quality of which was assessed by the Master of the Craft. If the work was satisfactory, the applicant was admitted to the Craft and allowed to carry on trade.

The gunmakers of London gained their craft independence in 1637 and in the preamble of the Charter, which is still in existence in the London Guildhall, the reasons for the foundation of the Gunmakers Company of London are set out.

'That divers blacksmiths and others inexpert in the art of gunmaking had taken upon them to make, try and proove guns after their unskilled way whereby the trade was not only much damnified, but much harm and damage through such unskilfulness had happened to His Majesty's subjects.'

Previously, the control of quality exercised by a craft association had in many instances extended only to the original 'proof piece' submitted by a prospective applicant. In many crafts this had been supplemented by snap checks taken by the craft masters and any work displayed for sale which was considered to be below the standard set could be seized. The London Gunmakers Charter went further than this.

In addition to the right of search, view, gauge, and proof during manufacture, all guns made within a ten-mile radius of the City of London and all imported guns had to be submitted for proof. The proof consisted in the barrels being fired in the rough state and finally in the finished state with a double charge of powder and ball. After proof, the barrels were impressed with the Company's mark, rough proof being indicated by the letter V beneath a crown, the mark for the final proof being a monogram of the letters G.P. (Gunmakers Proof) beneath a crown.

London proof marks.
Left: 1702. Right: c. 1800.

The proof of guns had been carried out by the Company since 1637 but it was not until 1713 that the Company established an official Proof House. The gunmakers of Birmingham lacked an official Proof House of their own and whilst this difficulty had been overcome to some extent by the establishment of private Proof Houses, the magnitude of their trade enabled them by Act of Parliament to 'erect and establish a proper Proof House' in 1813, despite considerable opposition from their London brethren. The Birmingham Proof House began operations on 16th March, 1814, taking for its mark the private proof mark of the Birmingham firm of Ketland, crossed sceptres surmounted by a crown. This mark

Birmingham proof marks.
Left: pre 1813. *Right:* post 1813.

was supplemented by the letter V for the view and letters B P C for the final proof mark.

Throughout the years, the rules of proof have been amended to meet changing conditions and additional or amended marks have appeared or been deleted. Due to these changes in markings, the proof impressions found on firearms are of considerable use in dating later weapons, and if a study of British Proof Marks is combined with that of other countries, not only approximate dates but also the origin of the firearm can often be decided. Not all countries established official Proof Houses, America being a notable exception.

Other marks found on guns, in addition to the maker's name and location, might include the barrel or lockmaker's marks and since

Left to right: Early private Birmingham mark; Utting, Birmingham, 1800; Thos. Richards, Birmingham, *c.* 1760.

the apparent maker was often the vendor and not the maker, a search for other markings may well bring to light the true origin of the weapon.

British guns which are silver or gold mounted provide the collector with an accurate means of dating by means of the Hall Marks. Although the use of precious metal on British firearms is the exception rather than the rule, the use of the Hall Mark is a valuable additional means of establishing the date of manufacture on those occasions when the collector is fortunate enough to encounter a weapon possessing such markings.

The name and address of the maker of the gun are usually found on the lock plate and barrel. With the aid of published lists of gunmakers' names and addresses, the period during which any particular maker worked can often be established and the later and more complete listings give, in addition, pertinent information concerning the maker's main activities should he have specialized in one type of arm. The absence of any maker's name from such listings does not mean that he was of little importance, since a considerable amount of work remains to be done before anything approaching a complete 'gunmakers' directory' could be completed. In the case of a collector who might specialize in local gunmakers, much additional information concerning location and the period during which they worked can be obtained by research amongst local historical documents and the general records of the community. In this task the Librarian or the Museum Curator will be able to provide a great deal of information of value to the specialized researcher.

Of interest in establishing past ownership of the piece are the crests which often were engraved on the escutcheon. Family crests are fully documented and the tracing of a particular example can often be both fascinating and rewarding.

Often the complete address of the maker cannot be found on the gun. The practice of furnishing guns complete with case and tools is often of help where a complete address of the maker is lacking, since it was the practice to insert inside the case a trade label which often provides a wealth of information. A note should always be taken whenever the collector has the opportunity of examining these labels, since the information gained may be of use in the future.

Gun cases, of importance in their own right, often contain powder and shot flasks as well as tools, the number and general excellence of which increased throughout the nineteenth century. Powder and shot flasks, besides being of value to muzzle-loading shooters, are of importance to collectors and the tools also of value, even if only as an exercise in finding out what was their original purpose.

The most important qualification for any gun collector is that he possesses a lively curiosity. The amount of money that can be diverted towards his collecting interests may be limited, the number of guns in his collection may be limited by considerations of space, but there is no limit to the amount of information that can be sought out, recorded and made available to others.

Continental proof marks. *Left to right:* Paris; St. Étienne; Tulle; Chatelleraut; Belgium; (Liége) post 1810.

Appendices

APPENDIX I

PROOF AND SERVICE LOADS FOR DOUBLE-BARRELLE MUZZLE-LOADING SHOTGUNS

No. of Gauge	Diameter of Bore by calculation	PROVISIONAL PROOF			DEFINITIVE PROOF				SERVICE CHARGE		
		Powder		Bullet	Powder		Shot		Powder		Sho
		grns.	drs.	grns.	grns.	drs.	grns.	oz.	grns.	drs.	grns.
4	1·052	928	34	1649	547	20	2041	$4\frac{2}{3}$	273	10	1531
5	·976	740	27	1315	426	$15\frac{9}{16}$	1623	$3\frac{17}{24}$	213	$7\frac{25}{32}$	1217
6	·919	612	$22\frac{1}{2}$	1090	357	$13\frac{1}{16}$	1367	$3\frac{1}{8}$	179	$6\frac{17}{32}$	1025
7	·873	525	$19\frac{1}{4}$	931	308	$11\frac{1}{4}$	1185	$2\frac{17}{24}$	154	$5\frac{5}{8}$	889
8	·835	481	$17\frac{1}{2}$	812	270	$9\frac{7}{8}$	1057	$2\frac{5}{12}$	135	$4\frac{15}{16}$	793
9	·803	394	$14\frac{1}{2}$	720	244	$8\frac{15}{16}$	967	$2\frac{5}{24}$	122	$4\frac{15}{32}$	725
10	·775	372	$13\frac{1}{2}$	646	219	8	875	2	109	4	656
11	·751	350	$12\frac{3}{4}$	586	191	7	765	$1\frac{3}{4}$	96	$3\frac{1}{2}$	574
12	·729	350	$12\frac{3}{4}$	535	178	$6\frac{1}{2}$	729	$1\frac{2}{3}$	89	$3\frac{1}{4}$	547
13	·710	328	12	493							
14	·693	306	$11\frac{1}{4}$	457	164	6	656	$1\frac{1}{2}$	82	3	492
15	·677	306	$11\frac{1}{4}$	425							
16	·662	295	$10\frac{3}{4}$	399							
17	·649	295	$10\frac{3}{4}$	374	150	$5\frac{1}{2}$	583	$1\frac{1}{3}$	75	$2\frac{3}{4}$	437
18	·637	273	10	352							
19	·626	241	$8\frac{3}{4}$	334							
20	·615	219	8	316	136	5	511	$1\frac{1}{6}$	68	$2\frac{1}{2}$	383
21	·605	219	8	300							

No of Gauge	Diameter of Bore by calculation	PROVISIONAL PROOF		Bullet	DEFINITIVE PROOF				SERVICE CHARGE			
		Powder		Bullet	Powder		Shot		Powder		Shot	
		grns.	drs.	grns.	grns.	drs.	grns.	oz.	grns.	drs.	grns.	oz.
22	·596	197	7¼	287 ⎫								
23	·587	197	7¼	274								
24	·579	186	6¾	262								
25	·571	186	6¾	251								
26	·563	186	6¾	242 ⎬	109	4	437	1	55	2	328	¾
27	·556	186	6¾	231								
28	·550	186	6¾	223								
29	·543	164	6	214								
30	·537	164	6	207 ⎭								
31	·531	164	6	200 ⎫								
32	·526	164	6	194								
33	·520	153	5½	188								
34	·515	153	5½	182								
35	·510	153	5½	177 ⎬	82	3	328	¾	41	1½	246	9/16
36	·506	153	5½	172								
37	·501	153	5½	167								
38	·497	142	5¼	162								
39	·492	142	5¼	158								
40	·488	142	5¼	154 ⎭								
41	·484	131	4¾	150 ⎫								
42	·480	131	4¾	146								
43	·476	131	4¾	142								
44	·473	131	4¾	139								
45	·469	120	4½	136 ⎬	55	2	219	½	27	1	164	⅜
46	·466	120	4½	133								
47	·463	120	4½	130								
48	·459	120	4½	127								
49	·456	120	4½	124								
50	·453	120	4½	122 ⎭								

PROOF AND SERVICE LOADS FOR MUZZLE-LOADING RIFLES

No. of Gauge	Diameter of Bore	Bullet for Provisional and Definitive Proof	POWDER, T.P.		SERVICE CHARGE	
			Provisional Proof	Definitive Proof	Powder	Bullet
	in.	grns.	grns.	grns.	grns.	grns.
4	1·052					
	1·000					
5	·976	1806	825	660	330	1400
6	·919					
7	·873					
8	·835					
9	·803	1533	550	440	220	1150
10	·775					
11	·751	1266	475	380	190	950
12	·729					
13	·710					
14	·693	973	300	240	120	730
15	·677					
16	·662					
17	·649					
18	·637					
19	·626	800	237	190	95	600
20	·615					
21	·605					
22	·596					
23	·587					
24	·579					
	·577					
25	·571					
26	·563					
27	·556					
28	·550	706	212	170	85	530
29	·543					
30	·537					
31	·531					
32	·526					
33	·520					
34	·515					

No. of Gauge	Diameter of Bore	Bullet for Provisional and Definitive Proof	POWDER, T.P.		SERVICE CHARGE	
			Provisional Proof	Definitive Proof	Powder	Bullet
	in.	grns.	grns.	grns.	grns.	grns.
35	·510					
36	·506	706	212	170	85	530
37	·501					
37	·500					
38	·497					
39	·492					
40	·488					
41	·484					
42	·480					
43	·476					
44	·473					
45	·469	640	212	170	85	480
46	·466					
47	·463					
48	·459					
49	·456					
50	·453					
	·450					
	·440					
	·430					
	·420	533	187	150	75	400
	·410					
	·400					
	·390					
	·380	347	187	150	75	260
	·370					
	·360					
	·350					
	·340					
	·330	247	100	80	40	185
	·320					
	·310					
	·300	214	68	54	27	160

Bibliography

BOOKS

ABELS, ROBERT: *Early American Firearms*, Cleveland, Ohio, 1950.

ANGIER, R. H.: *Firearms Blueing and Browning*, Samworth, S.C., 1936.

BARTLETT, W. A., and GALLATIN, D. B.: *Digest of Cartridges*, Washington, D.C., 1878. Reprint available from Pioneer Press, Harriman, Tennessee.

BLACKMORE, HOWARD, L.: *British Military Firearms, 1650–1850*, London, 1961.

BLANCH, H. J. A.: *Century of Guns*, London, 1909.

BOWMAN, H. W.: *Antique Guns*, Greenwich, Conn., 1954.

BRADBURY, FREDERICK: *Guide to Marks of Origin on British and Irish Silver Plate*, Northend, Sheffield, 9th ed., 1955.

CARY, A. MERWYN: *English, Irish and Scottish Firearms Makers*, Chambers, London, 1954.

CARMAN, W. Y. A.: *History of Firearms*, Routledge & Kegan Paul, London, 1955.

CHAPEL, CHARLES: *Gun Collecting*, New York, N.Y., 1939.

CHAPEL, CHARLES: *The Gun Collector's Handbook of Values*, San Leandro, Calif., 1940.

CLINE, WALTER: *The Muzzle Loading Rifle, Then and Now*, Huntington, W. Va., 1942.

DATIG, FRED A.: *Cartridges for Collectors*, Vols. I and II, Fadco Publishing Co., Calif., 1958.

DATIG, FRED A.: *The Luger Pistol*, Fadco Publishing Co., Calif., 1958.

DEANE, J.: *Deane's Manual of the History and Science of Firearms*, London, 1858. Reprint, Standard Publications Inc., Huntington, W. Va.

DILLIN, JOHN: *The Kentucky Rifle*, Washington, D.C., 1924.

DOWELL, WM. C.: *The Webley Story*, Holland Press, London, 1960.

DRUMMOND, J.: *Ancient Scottish Weapons*, London, 1881.

FFOULKES, CHARLES J.: *Inventory and Survey of the Armouries of the Tower of London*, London, 1916.

FREEMANTLE, T. F.: *The Book of the Rifle*, London, 1901.

FRITH, JAS. ANDREWS R.: *Antique Pistol Collecting*, Holland Press, London, 1960.

GEORGE, JOHN NIGEL: *English Pistols and Revolvers*. Small Arms Technical Publishing Co., Onslow County, N.C., 1938. Reprint, Spring 1961.

GEORGE, JOHN NIGEL: *English Guns and Rifles*, Stackpole Co., Harrisburg, Va., 1957.

GLENDENNING, IAN: *British Pistols and Guns, 1640–1840*. Cassell & Co. Ltd, London, 1951.

GRANT, JAMES R.: *Single Shot Rifles*, William Morrow & Co. Inc., N.Y.C., 1947. Reprinted 1959.

GRANT, JAMES R.: *More Single Shot Rifles*, William Morrow & Co. Inc., N.Y.C., 1959.

GREENER, WILLIAM: *The Gun*, London, 1835.

GREENER, WILLIAM: *The Science of Gunnery*, London, 1841.

GREENER, WILLIAM: *Gunnery in 1858*, London, 1858.

GREENER, WILLIAM WELLINGTON: *The Gun and its Development*, 9th ed., Cassell & Co., London, 1910.

GREENER, WILLIAM WELLINGTON: *Modern Breech Loaders*, Cassell, Petter & Galpin, London, 1881.

GROSE, — : *Military Antiquities*, London, 1801.

HARRIS, CLIVE: *A History of the Birmingham Proof House*, Guardians of the Birmingham Proof House.

HATCHER, JULIAN: *Pistols and Revolvers*, Small Arms Technical Publishing Co., Plantersville, S.C., 1935.

HAWKER, PETER WILLIAM: *Instructions to Young Sportsmen*, 5th ed., London, 1826.

HAYWARD, J. F.: *European Firearms*, H.M.S.O., London, 1955.

HELD, ROBERT, and JENKINS, NANCY: *The Age of Firearms*, Harper & Bro., N.Y.C., 1957.

JACKSON, H. J. WHITELAW: *C.E. European Hand Firearms*, Holland Press, London. Reprint 1959.

JEWITT, LLEWELLYN: *Rifles and Volunteer Rifles Corps*, London, 1860.

JOHNSON, T. B.: *The Shooters Companion*, London, 1819.

KARR, C. L., and KARR, C. B.: *Remington Hand Guns*, The Stackpole Company, Harrisburg, Pa., 1947.

LENK, T.: *Flintlaset*, Stockholm, 1939.

LEWIS, B. R.: *Small Arms and Ammunition in the United States Service*, Smithsonian Institution, Washington, D.C. Second Printing, 1960.

LOGAN, H. C.: *Cartridges*, Standard Publ. Inc., Huntington, W. Va., 1948. Reprinted 1959 by Stackpole Co., Harrisburg, Pa.

LOGAN, H. C.: *Hand Cannon to Automatic*, Standard Publ. Inc., Huntington, W. Va., 1944.

MCHENRY, R. C., and ROPER, W. F.: *Smith and Wesson Hand Guns*, The Stackpole Co., Harrisburg, Pa.

NEAL, W. KEITH: *Spanish Guns and Pistols*, G. Bell & Sons Ltd., London, 1955.

OMMUNDSEN and ROBINSON: *Rifles and Ammunition*, London, 1915.

PARSONS, JOHN E.: *The First Winchester*, William Morrow & Co., N.Y., 1955.

PARSONS, JOHN E.: *Henry Deringer's Pocket Pistol*, Morrow, N.Y., 1952.

PARSONS, JOHN E.: *The Peacemaker and its Rivals*, Morrow, N.Y., 1950.

POLLARD, H. B. C.: *The Book of the Pistol and Revolver*, London, 1917.

POLLARD, H. B. C.: *A History of Firearms*, London, 1926.

POLLARD, H. B. C.: *Automatic Pistols*, London.

POLLARD, H. B. C.: *Shot Guns*, London, 1923.

REID, A. J. F.: *The Rev. Alexander John Forsyth*, Aberdeen University Press, 1909. Reprinted, 1955.

REYNOLDS, E. G. B.: *The Lee Enfield Rifle*, H. Jenkins, London, 1960.

RILING, RAY: *The Powder Flask Book*, Robt. Halter, New Hope, Pa., 1953.

SERVEN, JAMES E.: *Colt Firearms*, Published by the Author, Santa Ana, Calif., 1959.

SMITH, W. H. B.: *Pistols and Revolvers*, Military Service Publishing Co., Harrisburg, Pa., 1946.

SMITH, W. H. B.: *Rifles*, Military Service Publishing Co., Harrisburg, Pa., 1948.

SMITH, W. H. B.: *Small Arms of the World*, Military Publishing Co., Harrisburg, Pa., 6th ed., 1957.

SMITH, W. H. B.: *Mauser Rifles and Pistols*, Stackpole Co., Harrisburg, Pa., 1954.

Støckel, Johan F.: *Haandskydevaabens Bedømmelse*, 2 vols., Copenhagen, 1938–43.

Thierback, M.: *Die Geschichtliche Entwickeling der Handfeuerwaffen*, 3 vols., Dresden, 1886.

White, H. P., and Munhall, B. D.: *Centre Fire American and British Pistol and Revolver Cartridges*, Washington, D.C., 1950.

White, H. P., and Munhall, B. D.: *Centre Fire Metric Pistol and Revolver Cartridges*, Washington, D.C., 1948.

Williamson, Harold F.: *Winchester: The Gun that Won the West*, Combat Forces Press, Washington, D.C., 1952.

Winant, Lewis: *Firearms Curiosa*, Arco Publishers Ltd., London, 1956.

Winant, Lewis: *Early Percussion Firearms*, William Morrow & Co., N.Y., 1959, and Herbert Jenkins, 1961.

ADDENDUM

Woodend, Herbert: *Catalogue of the Enfield Pattern Room. British Rifles*, H.M. Stationery Office, London, 1981.

Wilson, R. L.: *Colt Pistols, 1836–1976*, Jackson Arms, Dallas TX, U.S.A., 1976.

Bailey, DeWitt & Nie, D. A.: *English Gunmakers*, Arms & Armour Press, London, 1978.

Schroeder, J. J.: *Gun Collector's Digest*, DBI Books, Northbrook, IL, U.S.A., 1985.

Boothroyd, G.: *The Handgun*, Cassell, 1971.

Boothroyd, G.: *The Shotgun*, A & C Black Ltd., London, 1985.

Boothroyd, G.: *Shotguns & Gunsmiths*, A & C Black Ltd., London, 1986.

Serven, James E.: *The Rare & Valuable Antique Arms*, Pioneer Press, Union City, TN, U.S.A., 1976.

Hawkins, Peter: *The Price Guide to Antique Guns and Pistols*, Antique Collector's Club, 1973.

Note: No price indication has been given since many of the books listed are now out of print. However, an increasing number of important books are now being reprinted at prices far below those asked for the originals.

PERIODICALS

Airgun World 10 Sheet Street, Windsor, Berks SL4 1BG.

American Handgunner 591 Camino de la Reina, San Diego, CA 92108, U.S.A.

American Rifleman Nat. Rifle Assoc., 1600 Rhode Island Ave., Washington DC20036, U.S.A.

AMI New Fashion Media, S.A., 60 Avenue Louise, 1050 Bruxelles, Belgium. (French Text).

Arms Collecting Museum Restoration Service, PO Drawer 390, Bloomfield, Ont., Canada.

Armes International 19 quai Alphonse Le Gallo, 92100 Boulogne, France. (French text).

Deutsches Waffen Journal Journal Verlag Schwend GmbH, Postfach 100340, D7170 Schwabisch Hall, West Germany. (German text).

The Gun Report World Wide Gun Report Inc., Box 111, Aledo, IL61231, U.S.A.

Guns Review Ravenhill Publishing Co., Ltd., Box 35, Standard House, Bonhill St., London EC2A 4DA.

Guns Guns Magazine, 591 Camino de la Reina, San Diego, CA 92108, U.S.A.

Man at Arms Box 460, Lincoln, RI 02865, U.S.A.

Schweizer Waffen-Magazin Orell Fussli Zeitschriften, Postfach 1459, 8036 Zurich, Switzerland. (German text).

Shooting Times & Country Magazine 10 Sheet Street, Windsor, Berks SL4 1BG.

TACARMI Via E DeAmicis 25, 20123 Milano, Italy. (Italian text).

Gunsmiths and Gunmakers of the United Kingdom, 1908

Author's Note

Over the years a number of 'Gunmakers Lists' have been published and more recently Bailey & Nie published their *English Gunmakers* which provided much needed information on 18th and 19th century British gunmakers in the Birmingham area and the provinces. No complete list has ever been compiled although a start was made by A. Merwyn Carey in his *English, Irish and Scottish Firearms Makers* published in 1954. The list 'Gunsmiths and Gunmakers of the United Kingdom, 1908' is, to the best of my knowledge, unpublished. It was given to me many years ago by Miss Betty Brown (now Betty Porter) when she was a Director of Atkin, Grant and Lang. To the best of her belief the list was obtained, along with other material, by her uncle, W. R. H. Robson, the Managing Director of Atkin, Grant & Lang and a man whose interest in, and knowledge of, the gun trade was extensive. The list has been left in its original form; the letters 'N.B.' for example mean 'North Britain', more properly, Scotland, but one or two obvious errors have been corrected and, no doubt, others remain.

It is possible that readers may be puzzled by the letters 'S.O.' and 'R.S.O.' which are included in some of the addresses. I am informed that these letters mean Sub Office and Railways Sub Office.

The more important of the gunmakers are marked with a ● but it should be noted that the list includes vendors of guns, the names and addresses which have often puzzled those who seek information since the directories of the period would not list these names under gunmakers but under their main business which, in many instances was Ironmonger.

Abingdon Works Co., Ltd., (Thomas Mabbutt, Man Director) 94, 95, 96 Bath Street and Shadwell Street, Birmingham.
Adams & Tait, 1 New Buildings, Price Street, Birmingham.
Adams, Samuel, Columbia Building, 30 Brunswick Street, Liverpool.
Adkin, Henry and Sons, 57 High Street, Bedford.
Adsell, Thomas and Son, 101 High Street, Guildford.
Agnew and Son, 79 South Street, Exeter.
Airey, T. R., South Anston, Sheffield.
Aitken and Son, M., Crieff, N.B.
Akrill, Henry Esau, Market Place, Beverley, Yorkshire.
Allan, Arthur, 144 Trongate Street, Glasgow.

187

Allport, John, 26 Beacon Street, Lichfield, Staffs.

Allendorf and Wright, Vesey Street and Loveday Street, Birmingham.

Anderson, Henry F., Market Place, Bedale, Yorks.

Anderson, John, 52 Market Place, Malton, Yorks.

Andrews, Charles William Ltd., 13 Bath Street, Birmingham and Great
    Winchester Street, London

Andrews, C. W., Ltd., 5 & 6 Great Winchester Street, London E.C.

Andrews, Thomas, 2 Green's End, Woolwich, London S.E.

Anson, Edward & Co., 14 Steelhouse Lane, Birmingham.

Armfield, Stephen, 6 Sand Street, Birmingham.

Armoury Co., (The), 40 Dock Street, Dundee.

Armstrong, Stevens & Son,.Whittall Street, Birmingham.

Armstrong & Co., 115 Northumberland Street, Newcastle-on-Tyne.

● Army & Navy Co-operative Society Ltd., 105 Victoria Street, London
    S.W.

● Atkin, Henry, Jermyn Street, London S.W.

Atkinson and Griffin, 58 Highgate, Kendal.

Atkinson, William, & Sons, 20 Market Street and North Road, Lancaster,
    and 11 Skipton Street, Morecambe.

Austin, T. C., 16 Welselry Road, Ashford.

Baker, Joseph, Norwich Street, Fakenham, Norfolk.

● Baker, F. T., 20 Glasshouse Street, London W.

Barclay, T., 9 Bath Street, Frome.

Barham, Henry, Sun Street, Hitchin, Herts.

Barnes, Alfred A., Market Place, Ulverston, Lancs.

Barnett, T. E., and Sons Ltd., Duncan Street, Leman Street, London E.

Barrett and Son, 48 & 49 High Street, Burton on Trent.

Bartram, Geo. Thos. Thorpe, 33, 35 & 44 Bank Street, Braintree.

Bate, Geo., 132 Steelhouse Lane, Birmingham.

Bates, A. T., 23 Harbour Street, Whitstable, S.O., Kent.

Bates, Alfred, 22 Sun Street, Canterbury.

Bates, George, 48 Sea Side Road, Eastbourne.

Batty, J. E., Crowie, Doncaster.

Bayliss, Thomas, Back of 28 Whittall Street, Birmingham.

● Beesley, Frederick, 2 St. James' Street, London S.W.

Bell Bros., 93 Waterloo Street, Glasgow.

Bell, Henry, 23 New Buildings, Price Street, Birmingham.

Bellman, Carl, 8 St. Mary's Row, Birmingham.

Benbow, John Griffiths, 25 Bailey Street, Oswestry, Salop.

● Bentley & Playfair Ltd., Summer Lane, Birmingham.

Bentley & Playfair Ltd., 60 Queen Victoria Street, London E.

Berry, Joseph, Bridge Place, Worksop, Notts.

Bircham, Charles Octavius, and Son, 124 Poplar High St., London E.

Birmingham Gun and Cycle Co., (The), 15 St. Mary's Row, Birmingham.

Birmingham Metal and Munitions Co., Ltd., (The), Adderley Road, Saltley, Birmingham.
- Birmingham Small Arms Co., Ltd., Armoury Road, Smallheath, Birmingham.
Birmingham Small Arms Co., Ltd., 5 & 6 Gt. Winchester St., London E.C.
Blake, James (dealer), 12 Square, Kelso, Roxburghshire.
Blakemore, Edward, 8 Sand Street, Birmingham.
Blakemore, Thomas, 16 Weaman Street, Birmingham.
Blakemore, V. & R., 86 Leadenhall St., London E.C.
- Blanch, John, & Son, 29 Gracechurch Street, London E.C.
- Bland, Thos., & Sons, 41, 42 & 43 Whittal St., Birmingham and 2 King William Street, Strand, London.
Blankensee, M., and Son, Bristol.
Blenheim Engineering Co., Ltd., Tunnel Avenue, Greenwich, London S.E.
Blissett & Son, 36 South Castle Street, Liverpool.
Bond, George Edward & Son, Castle Street, Thetford, Norfolk.
- Bonehill, Christopher Geo., Belmont Row, Birmingham.
Booth, J., 26 Antrobus Street, Congleton, Cheshire.
- Boss & Co., 73 St. James' Street, London S.W.
Boston, J., Wood Street, Wakefield.
- Boswell, Charles, 126 Strand, London W.C.
Bott, J., & Son, 7 St. Mary's Row, Birmingham.
- Bourne, Joseph & Son, 7 St. Mary's Row, Birmingham.
- Bozard & Co., 8 Craven Street, Strand, London W.C.
Bradbury, Thomas, 61 Campo Lane, Sheffield.
Braddell, Joseph & Son, 21 Castle Place, Belfast.
Braendlin Armoury Co., Ltd., 55 Loveday Street, Birmingham.
Brander Bros., Gordon Street, Huntley, N.B.
Brewster, Jas. B., Stratton St. Mary, Long Stratton, Norfolk.
Brown, J., Morpeth.
Bryson, R., London Street, Glasgow.
Burgess & Co., Malvern Wells.
Burns, George, 31 Loveday Street, Birmingham.
Burrows, James, 116 Fishergate, Preston.
Burrow, J., 19a Lowther Street, Carlisle.
Burton, Frederick Matthew, 7 Purfleet Street, Lynn, Norfolk.
Busk & Paterson Ltd., 66 & 68 Union Street, Southwark, London, S.B.

Calder, William, 30 Guild Street, Aberdeen.
Canaway, Robert, 17 Winchester Street, Salisbury.
Carr Bros., 3a Market Street, Huddersfield.
Carr, James, & Sons, 10 & 11 St. Mary's Row, Birmingham.
Carr & Co., 4 Lower Parliament Street, Nottingham.
- Cashmore, William, 130 & 131 Steelhouse Lane, Birmingham.

Chalkley, W., The Square, Winchester.

Chamberlain, Arthur, 18 Queen Street, Salisbury.

Chamberlain, Edward, Winchester Street, Andover, Hants.

Chambers, W. Robert, 22 Walcot Street, Bath.

Chambers, Septimus, 63 Broad Street, Bristol and 21 Castle Street, Cardiff and at Shepton Mallet.

Chappell, Mrs. E., Thoroughfare, Harleston, Norfolk.

Charlish, R., Earsham Street, Bungay.

● Churchill, Edwin John, 8 Agar Street, Strand, London W.C.

● Clabrough, J. P., and Johnstone, 3 Price Street, Birmingham.

Clark, William, 73 Bath Street, Birmingham.

Clarke, Henry & Sons, 38 Gallowtree Gate, Leicester.

Clarke, Frank (factor), Great Charles Street, Birmingham.

Clarke, Henry W., 12 Queen Street, Newton Abbot, Devon.

Clarke, Albert Edward, 54 Strand, London, W.C.

Climie, Robert, & Son, 20 West Blackhall Street, Greenock.

Clisby, Fred Kent, Chapel Street, Great Marlow, Bucks.

Clough, Thomas, & Son, 52 High Street, Lynn, Norfolk.

● Cogswell & Harrison Ltd., 226 Strand, London W.C., and 29a Gillingham Street, London S.W.

Cole & Son, 33 Market Place, Devizes, Wilts; 116 Peascod Street, Windsor; 21 Pembroke Road, Portsmouth and 89 High Street, Cheltenham.

Cole, Francis John, 171 Crickdale Street, Cirencester, Gloucester.

Collie, William, 10 High Street, Montrose, Forfarshire.

Colt Gun & Carriage Co., Ltd., 34 Victoria Street, London S.W.

Colt's Patent Fire Arms Manufacturing Co., 26 Glasshouse Street, Regent Street, London W., and 15a Pall Mall, London S.W.

Conyers, John & Son, Market Place, Pocklington, and 71 Middle Street, South Driffield, Yorks.

Conyers, Arthur, 71 East Street, Blandford, Dorset.

Cooper, Charles H., Staniforth Street, Birmingham.

Cox & Macpherson, 62 High Street, Southampton.

Cox & Son, 28 High Street and 7 Bernard Street, Southampton.

Cox, D., Newtown, Newbury.

Cox, Frederick, 15 Weaman Street, Birmingham.

Cranmer, Samuel, Melton, Woodbridge, Suffolk.

Crawford, Charles H., 72 Weaman Street, Birmingham.

Creighton, G., 8 Warwick Road, Carlisle.

Cresswell, Walter, 16 Dean's Building, Weaman Street, Birmingham.

Crockart, David, & Co., 35 King Street, Stirling, N.B.

Crockart, D. B., 33 County Place, Perth, N.B.

Crockart, Jas., & Son, 26 Allan Street, Blairgowrie, Perthshire.

Cross & Co., 4 Price Street, Birmingham.

Culling, John Thos., 19 Little Church Street, Wisbech, Cambridgeshire.

Dadley, Thomas Alex., Market Place, Stowmarket, Suffolk.
Dainteith, Thomas, 121 Bridge Street, Warrington.
Darlow Ltd., Orford Hill, Norwich; Midland Road, Bedford, and Guildhall
    Street, Cambridge.
Doyle, W. & Co., Church Court, Dublin.
Davie, Francis, 157 High Street, Elgin, N.B.
Davidson, Edward, Market Place, Kettering.
Davies & Cockayne, Potter Street, Birmingham.
Dean, Henry, 71 North Road, Durham.
Dickins, John T., 69 Bridge Street, Northampton.
● Dickson, John & Son, 63 Princes Street, Edinburgh.
Diss, Fred M., 5 Pelham's Lane, High Street, Colchester.
Dixon & Co., 34 Lozells Road, Birmingham.
Dodd, Thomas (finishers), 126 Steelhouse Lane, Birmingham.
● Dougall, James D., & Sons, Gordon Street, Glasgow.
Doyle W., & Co., Church Street, Dublin.
Draper, J., 24 Town Hall Square, Bolton.
Duerden, Nathan, 6 Bradley Road, Nelson.
Duff, P., Ballygawley, R.S.O., Tyrone.
Dunne, John, 10 Russell Street, Tralee.
Dyke, Frank & Co., 5 St. George's Avenue, London E.C.
Dyson, Lewis, 3a Market Street, Huddersfield.

Eaton & Co., Ltd., (dealers), High Street, Market Harborough,
    Leicestershire.
Ebrall Brothers, 4 Wyle Cop, Shrewsbury.
Edwards, C. G. & Sons, 2 George Street, Plymouth.
Edwards, Walter & Co., 4 Whittall Street, Birmingham.
Edwards, W. H., & Co., Ltd., 32 & 33 Weaman Street, Birmingham.
Edwards, Benjamin, 50½ Newton Street, Birmingham.
Edwards, R. F., Hockerill, Bishops Stortford.
Edwards, Herbert, 64 Commercial Street, Newport, Mon.
Edwards, John, 34 Upper Castle Street, Tralee.
Ellis Bros., 16½ St. Mary's Row, Birmingham.
Ellis, Edward, South Quay, Wicklow.
Emslie, Samuel, 20 Barrack Street, Dundee.
Enos, James, & Co., 32½ Weaman Street, Birmingham.
● Erskine & Sons, Victoria Street, Newton Stewart, Wigtownshire.
Esser-Barratt Repeating Arms Co., New Summer Street, Birmingham.
Evans, C., 19 Lion Street, Brecon.
Evans, Thomas, 16 Weaman Street, Birmingham.
Evans, B., & Co., Ltd., 126 Temple Street, Swansea.
Evans, William, 63 Pall Mall, London S.W.
Evans, William, 47 Tullow Street, Carlow.

Ewen, James Walker, 20 Carmelite Street, Aberdeen.

Farmer, Richard, 12 North Street, Leighton Buzzard, Beds.
Field, Alfred & Co., 77 Edmund Street, Birmingham.
Field & Son, T., Aylesbury.
Field Rifle Co., Cambridge Street, Birmingham.
Fitchew, Arthur T., 75 High Street, Ramsgate.
Fletcher, Frederick S., 158 Westgate Street, Gloucester.
Fletcher, Walter, 46 Wilson Street, Finsbury, London E.C.
Flint, John & Co., 17 Essex Quay, Dublin.
• Ford, Wm., 15 St. Mary's Row, Birmingham.
Forrest & Sons (dealers), 35 Square, Kelso, Roxburghshire.
Fox, Isaac, 4 Upper Bridge Street, Canterbury.
Frampton, Mrs. Eliza, 10 Sussex Road, Nottingham.
Francis, Chas., 9 Long Causeway, Peterborough, Northants.
• Fraser, Daniel & Co., 4 Leith Street Terrace, Edinburgh.
Freeman, W., 148 Charles Street, Birmingham.
Freeth, John, 19 Whittall Street, Birmingham.
Fry, John, 17 Sadlergate, Derby.
Furlong, Francis Robert, King Street, Saffron Walden, Essex.

Gale, Edward, 20 Joy Street, Barnstaple, Devon.
Gallyon & Sons, 66 Bridge Street, Cambridge.
Garden, William, 122½ Union Street, Aberdeen.
Garrett, Frank, 7½ Bath Street, Birmingham.
Geering, Lewis, 12 Malling Street, Lewes.
George, William John, 192 Snargate Street, Dover.
• Gibbs, Geo., 39 Corn Street (works at St John's Bridge), Bristol and 35
    Saville Row, London W.
Gibbs, Geo., 35 Saville Row, London W.
Giles, J. 23½ Weaman Street, Birmingham.
Gingell, William, Golding's Hill, High Road, Loughton, S.O., Essex.
Glanville, R. W., 6 Wellington Street, Woolwich.
Golden, William, 6, 8, 10 & 12 Cross Church Street, Huddersfield.
Gow, John R., & Sons, 12 Union Street, Dundee.
Graham, John, & Co., 27 Union Street, Inverness.
Graham, George P., Station Street, Cockermouth, Cumberland.
• Grant, Stephen, & Sons, 67a St James' Street, London S.W.
Gray D., & Co., 36 Union Street, Inverness.
Gray, R. M., & Co., 6 Station Road, Walthamstow, London N.E.
• Green, Edwinson Charles & Son, 87 High Street, Cheltenham, and
    Northgate Street, Gloucester.
Green, J., 33 Loveday Street, Birmingham.
Greener, William W., 22 St Mary's Row, and 61 & 62 Loveday Street,

Birmingham; 19 Paragon St., Hull; and 68 Haymarket, London S.W.
Greener, William Wellington, 68 Haymarket, London S.W.
Gregson, James, 59 Penny Street, Blackburn.
Grice, J., 1 Court, Weaman Street, Birmingham.
Griffiths, Charles S., Belmont Bridge, Skipton.
Griffiths, J., Dudley.
Griffiths, W. J., 87 Bridge Street, Deansgate, Manchester.
Griffiths, William, 5 Bridge Street, Worcester.
Griffiths, William, 16 Weaman Street, Birmingham.
Gundy, Joseph, 19 Whittall Street, Birmingham.

Hadfield, Frederick, 31½ Whittall Street, Birmingham.
Hall, Christopher, Market Place, Knaresborough, Yorks.
Hall, Henry, 13 Court, Price Street, Birmingham.
Halle Automatic Fire Arms Syndicate, Ltd., (The), 18 St. Helen's Place, London E.C.
Hammond Bros., 40 Jewry Street, Winchester.
Hanson, John Robert, 1 Cornhill, Lincoln.
Harcourt, Harry, 7 & 9 Market Hill, Maldon, Essex.
Hardy Bros., London and North British Works, Alnwick, Northumberland.
Hardy, Harry, 17½ Whittall Street, Birmingham.
Hardy, John Charles, West End, Holbeach, R.S.O., Lincs.
Harkness, W. J., George Street, Templemore.
Harkness, William, 46 Castle Street, Nenagh.
● Harkem, Joseph & Son, George Street, Edinburgh.
Harold, J. O., Mallory.
Harper, Albert J., Steelhouse Lane, Birmingham.
Harper, John, 124½ Steelhouse Lane, Birmingham.
Harrison, Thomas, 8 Bank Street, Carlisle.
Harvey & Son, 32 Whittall Street, Birmingham.
Hawkes, Thos., Harper's Building, Weaman Street, Birmingham.
Hawkins, Jacob, South Street, Ilkeston, R.S.O., Derbyshire.
● Hellis, Charles, 119 Edgeware Road, London W.
Helyar & Sons, 93 Middle Street, Yeovil.
Henderson, Thomas, G., Highland Club Buildings, Inverness.
● Henry, Alexander & Co., 18 Frederick Street, Edinburgh.
Henry, Alexander, 89 Leith Walk, Edinburgh.
Hensman, W., 19 Bridge Street, Boston, Lincs.
Hepplestone, Thomas, 25 Shudehill, Manchester.
Higham, E. & G., 4 Adelaide Buildings, 4 Chapel Street, Liverpool.
Higham, George G., 24 Berriew Street, Welshpool, N. Wales.
Higham, George Garnett, 3 Bailey Street, Oswestry, Salop.
Hill and Smith, 13 Court, Price Street, Birmingham.
Hill, Arthur, Market Place, Horncastle.

Hill, Joseph, Anderson's Square, Whittall Street, Birmingham.
Hinton, George, 5 Fore Street, Taunton.
Hobson, John, 63 Regent Street, Leamington.
Hodges, G., Westbury, Sherbourne, Dorset.
● Hodges, Edwin Charles, 8 Florence Street, Islington, London.
Hodges, Lionel, 18 Charterhouse Buildings, London E.C.
Hodgett, Joseph, 13 Court, Price Street, Birmingham.
Hodgson, Francis, 1 Market Place, Bridlington, Yorks.
Hodgson, Henry, 26 Westgate Street, and 55 Butter Market, Ipswich.
Hodgson, Jesse Parker, 27 Mercer Row, Louth.
Hodgson, William, Middle Street, Ripon, Yorks.
● Holland & Holland Ltd., 98 New Bond Street, London S.W.
● Hollis, Isaac & Son, Lench Street, Birmingham.
Hollis, A., & Son, 28 Victoria Street, London S.W.
Hollis, Isaac & Sons, 9 New Bread Street, London E.C.
● Holloway, Geo. & Sydney, Imperial Works, Vesey Street, Birmingham.
Holloway & Co., Vesey Street, St. Mary's, Birmingham.
Holmes, Henry Charles, 15 Bath Street, Birmingham.
Horner, Henry B., Vesey Street, St. Mary's, Birmingham.
Hooke, Theodore, 38 & 39 Pavement, Liverpool.
Hooton and Jones, 60 Dale Street, Liverpool.
Hooton, William M., 15 South Gate, Sleaford, Lincolnshire.
● Horsley, T., & Son, 10 Coney Street, York.
Horton, William, 98 Buchanan Street, Glasgow.
Howe, James, 5 Long Wyne Street, Colchester.
Hughes, J., & Sons, 18 Bath Street, Birmingham.
Hughes, Robert & Sons, 100 Moland Street, Birmingham.
Hughes, Robert & Sons, 46 Fenchurch Street, London E.C.
Humphrey, G., & Co., 166 High Street, Sevenoaks, Kent.
Hume, George, 6 Loreburn Street, Dumfries, N.B.
Hunter & Vaughan, 63 Broad Street, Bristol.
Hunter and Sons, 62 Royal Avenue, Belfast.
Hussey, Henry Joseph, 81 New Bond Street, London W.
Hutchings, James, 9 Bridge Street, Aberyswyth, S. Wales.
Huthrings, F. W., & Co., 2 Gothic Arcade, Snowhill, Birmingham.

● Ingram, Charles, 18b Renfield Street, Glasgow.

Jackson, Samuel, 7 & 8 Church Gate, Low Pavement, Nottingham.
James, William & Enos, & Co., 38 Staniforth Street, Birmingham.
James & Reynolds, 8 George Street, Minnories, London E.C.
Jeffery, William & Son, 12 George Street, Plymouth.
Jeffery, Charles, High East Street, Dorchester.
Jeffery, Richard, 15 Borough, Farnham, Surrey.
Jeffery, Samuel Richard, 137 High Street, Guildford.

- Jeffrey, W. J., & Co., 60 Queen Victoria Street, London E.C., and 13 King Street, St. James's, London S.W.

Jefferies, L., (jnr.), 28 (back of) Whittall Street, Birmingham.

- Jefferies, Lincoln, 121 Steelhouse Lane, Birmingham.

Jenvey & Tite, 20 Watergate, Grantham.

Jewson, Alfred J., 1 Westgate, Halifax.

Johnson, Thomas & Son, Market Place, Swaffham, Norfolk.

Jones, Horatio, 25 High Street, Wrexham, N. Wales.

Jones, Robert, 42 Manchester Street, Liverpool.

Jones, William Charles H., 35 Park Street, Newtown, N. Wales.

Jones, William P., 25 Whittall Street, Birmingham.

Kavanagh, William & Son, 12 Dame Street, Dublin.

Keegan, L., 35 Upper Ormond Quay, Dublin.

Kennedy, W., & Son, 22 Bath Street, Birmingham.

Kerr, Thomas, Stranraer, N.B.

Kerr, Charles, 74 Hanover Street, Stranraer, Wigtownshire.

King, W. T., Market Place, Oundle.

King, Wm., Son & Co., 27 Oxendon Street, Haymarket, London S.W.

Kirk, James, Union Buildings, 36 Smith Street, Ayr, N.B.

Knight, Peter, 22 Carrington Street, Nottingham.

Knox, H. A., & Co., Ltd., 222 & 224 Borough High Street, London S.E.

- Lancaster, Charles, 11 Panton Street, Haymarket, London S.W.

Lane Bros., 45a New Church Street, Bermondsey, London S.E.

- Lang, Joseph & Son Ltd., 102 New Bond Street, London W.

Langley, James John, 31 Park Square, Luton, and Flander's Buildings, Hitchin, Herts.

Law, Thomas, (jnr), 17 King Street, Castle Douglas, N.B.

Lawson, James, 70 Argyle Street, Glasgow.

Lee, William, 28 Lancaster Street, Birmingham.

Leech, William & Sons, Conduit Street, Chelmsford.

Leeson, William Richard, 38 Bank Street, Ashford, Kent.

Lemon, John & Son, East Bridge Street, Enniskillen.

Leonard, H., Lench Street, Birmingham.

Leonard & Walker, Harper's Building, Weaman Street, Birmingham.

Leonard, Denis & Co., 67 William Street, Limerick.

Le Personne, L., & Co., 99 Cannon Street, London E.C.

Lewis, Charles E., High Street, Alford, Lincs.

Lewis, Geo. Edward, 32 & 33 Lower Loveday Street, Birmingham.

Lightwood, Joseph Birks, 50 Weaman Street, Birmingham.

Lilley, George, 19 Whittall Street, Birmingham.

Lingard, Ebenezer & Co., 144 Victoria Street South, Gt. Grimsby.

Linnington, J. Henry, 107a St. James' Square, and 24 Union Street, Newport, Isle of Wight.

Linscott, Tom, John Street, Exeter.
Linsley Bros., Lands Lane, Leeds, and 53 Tyrell Street, Bradford.
Little & Son, 14 Silver Street, Yeovil, Somerset.
Littleford, Alfred Thomas, 2 Market Place, Cirencester, Gloster.
Littlejohns & Co., 100 Gray's Inn Road, London W.C.
Liversidge, Chas. Frederick, 29 Market Street, Gainsborough, Lincs.
Lloyd & Son, 2 Station Street, Lewes.
Lloyd, Henry John, Davygate, York.
London Armoury Co., Ltd., 1 Laurence Pountney Hill, London E.C.
London Small Arms Co., Ltd., Old Ford Road, Bow, London E.
Longmore, John James, 31½ Whittall Street, Birmingham.
Loughlan Michael, North Main Street, Youghal.
Lowbridge, Phillip, 16 New Buildings, Price Street, Birmingham.

McCall, W., & Co., 23 Castle Street, Dumfries, N.B.
McCririck, James, & Sons, 72 Sandgate, Ayr, N.B.
McCririck & Sons, 6 John Finnie Street, Kilmarnock, N.B.
McLagan, Peter, 33 County Place, Perth.
MacLeod, John, Tarbert, Loch Fyne, Argyllshire.
Maleham, C. H., 12 Princes Street, Hanover Square, London W.
● MacNaughton, James, & Son, 36 Hanover Street, Edinburgh.
MacNaughton, P., & Son, Grantully, N.B.
McNaughton, James, 44 George Street, Perth.
Macpherson, John, 24 Church Street, Inverness.
Maleham, Charles Henry, 5a West Bar, Sheffield.
Malloch, Peter D., 26 Scott Street, Perth.
Manley, George & Son, 78 High Street, Birmingham.
Marks, James, 61 Queen Street, Portsea.
Marson, Samuel & Co., Great Western Gun Works, Lower Loveday Street, Birmingham.
Marson, John, 14 Weaman Street, Birmingham.
Martin, Alexander, 20 & 22 Royal Exchange Square, Glasgow, and 128 Union Street, Aberdeen.
Mason, John, 35 Whittall Street, Birmingham.
Metcalfe, Robert, Market Place, Richmond, Yorks.
● Midland Gun Co., 77 Bath Street, Birmingham.
Middleton, Robert, 16 Weaman Street, Birmingham.
Midgley (Smith) & Co., 25 Sunbridge Road, Bradford.
Miles, William, Price Street, Birmingham.
Milburn & Son, Brampton, Cumberland.
Millichamp, Charles, High Street, Presteign, R.S.O., Radnorshire.
Mills, W., Stafford Street, Dunedin.
Mills, Mrs. Francis, 62 North Lane, Canterbury.
Mitchell, J., & Son, Midsteeple Street, Dumfries, N.B.

Monk, William H., 77 Foregate Street, Chester.
Montrieux, Theodore, 5 Whittall Street, Birmingham.
Moore (William) and Grey, 8 Craven Street, Strand, London W.C.
Morris, P., & Son, 4 High Street, Hereford.
Morrow & Co., 22 Horton Street, Halifax; 60 Station Parade, Harrogate,
    York; and 27 Queen Victoria Street, Leeds.
Morton, W., & Sons, 17 Patrick Street, Limerick.
Morton, William & Son, 53 George Street, Cork.
Mountstephen, John Henry, Fleet Street, Torquay; and 1 Radford Place,
    Plymouth.
Murray, David (jnr), 23a St. David Street, Brechin, Forfarshire.
Murray, Thomas W., & Co., 87 St Patrick Street, Cork.

Naylor, Clement, 34 West Bar, and 6 Woodhead Road, Sheffield.
Neal, Edward, 19 Whittall Street, Birmingham.
● Needham, Joseph Vernon, Loveday Street, Birmingham.
Nelson, Frank Horatio, Broad Street, Chipping Sodbury, R.S.O., Glos.
Nelson, Francis, 32 Castle Street, Sligo.
Nestor, Augustine, 28 & 33 George Street, Limerick.
Nettleship & Co., Bondgate, Alnwick.
Newington, H., High Street, Wadhurst, Sussex.
Newnham Ltd., 29 Commercial Road, Landport, Portsmouth.
Nichols, Alma (dealer), Stalham, Norwich.
Norman, Benjamin, Church Street, Framlingham, R.S.O., Suffolk.
Northern Gun Co., 97 Bondgate, Darlington.

Oakes, M. A., 18 Market Square, Horsham, Sussex.
O'Brien, John, 17 Patrick Street, Limerick.
O'Connor, W., 3 Nelson Street, Tralee.
O'Hagan, Patrick, Beaverbank, Edinburgh.
Oldbury, John, 8 Sand Street, Birmingham.
● Osborne, Charles & Co., Ltd., 12, 13 & 14 Whittall Street, Birmingham;
    Sandgate Street, Birmingham; and 2 Great Scotland Yard, London S.W.

Palmer, W. & H. E., 85 High Street, Rochester.
Palmer, Augustus, 31 Preston Street, Faversham.
Palmer, Edward, 35 High Street, Stroud.
Palmer, George, 29 High Street, Sittingbourne.
● Pape, William R., 21 Collingwood Street, Newcastle-on-Tyne.
Parker, Alfred G., & Co., Ltd., 264 Lichfield Street, Birmingham.
Parkes, J. C., & Son, 110–111 Coombe, Dublin.
Parkinson, John, 17 Arran Quay, Dublin.
Parson, John & Son, 25 High Street, Southampton.
Percy, Joseph, 48 King Street West, Manchester.
Phillipson, William, 78 Weaman Street, Birmingham.

Pierpoint, Edward J., 1 New Buildings, Price Street, Birmingham.
Pinion, G., 1 Carlton Villas, Rosemont Road, Richmond, Surrey.
Playfair, Charles & Co., 142 Union Street, Aberdeen.
Pollard, Herbert Edward & Co., 62 Broad Street, Worcester.
Pollard, William Hebdon, 63 King William Street, London E.C.
● Powell, William & Son, Carr's Lane, Birmingham.
Powell, E., 12 Grove Hill Road, Tunbridge Wells.
Powell, Frank, 99 High Street, Tonbridge, Kent.
Pullan, H., Linden Works, Cirencester.
Pulvermann, Martin & Co., 26 Minories, London E.
● Purdey, James & Sons, Audley House, South Audley Street, London W.

Quinton, A., 40 South End, Croydon, London.

Radcliffe, Kenneth Dudley, 150 High Street, Colchester.
Ramsbottom, R., 81 Market Street, Manchester.
Rawcliffe & Waldron, 211 Newhall Street, Birmingham.
Rawcliffe & Waldron, 10 St Dunstan's Hill, London E.C.
Ray, T., & Co., 68 Lowfield Street, Dartford.
Reilly, E. M., & Co., 205 Oxford Street, London W.
Rhodes, Frank, 5 North Street, Scarborough.
● Richards Westley & Co., Ltd., 12 Corporation Street, Birmingham; and
    New Bond Street, London W.
Richards, William, 44 Fishergate, Preston.
Richards, William, 1 Tithebarn Street, Liverpool.
Richardson, George, Benjamin Bank, Barnard Castle.
Rickarby, A. G., 12–16 New Rents, Ashford, Kent.
● Rigby, John, 1 & 2 Ham-yard, Gt. Windmill Street, London W.
Roberts, Edgar, 22 Weaman Street, and 5 Steelhouse Lane, Birmingham.
Roberts, Joseph T., 22 Weaman Street, and 5 Steelhouse Lane,
    Birmingham.
Robertson, Alexander & Son, Bridge Street, Wick, Caithness-shire.
Robinson, Henry James, 5 Court, Price Street, Birmingham.
Robinson, Robert, 7 Queen Street, Hull.
Rodda & Co., Stafford Street, Birmingham.
Rogers, J., 4 Price Street, Birmingham.
Roper, Robert, Son & Co., Ltd., 39 Sheaf Street, Sheffield.
● Rosson, Charles, 4 Market Head, Derby; and 13 Rampant Horse Street,
    Norwich.
Rowe, James, 62 High Street, Barnstaple, Devon.
Royal Small Arms Factory, Enfield Lock, Enfield, Ponder's End.
Rudd, Arthur James, 54 London Street, Norwich; and 17 Regent Street,
    Great Yarmouth.
Russam, J., & Son, Weaman Street, Birmingham.
Russell, Alexander John, 32 High Street, Maidstone.

Rutt, Alfred H., George Row, Northampton.
Ryland, Charles, Weaman Street, Birmingham.

Sanders, Alfred, 79 Bank Street, Maidstone.
Saunders, John, 26a Loveday Street, Birmingham.
Schwarte & Hammer, 6 Lime Street, London E.C.
Scotcher & Son, Bury, Suffolk.
Scott, Martin, & Sons Ltd., 13 St. Mary's Row, Birmingham.
• Scott, W., & Co., Lancaster Street, Birmingham.
Scott & Co., 19 Marton Road, Middlesborough.
Scott, Frederick C., Bath Street, Birmingham.
Scott, W. & C., & Son, 8 Shaftsbury Avenue, London W.
Sell, John Tucker, 10 Potter's Street, Bishop's Stortford.
Sellars & Co., 83 High Street, Elgin, N.B.
Shand, William, 3 King Street, Towerhill, London E.
Silver, S. W., & Co., and Benjamin Edgington Ltd., Sun Court, 6 Cornhill,
    London.
Simkin, J., & Son, 3 Church Street, Bolton.
Simonon, Noel, 47 Loveday Street, Birmingham.
Slingsby Brothers, 10 High Street, Boston, Lincs.
Slingsby, Mrs. Emma, 44 Lowerhead Row, Leeds.
Small, Peter, 38 Pilgrim Street, Newcastle-on-Tyne.
Smallwood, Samuel, Milk Street, Shrewsbury.
Smith, Alfred, and Son, 28 Whittall Street, Birmingham.
Small, Charles, and Sons, Khama Gun Works, 25 Weaman Street,
    Birmingham.
Smith, Charles, and Sons, 47 Market Place, Newark.
Smith, Charles Hubert, & Co., 123 Steelhouse Lane, Birmingham.
Smith, Samuel, & Son, Gun Barrel Works, Witton Road, Aston Park,
    Birmingham.
Snowie, Hugh, & Son, 30 Church Street, Inverness.
• Southgate, Thomas, 6 Burton Crescent, London W.C.
Sparrow & Baker, High Street, Epsom, Surrey.
Spence, R., & Co., Richmond, Yorks.
Spencer, Charles, Field Street, Richmond, Yorks.
Spencer, William, 31½ Whittall Street, Birmingham.
Srawley, Joseph William, 31½ Whittall Street, Birmingham.
Stacey and Co., 17 & 19 Settle Street, London E.
Starret, G., 51 Spring Street, Hull.
Stensby, Thomas, 6 Withy Grove, Manchester.
Stoakes, K., & Co., 8 George Street, Hastings.
Stoakes, John, 27 St. Peter's Street, Canterbury.
Stokes, Frederick Henry, Clyde Works, Weaman Street, Birmingham.
Stovin, William, 4 Westgate, Grantham.
Styles, J. G., & Co., 97 Spencer Street, Birmingham.

Tannahill, Andrew, 1 Old Smith Hills, Paisley, N.B.
Tarrant, Elijah, 16 Sussex Street, Cambridge.
Taylor, Richard, 13 Court, Price Street, Lancaster Street, Birmingham.
Thacker, Thomas, 28 New Buildings, Price Street, Birmingham.
Thompson, Herbert, 22 West Street, Boston, Lincs.
Thompson, W., 149 Great Charles Street, Birmingham.
Thompson, Wm. Frederick, (back of) 28 Whittall Street, Birmingham.
Thompson, J. D., 31 Whittall Street, Birmingham.
Thompson, E., Essex Quay, Dublin.
Thornhill, William, Harper's Building, Weaman Street, Birmingham.
Tilney, Robert & Son, Smallgate Street, Beccles, Suffolk.
Tims, Frederick Hope, Cathedral Lane, Truro.
Tisdall, John, 8 South Street, Chichester, and High Street, Arundel, Sussex.
Titterton, Frank, 19 Whittall Street, Birmingham.
Todd, Wm., Oundle.
● Tolley, Jas. and Wm., Ltd., 18 Loveday Street, Birmingham.
Townend, R., High Street, Burford.
Townsend and Williams, 11 Sand Street, Birmingham.
Tranter Bros., 18 Sand Street, Birmingham.
Trimm, Frederick, Dean's Building, Weaman Street, Birmingham.
Troughton, Stephen, 24 Caunce Street, Blackpool.
Trulock Brothers, 13 Parliament Street, Dublin.
Trulock, Harris and Richardson Ltd., 9 Dawson Street, Dublin.
Tulloch, W., & Co., 4 Bishopsgate Churchyard, New Broad Street, London
    E.C.
Turner, Thomas and J. S., Ltd., Fisher Street, Birmingham.
Turner, Thomas and Sons, Market Place, Reading; and 86 Northbrook
    Street, Newbury, Berks.
Turner, Henry Arthur, High Street, Marlborough, Wilts.
Tuthill, Joseph, 134 North Main Street, Youghal.

Usher, Horace, 105 High Street, and Bank Street, Sevenoaks.

Veals, S., and Son, 3 Towerhill, Bristol.
Venables, John, and Son, 99 St Aldate's Street, Oxford.
Vickers, Sons, and Maxim, Ltd., Erith, S.O.; Crayford, S.O.; Dartford,
    Kent; and Victoria Street, Westminster (T.A. "Vickers, Erith". Tel. No.
    68 Erith).

Wakefield, W. H., and Co., 3 Price Street, Birmingham.
Wales, Durrant, 16 Regent Street, Yarmouth, Norfolk.
Walker, Geo., 95 Weaman Street, Birmingham.
Wallace, William, 66 King Street, Wigton, Cumberland.
Wallis Brothers, 156 High Street and 4 Corporation Street, Lincoln.
Wanless Brothers, 20 Norfolk Street, Sunderland.

Ward, H. Arthur, Alpha Works, 99 Snowhill, Birmingham.
Ward and Sons, 2 St. Mary's Row, and 24 to 27 Bath Street, Birmingham.
Ward, Peter, Henfield, Sussex.
Warrick, J., & Co., 34 St. Mary Butts, Reading.
Warrilow, James Bakewell, Railway Works, Chippenham, Wilts.
Watkins and Co., 75 High Street, Banbury, Oxon.
Watson and Co., 19 Inglis Street, Inverness.
Watson and Stewart, 68 Murraygate, Dundee.
Watson, Rowland, Victoria Gun Works, Whittall Street, Birmingham.
Watson, W. G., Market Place, Bedale.
Watson Brothers, 29 Old Bond Street, London W.
● Webley and Scott Revolver and Arms Co., Ltd., 81 to 91 Weaman Street,
    Birmingham.
Webley and Scott Revolver and Arms Co., Ltd., (The), 7 Shaftsbury
    Avenue, London W.
Weekes, Charles and Co., 27 Essex Quay, Dublin.
West and Son, Retford, Nottinghamshire.
● Westley-Richards & Co., Ltd., Bournbrook; 12 Corporation Street,
    Birmingham, and 178 New Bond Street, London W.
Weston, C. & H., High Street, Hailsharp, Sussex.
Weston, Charles and Herbert, 7 New Road, Brighton.
Wheatley, George, Hitchin Street, Biggleswade, Beds.
Wheelock, John, Main Street, Wexford.
Whitby, Henry Albert, 61 Weaman Street, Birmingham.
Whitaker & Co., 14 William Street, Limerick.
Whitehouse, E., & Co., Melton Mowbray.
Whistler, Edward & Co., 11 Strand, London W.C.
Whitehouse, J. E., High Street, Oakham.
White and Woodyett, (back of) 28 Whittall Street, Birmingham.
Widdas, George A., 31 Charles Street, Shipley, Yorks.
Wiggett, James & Sons, 10 Vesey Street, Birmingham.
Wild, Thomas J. William, 10 Whittall Street, Birmingham.
Wilkes, John, 1 Lower James Street, Golden Square, London W.
Wilkinson, T. H., Thurlestone, Yorks.
● Wilkinson Sword Co., Ltd., (The), 27 Pall Mall, London S.W., and
    Southfield Road, Acton, London W.
Wilcocks, J. William, 14 St. Mary Street, Stamford.
Williams, A. D. & Co. Ltd., 12 Weaman Street, Birmingham.
Williams, James & Co., 1 Great Hampton Street, Birmingham.
Williams and Powell, 27 South Castle Street, Liverpool.
Williams, Frederick William, 32 & 33 Weaman Street, Birmingham.
Williamson and Son, 34 Bull Ring, Ludlow, Salop.
Williamson Chas. Wm., 3 Bridge Road, Stockton-on-Tees.
Williamson, D., 3 Waterloo Road, London S.E.

Williamson, Dudley, George Street, Kettering.
Williamson, William, 72 High Street, Bridgnorth, Salop.
Willis, George, 1 New Buildings, Price Street, Birmingham.
Wilson, Edwin, 13 Rampant House Street, Norwich.
Wilson, James, Goodramgate, York.
Woffindin, John, Market Place, Market Rasen, Lincs.
● Woodward, James & Sons, 61 St. James' Street, London S.W.
Wright and Currey, 1 Churchgate, Spalding, Lincs.
Wright, E. J., 1 North Mews, High Street, Southend on Sea.
Wright, Job, 13 Court, Price Street, Birmingham.
Wright, J., 1 High Bridge House, Spalding.

Yarnold, William, 31½ Whittall Street, Birmingham.

Index

Index

205